MORALITY STORIES

MORALITY STORIES

Dilemmas in Ethics, Crime & Justice

FOURTH EDITION

Michael Braswell

Joycelyn Pollock

Scott Braswell

CAROLINA ACADEMIC PRESS

Durham, North Carolina

Library of Congress Cataloging-in-Publication Data

Names: Braswell, Michael, author. | Pollock, Joycelyn M., 1956- author. |
Braswell, Scott, 1971- author.
Title: Morality stories : dilemmas in ethics, crime & justice / Michael
Braswell, Joycelyn M. Pollock, Scott Braswell.
Description: Fourth edition. | Durham, North Carolina : Carolina Academic
Press, [2017] | Includes bibliographical references and index.
Identifiers: LCCN 2017013430 | ISBN 9781531005061 (acid-free paper)
Subjects: LCSH: Criminal justice, Administration of--Fiction. | Didactic
fiction, American.
Classification: LCC PS3602.R388 A6 2017 | DDC 813/.6--dc23
LC record available at https://lccn.loc.gov/2017013430

eISBN 978-1-53100-507-8

Carolina Academic Press, LLC
700 Kent Street
Durham, North Carolina 27701
Telephone (919) 489-7486
Fax (919) 493-5668
www.cap-press.com

Printed in the United States of America

To Richard Quinney
and the stories he writes with words and photographs

Contents

Acknowledgments ix

Foreword xi

Preface xv

Part One · Stories and Moral Dilemmas: An Introduction 3
A Framework for Ethical Analysis 5
Three Ethical Models 7
Duty-Based Ethics 7
Utilitarianism 8
Peacemaking Ethics 9
Three Contexts for Taking Moral Action 9
Back to the Beginning 10

Part Two · Loyalty and Personal Relationships 13
1 · Second Street 15
2 · Sarah Salvation 25
3 · Black and Blue 31
4 · A Difficult Choice 43
5 · Rosy 53
6 · Amnesia of the Heart 61
7 · Stray Dogs 67
8 · The End Is Near 77

Part Three · Duties to Self and Others 83
9 · Invisible Boy 85
10 · Special of the Week 97
11 · Rasheed's Ticket 105
12 · Crazy Times 113

13 · The Big Picture   117
14 · Short-Cut   129
15 · It's Too Bad about Tommy   135
16 · Truth Teller   141

Part Four · Justice and Redemption   147
17 · The Open Door   149
18 · Dead Man's Parade   157
19 · The Clock Maker   165
20 · Best Intentions   179
21 · The Price of Justice   191
22 · The Mercy Seat   203
23 · The Cracker Jack Gospel   217
24 · As Is   223

References   231

Index   233

ACKNOWLEDGMENTS

"Dead Man's Parade" and "The Clock Maker" were previously published in *Remembering Peleliu*. For this edition, we want to thank Beth Hall and the CAP staff for their help. We want to thank Susan Braswell for her help in getting this edition ready for press. We also want to acknowledge that while historical and news events may have inspired aspects of some of the stories, the stories and characters depicted in them are fictional.

FOREWORD

From the second and third editions:

I read the stories in this collection over the course of several evenings, while sprawled comfortably on my living room couch. I found that I was taking the themes of what I had read to bed with me, staying awake longer than I cared to and wondering about the likely outcomes of this or that story, pondering what I thought might be the "correct" resolution and then imagining what I myself might have done—or not done—had I been faced with the same set of circumstances. I was particularly intrigued by my response to "Rosy," the portrayal of the border patrol trainee who finds an extraordinarily *simpatico* girl of about his own age in the poor Mexican family that he has been assigned to live with in order to improve his Spanish. I was at first certain that I would have behaved differently than he did, but, thinking about it some more, I wasn't certain. The stories have that kind of effect; they fuel self-examination.

The events portrayed in *Morality Stories* will fascinate persons concerned with human goodness and human evil. The book's moral is translucent: "An evil act doesn't necessarily make a person who committed it evil," the authors declare in a thematic statement. I found the stories exceptionally interesting and provocative. Often the writers deliberately tease us by raising questions and letting them hover unanswered. In "Stray Dogs," for instance, we wonder what the preacher has in mind when he doubts Laney's claim that he threw the bricks at the display window of Cook's Dimestore Dream because he wanted a warm place to stay on Christmas Eve. What might the "true" reason have been? And why does the preacher say that the Dream deserved that brick and more? What is the meaning of Sergeant Hollis Rivers' cough? Is it serious and does it influence his actions? And what words were written underneath the picture that Laney tried to read but could not see clearly enough to make them out?

I was intrigued by the fact that in a number of stories it is a throwaway observation of strangers that sets in motion reactions from those who hear the words and then reflect on how they apply to their own situation. A waitress, adept at jollying customers, suggests that "sometimes you gotta do something risky to make sure you're still alive," and her homeless customer, down and out, makes a move that at least holds some hope for turning his dreary life around.

These are artfully constructed portrayals of people who come across as real folks with real problems and, for some, immediate ethical dilemmas that require resolution. At times, there is a change of pace in the stories with the recital tending toward understatement, such as in the moving description of the prison inmate who receives a gift from a totally unlikely source. The donor is asked why he did what he did; the question puzzles him (as it puzzles us as well) and he can offer only a laconic uninformative response before dropping the subject and moving along.

The prison stories are a sub-group of tales. They are marked by an exceptionally clear-eyed rendition of the aura and the undertones of life on a cell block and the verbal thrusts and jabs of the prisoners. The lesson is that even among some of those who appear to be the worst, there are human beings who are decent, even admirable persons. In several instances, prison guards, who have close contact with inmates, come to understand their humanity and to forgive the awful deeds that brought them to where they are. The "Mercy Seat" demonstrates that the death penalty can catch in its lethal embrace persons who have earned the opportunity to remain alive. The story brings to mind the wisdom of Winston Churchill: "The mood and temper of the public with regard to the treatment of crime and criminals is one of the most unfailing tests of the civilization of any country."

I would be hard-pressed to decide which story I liked best. Each in its own way set me to thinking, but I suspect that it was the riddle of the grandfather who refused to open doors for others or to allow others to open doors for him that made the deepest impression. The tenderness between the old man, the boy grandchild, his namesake, is conveyed with great sensitivity and the moral power of the story leaves indelible memories. Life is made up of choices, and the vital ones that we make will mark us for the remainder of our time on earth.

Science and morality often are said to exist in distinctively different realms. Science seeks objectivity and presents a façade of detachment and neutrality. This façade has been satirized by one writer who wondered whether if her husband and a grizzly bear were locked in mortal combat, she was required to say: "C'mon husband, c'mon bear."

Many scientists say that the application and the consequences of what they learn is the business of others, perhaps one of those touchy-feely people who deal with concepts such as goodness and decency. Such ideas faded in the wake of construction of atomic weapons. The scientists who had unraveled the mysteries that led to the production of the atomic bomb began to wonder how much responsibility they ought to assume when their invention was dropped on Hiroshima and Nagasaki, producing thousands of civilian deaths. The horrors produced by the atomic bombs were brilliantly brought home not by sterile medical reports or long-term longitudinal studies of the results of exposure to radiation from atomic fusion. The fiction and non-fictional portrayals, such as Nevil Shute's *On the Beach* and John Hersey's *Hiroshima* provided much more compelling accounts than those found in the medical and social scientific probes. Similarly, to read the opening pages of Ernest Hemingway's *A Farewell to Arms* is to experience the Italian army's retreat at Caporetto in a manner that no scientific inquiry could convey.

The stories that follow, written by Michael Braswell, Joycelyn Pollock, and Scott Braswell, are of a kind with these classics. They put you in touch with important life experiences of people, sometimes people like yourself, who are confronted with situations that require a degree of moral and ethical courage. *Morality Stories* allows you to share their experiences, debate within yourself and with others the issues that are raised as they relate to your life and your hopes, ideals, and expectations.

Gilbert Geis
University of California, Irvine

PREFACE

"Imagination and fiction make up more than three-quarters of our real life."

Simone Weil

"The Possible's slow fuse is lit by the imagination."

Emily Dickinson

Our goal in this edition of *Morality Stories* is to continue the tradition of telling stories about experiences where personal and social justice meet, often in the context of criminal justice. Gandhi wrote, "I have always felt that the true textbook for the pupil is the teacher" (Maggio, 1997: 34). It is the teacher then, who translates the insights and truth found in the big ideas and stories hidden in both fiction and nonfiction writing. The literature of criminal justice, criminology and sociology whether found in academic textbooks, novels or short stories offer fertile ground for unexpected lessons that draw us into the mystery of what justice is and is not— and how it squares with consequences, compassion and redemption on a personal, social and systemic level.

The story is the thing. The lessons that need to be learned are embedded in the byways and tall weeds more often than on the main road. And the truth of the matter often slips in through the back door, sneaking up on us from behind and surprising us with delight, horror or both at once. In the best of circumstances, there is a kind of transparency on the bridge of learning between student and teacher where both contribute insights to the questions and possible solutions a story offers. As Gil Geis alludes to in the "Foreword," such an experience enables both student and teacher to become more than the stories they tell, filling them with a conscious sense of wonder—of questions that can never be fully answered, but only lived out through one's best intentions put into action. Questions like "what is justice?"; "what does it mean to be a just and moral person?"; "what should we do with the 'least of those' in our society?"; and "where does justice meet mercy and compassion?" haunt us as we wrestle with the choices we make as individuals and as a society.

We offer six stories new to this edition. One examines how young boys become aware of class and territorial differences at an early age. Armed with air rifles and bicycles, it is a hop, skip and a jump before they are terrorizing a hapless victim they perceive to be a member of the upper crust of their neighborhood. Two of the stories address issues in contemporary policing, one regarding the pressures on marriage and family relationships and the other, challenges in keeping the peace during volatile times of unrest and protest. Another story explores how a clockmaker who was a concentration camp doctor during the holocaust of WWII tries to morally justify his treatment of helpless victims to a young journalist while he awaits deportation to face trial for war crimes. Finally, there is also a story that examines racial prejudice from a historical perspective when two decorated black soldiers return to the Jim Crow South where they are met with derision and disrespect.

Given all the questions and possibilities a meaningful and creative narrative provides, a good story never really ends. More than that, the Student in charge is not just teaching students about criminal justice, criminology and social justice, but about the larger landscape of life itself—about how they can make a difference in the world around them.

Michael Braswell
Joycelyn Pollock
Scott Braswell

MORALITY STORIES

PART ONE

Stories and Moral Dilemmas:
An Introduction

Since the written word appeared and human beings learned to read, write and communicate, literature has reflected our struggle with moral dilemmas. The ancient parables of religious Masters, *Aesop's Fables, The Scarlet Letter* and *Crime and Punishment* all wrestle with the existential and ethical dilemmas inherent in social and political life. We explore the human condition through our narrative.

> Deprive children of stories and you leave them unscripted, anxious stutterers in their actions as well as their words. Hence there is no way to give us an understanding of any society, including our own, except through the stock of stories which constitute its initial dramatic resources. Mythology, in its original sense, is at the heart of things. Each of us has our own story to tell, a framework which gives meaning and direction to the events and goals of our lives (MacIntyre, 2001: 6).

The literature of fiction has offered a unique and dynamic way of examining moral and ethical decision-making. Whether contemplating Shylock's desire for just retribution in the form of his "pound of flesh" in Shakespeare's *Merchant of Venice* or observing the violence and irony of racial and social class prejudice in the short stories of Flannery O'Connor, the reader is touched by the characters and story emotionally as well as intellectually. There are lessons to be learned through the eyes of heroes, villains and spectators alike. For instance, the motivations of villains who bring physical and psychological harm to unsuspecting or powerless victims may be just as murky as the choices of apathetic bystanders who omit to do the good that they could do, thus allowing another person's violent intent to become a tragic reality.

In a moral context, each of us at one time or another has played out the role of hero, villain, victim or spectator in life situations. We may or may not have robbed someone of their money at gunpoint, but we have more than likely participated through gossip or idle chatter in robbing someone of their good reputation. We may or may not have been the victim of a criminal assault where an injury occurred, but all of us on occasion have experienced emotional injury through a betrayal of trust and a broken heart. And of course, all of us have been spectators and bystanders in the unfolding story of life. There have been times when we chose not to speak up or intervene, perhaps not in the course of an actual crime being committed, but most certainly when a moral offense was being perpetrated. When someone absent was being ridiculed or slandered, most of us have at times, remained silent when we could have corrected the cruel conversations of others. There are also the more pleasant and encouraging memories, the occasions when we did the right thing.

Fiction and nonfiction literature have provided valuable contributions to the study of justice, morality and ethics (Maas, 1973 and 1983; Masters, 1997; Lozoff, 1988; Carlson and Hawkins, 1994; and Tannebaum, 2000). In the arena of social and criminal justice, creative fiction is a particularly well-suited means through which the ethical and moral dimension of living as responsible persons can be explored. In Harper Lee's classic novel, *To Kill A Mockingbird,* we can observe the courage of a white attorney, who defends a black man falsely accused of assault by a young woman in the Deep South. In Arthur Miller's *The Crucible,* moral injustice on personal, social and judicial levels result in the death of innocent victims in the Salem Witch Trials of 1692. In a more contemporary vein, novels such as *The Prince of the City,* by Robert Daly, is a thinly veiled account of the personal costs of a real New York City detective who sinks into corruption and then becomes a whistle blower. The work of author-attorneys such as Scott Turow and John Grisham examine issues including corporate and judicial corruption and the personal ethics of attorneys. From a more academic perspective, Norval Morris wrote *The Brothel Boy and Other Parables of the Law,* a work of fiction where an inspector in Burma in the 1920s was confronted with cases addressing a variety of legal and moral issues, including insanity, criminal responsibility and domestic violence. Fictional "hypotheticals" have also been used to illustrate ethical issues in more traditional academic textbooks on ethics (Pollock, 2012).

Creative fiction not only allows the reader to explore the moral dimension of life, but also has the potential to become a catalyst in righting wrongs and restoring health and balance. Novels and short stories may both convict and heal. Maya Angelou, in discussing her years of silence following being raped as a young girl, talked about the therapeutic effects of reading and reflecting upon what she read. In reading about the struggles of others and how they dealt with and overcame their suffering, the characters in the stories became an example and source of encouragement to her as she faced her own difficult experiences and emerged as someone with a sense of positive purpose who had something important to say (Angelou, 1983).

The collection of original short stories in this volume attempt to explore the personal, social and criminal justice aspects of human interaction where moral choices made and not made are examined. Personal and social injustice is addressed through stories about homelessness, emotional neglect and family violence. Stories more specific to criminal justice themes include such issues as defending the guilty, criminal culpability, police brutality, juvenile offenders, reintegration and capital punishment. At this point, it seems useful to provide an ethical framework for exploring the moral dilemmas and meanings the stories offer.

A Framework for Ethical Analysis

What does it mean to be a moral or ethical person? Can one be moral and just without being compassionate? Can even a just or ethical person experience moral lapses that result in wrongdoing? Can a person who has demonstrated little integrity or caused great harm change? Can such a person be restored and do something good? Does everyone have the potential to be moral and compassionate, as well as unethical and selfish?

Wisdom and religious traditions teach us to treat others the way we want to be treated, that our deepest selves are expressed by how we respond to the "least of those," whether they live on the street, in prison, or in our own families. Such traditions maintain that we are all connected in ways both apparent and hidden. Our legal justice system is primarily concerned with those among us who break the law and do harm to others. Moral and religious values go a step further by also holding us accountable for failing to do the good that we could do and, as a result, allowing unnecessary suffering and harm to exist.

Pollock (2012: 8) reminds us that the words *morals* and *ethics* are often used in everyday conversation. She gives an example by writing,

> When public officials use their offices for personal profit or when politicians accept bribes from special interest groups, they are described as unethical. When an individual does a good deed, engages in charitable activities or personal sacrifice, or takes a stand against wrongdoing, we might describe that individual as a moral person.

It is interesting to note that when a public official or politician is confronted by the news media about an act most persons would consider unethical, they often respond, "I have done nothing *illegal!*" While the terms moral and ethical have similar meanings, neither is a synonym for legal. In our culture, we often seem to confuse what is moral or ethical with what is legal. For example, an unscrupulous attorney may allow one individual to legally deceive another person and acquire all of that person's property and assets. While such an action might be viewed by the rest of us as being very unethical, it could still fall within what the law allows. Conversely, an illegal action could be viewed by many persons as being highly moral and ethical, examples being marching with Martin Luther King, Jr. in a civil rights demonstration or hiding Jews from the Gestapo during World War Two.

Our moral and ethical beliefs often come from the values we hold to be important. Our values often come from our parents and other persons significant in our lives, as well as the experiences we have shared with them. Our values tend to be more general and relative while morals and ethics are more prescriptive in nature. We may believe honesty is an important value and, therefore, our moral belief system might include a rule that prohibits lying. Moral actions and personal values often come into conflict with one another. For example, as a student you may place a high value on both academic success and honesty. When confronted with an opportunity to cheat and improve your grade in a class, you are faced with a conflict regarding your values and moral choices. What would you do if there was a high probability of your not being caught? What if your graduation from college depended upon the grade you received? Our values help shape our moral beliefs, which in turn, shape our ethical decision-making.

> Moral standards derive from the value one places on such things as honesty, integrity, and trust. However, universalists would not hesitate to add that all values are not equal. Valuing money over life, for instance, would be wrong, as would valuing pleasure over charity (Pollock, 2004:12).

Three Ethical Models

Duty-Based Ethics

Immanuel Kant's approach to ethics is often referred to as "deontological," meaning the moral intentions of our actions are more important than their consequences or outcomes. He believed that we should act out of a "sense of duty." In addition, we should behave as though our actions were a "universal law," applying equally to everyone. In other words, we should not behave toward others in ways we would not be willing to be subjected to ourselves. Using the previous example of cheating, under Kant's approach, we cannot choose to cheat on an exam or cheat someone out of their property (even if done legally), unless we are willing to agree it is "right" or "good" for the same to happen to us. Another example would be that unless we are willing to be ridiculed and made fun of, we cannot ridicule and make fun of others, even if everyone else is doing it. In sum, Kant would contend it is important that every act we take conform to this standard of "universal law", no matter what the consequences and no matter what it costs us.

Utilitarianism

"Utilitarianism" is the term used to identify Jeremy Bentham's approach to ethics and morality. Rather than emphasizing one's individual sense of duty and moral intentions as did Kant, Bentham focused on the outcomes or consequences of one's actions. "Good" is defined as the greatest good for the majority. For example, cheating on an exam or unethically gaining someone else's property might benefit me, but what would be the cost to the other students in the class or to the other members of my community? I might receive a higher grade, but the teacher might discover that cheating occurred and penalize the entire class. Unethically acquiring another person's property could substantially diminish other community members' confidence in the law and justice system, possibly resulting in one or more of them attempting to "take the law into their own hands" under similar subsequent circumstances. While Bentham might agree that individual rights and responsibilities are important, he would contend that the greater good for the majority is more important.

One of the phrases associated with utilitarian ethics is "the ends justify the means." Basically, the idea is that if one has a good "end" in mind, then committing acts that would otherwise be wrong may be ethically justified. The trouble with this approach, however, is that we might create a greater, unintended harm from "bad means" that we performed for a "good end." For instance, police officers who lie on the stand in order to obtain a conviction in one case risk losing their credibility in all other cases, resulting in a much greater harm to society than the release of one criminal.

Peacemaking Ethics

"Peacemaking" is an approach to ethics and morality inspired by ancient wisdom traditions and contemporary advocates such as Gandhi, Martin Luther King, Jr. and Mother Teresa. Peacemaking would find elements of both Kant's and Bentham's approach valuable, but would place a greater priority on serving and caring for those who are less fortunate. The goal of peacemaking is to relieve suffering through compassionate service and loving kindness. Each person is responsible to commit to such action whether he or she accepts such a responsibility or not. Three core elements of the peacemaking approach are "connectedness, care and mindfulness" (Braswell, McCarthy and McCarthy, 2012).

Connectedness essentially refers to the belief that everyone is connected to each other and to their environment. In other words, "we are all in it together," including the privileged and the outcasts, civic leaders and prisoners. What we do to the environment or someone else, we do to ourselves. The ethic of care encourages us to be more compassionate as we attempt to alleviate suffering wherever we find it. Such action provides meaning and fulfillment in our lives. An interesting irony is that the more we do for others, the more empowered we feel. Mindfulness is about learning how to "pay attention" to what is going on around us. When we become more mindful, we become more aware of our opportunities for service in ways both large and small (Braswell, McCarthy and McCarthy, 2012).

Three Contexts for Taking Moral Action

The first context is the *personal*. It is important that we take our lives personally rather than simply "going along to get along." What are our values? What exactly do we believe in? What are our personal ideas and feelings about justice, morality and ethics? What are we as individuals willing to sacrifice for what we believe in? We cannot control what others do, but we can do what is within our power. In fact, that often turns out to be enough to make a difference. Examples include voting in elections (every vote does count), volunteering where we are needed and speaking up for what we believe in.

The *social* context refers to the community we live in and the groups of people we affiliate with (our family, friends, neighbors, and classmates). Our social relationships influence us as we influence them. As we can observe in the moral lives of such persons as Gandhi, Martin Luther King, Jr. and Mother Teresa, one committed person can have an amazing impact on a corrupt community. One honest and ethical police officer can create a positive impact in a corrupt law enforcement agency.

The third context involves the *justice process*. It is no secret that morality and ethics cannot be legislated. Regardless of laws passed, there will always be someone who is prejudiced against others because of their color, ethnicity, gender, or for some other reason. There will always be persons who will lie, cheat or steal someone else's opportunity or property. While neither laws nor our criminal justice system can force us to be moral, ethical individuals do have an impact on their communities, which in turn influences the nation and culture, including our system of justice. While perhaps not perfect, civil rights today are more of a reality than they were 100 years ago. For example, women now have the right to vote and have greater self-determination because of selfless and committed people who worked and sacrificed for these causes. Sacrifices of some moral pioneers included their very lives in some tragic cases (Braswell, McCarthy and McCarthy, 2012).

Back to the Beginning

For better or worse, it comes back to each of us. Our personal sense of morality and compassion is where we begin—inside our own skins. Do we do the good we are able to do wherever we find ourselves? When we fail to support what is right or commit wrong-doing ourselves, do we accept responsibility for our actions and try to make things right to the best of our ability? Or do we blame others and look for ways to avoid taking responsibility for what we have done or left undone? Do we make a genuine effort to learn from the suffering we have experienced and contributed to, or do we attempt to suppress the lessons such suffering offers us? Do we expect forgiveness when we err but show little compassion for those who have hurt our feelings or have harmed us in some way? It is worth remembering that all our experiences, both good and bad, are grist for our lives.

Persons who are morally responsible and compassionate encourage the communities they work and live in to become more just and merciful. While the process starts with each of us, our larger goal is, as Martin Luther King, Jr. suggests, "a community at peace with itself" and a world that is becoming more just.

We hope the stories in this book will help you think and feel more deeply about what it means to be a moral person who acts in ethical ways. Like the characters in the stories, we are all flawed and wounded in one way or another. And like them, each of us has the capacity to do both good and bad. If we are open to listening, learning and understanding, we have the opportunity to change our perceptions of the world. In doing so, we may even come to make a difference not only in the lives of those around us, but in our own as well.

PART TWO

Loyalty and Personal Relationships

Personal relationships involve emotional investment and sacrifice. Relationships also include responsibilities, choices and consequences—sometimes unintended. Sometimes the responsibilities seem to be more than we can handle. On the other hand, when we cut ourselves off from others we are in relationships with, those relationships can end through causes and circumstances which are beyond our control. When that happens, we may find ourselves adrift—without direction or purpose.

Second Street is a story about how social and economic differences can affect the interaction between younger children. Three young boys harass a boy who lives on a different street than they do and who comes from a more economically advantaged family.

Sarah Salvation examines the plight of a homeless veteran with a drinking problem who is at the end of his rope. He wanders into a rundown diner and experiences the special effect a waitress has on him and the other customers.

Black and Blue is a story about a rookie police officer who has to choose sides when his partner roughs up a young driver. Until now, the young officer has looked up to his partner who is also his Field Training Officer. He doesn't want trouble on the job, but he also wants to do the right thing.

A Difficult Choice explores the challenges a female police officer faces both on the job and at home. The officer in this story is dealing with a young boy who is threatening to kill himself, but won't reveal the ones who have been bullying and torturing him on his way to school each day. In addition, the officer's husband has become increasingly concerned about the risks and potential dangers associated with her job.

Rosy is about a budding romantic relationship between a border agent and Rosy, a young Hispanic woman whose family was part of a college immersion program designed to help him learn Spanish. The agent eventually succumbs to peer pressure from his fellow agents, some who have strong prejudicial feelings and attitudes about Hispanics in general and even moreso regarding those who cross the border illegally.

Amnesia of the Heart addresses a problem present in many demanding professions where a person is married more to his work than to his family. In this story, a retired FBI agent whose wife has died is estranged from his daughter who is married and has young children. Although he put his career before his family, his daughter wants him to visit for the holidays. He is unsure about what to do.

Stray Dogs illustrates how a lonely, homeless boy commits a minor crime in order to spend Christmas out of the cold.

In *The End is Near* a Wall Street hedge fund manager has a crisis of conscience when he meets an elderly street preacher and has to decide whether or not he will cooperate with criminal justice authorities.

1

SECOND STREET

"It's a damn hot day," Big M exclaimed while straddling his three speed Schwinn in the alleyway between First and Second Street.

"Damn hot," repeated Little M, his nine year-old brother, standing beside him. Little M never really talked much until Big M spoke. Then he simply repeated in some form or fashion whatever this older brother said. Nobody really knew how the two brothers got to be known as Big M and Little M. The older brother was eleven, short and stocky while his younger sibling was tall and skinny. Their given names were Marvin and Theodore, respectively. Their mother called them Marty and Ted while their father succumbed to neighborhood tradition and referred to them as Big M and Little M except when he was mad.

Then he simply bellowed their gender, "Boy."

The two brothers lived on Second Street, one of four streets that made up Magnolia Estates in the small South Georgia town of Mulberry. It was a nice enough neighborhood although the six-room, shingle-sided tract houses could hardly be called estates and no one ever remembered seeing a magnolia tree. Rumor had it that Hubert Holbrook, the developer, did cut down two magnolia trees that interfered with some road grading when he first started developing the neighborhood.

Magnolia Estates was referred to by real estate brokers as a nice, middle class neighborhood. It was true that most families who lived there thought of themselves as middle class. In reality, except for First Street, everybody else was on the low side of middle class. First Street was different. It faced the paved two-lane highway that connected Mulberry with Newberry, twenty miles away. The people who lived on First Street were honest-to-goodness middle class although they thought of themselves as upper-middle class. Their houses were made of brick or wood siding and had garages and brick barbecue pits. Two families on First Street even had above-ground swimming pools. Hot summer days found those pools full of yelling, splashing First Street children, while their mothers sat in folding chairs or reclined on beach towels trying to get the beginning of a tan before their annual three-day, Panama City beach vacations. Second through Fourth Street children were not invited. They had to settle for playing with a water hose, running through their Mom's sprinkler system, or taking their chances in a nearby creek or fishing pond. Maybe that's why on a humid night in mid-July, Big M and Jimmy Simpkins, his best friend who lived on Third Street, punched a dozen or more holes through each of the pools sidewalls while Little M stood watch in the alleyway.

Big M, Little M and Jimmy Simpkins were inseparable whenever they weren't in school. They were three boys like all other nine to eleven year olds experiencing the long, hot, slow summers of South Georgia. Whether sneaking around in someone's yard when the occupants weren't home or exploring the oak and yellow pine forests that surrounded them, each day was a new adventure. Had it not been for two inventions these three young boys and countless others like them would have perhaps, spent their summer days more productively.

The BB gun and the bicycle transformed young boys from the artistry of crayons and coloring books to marauding bandits, on the move and ready for action. With their three-speed Schwinns and Daisy rapid-fire, lever-action BB guns, Big M, Little M and Jimmy Simpkins defended their turf ruthlessly, especially when it came to any hapless kids who ventured from First Street. The streets were for cars and adults, but the alleyways were their domain, a kind of no-man's land fraught with danger and surprise attacks.

Leaning on his bicycle's handle-bars, Big M turned to his little brother and whispered, "I think I see Billy Ray Wilson. I bet he's gonna try and catch some minnows. Ride over to Jimmy's and the two of you meet me at the creek."

Little M nodded his assent with the seriousness of a special agent carrying out a dangerous assignment. He left in a cloud of dust, his skinny legs pedaling as fast as they could toward Jimmy's house.

Big M carefully loaded the BB's into his Daisy with delicate precision. His lips curled into a smile as he thought about his prey, Billy Ray Wilson, and the fun he and his compadres were going to have. Mr. big-shot, Billy Ray Wilson, was about to learn a thing or two. His fancy, chrome-fendered bicycle with the genuine leather saddle bags wouldn't do him any good when Big M and the boys got hold of him. It didn't matter if he and his chiropractor father, mother, and little sister lived in the biggest house on first street or not. When he used the alley or "thunder road" as Jimmy liked to call it, he was dead meat.

Big M wasn't really a bad kid. His parents' friends referred to him as a "spirited child." Adults who weren't acquainted with his parents called him a "little devil" or worse. In today's world a psychologist would probably describe him as an Attention Deficit-Hyperactive child. In the sixties there wasn't any Ritalin or related drugs, only keen switches at the hand of his mother to settle him down or a foot in his behind from his father to put the fear of the Lord into him. Big M once mentioned to his best friend Jimmy that he did not know the Lord well enough to be afraid of him, but he sure was afraid of his Daddy.

A bicycle, a BB gun and a couple of followers brought out the predatory instincts Big M possessed. He liked dangerous situations. The only thing he liked better than walking on the edge of danger himself was instilling fear and terror in others. Whatever the case, on that day, things didn't look good for Billy Ray Wilson. Big M's eyes narrowed as he chuckled to himself, peddling his bicycle ever faster toward the creek.

Billy Ray was bending over the creek, carefully working his minnow net through its waters when he heard the boys come up behind him. Big M stood in the middle of the path that led to the creek, flanked on both sides by Little M and Jimmy. Holding his Daisy air rifle in his left hand and wearing a pair of red-frame, superman sunglasses, Big M, who always had a flare for the dramatic, was more than a little cocky. Jimmy also looked confident, but not Little M. He shifted his weight from one foot to the other and held his BB gun as though he was afraid it might go off.

"Billy Boy, what do you think you're doing, riding down our alley and messing in our creek," Big M said in his most menacing voice.

"Yeah, who gave you permission, Silly Billy," chimed in Jimmy Simpkins.

"Yeah, Billy Boy," echoed Little M, who seemed to be gaining more confidence by the moment.

Billy Ray Wilson stumbled backwards, knocking over his minnow bucket. Beads of sweat began to break out on his forehead.

"I ain't doing nothing but trying to get me some minnows. This here's public property." Conjuring up all the false courage he could muster, Billy Ray continued, "It's a free country. My daddy said I could ride in the alley anytime I wanted to."

Big M inched towards Billy Ray, holding his air rifle with both hands. "Is that so, Billy boy? Your daddy's full of cow manure. He ain't even a real doctor."

"He is so a real doctor!" Billy Ray retorted, his red face raining sweat.

Almost in unison, Little M and Jimmy shouted at Billy Ray, "You're full of cow manure. Big M, let's make him eat boogers like we did last time!"

"Maybe later, but not just yet." Big M cocked his lever-action rapid-fire Daisy. "First, we need to teach Billy Boy a lesson for trespassing on our private property. "

Jimmy and Little M responded with a resounding "Yeah, that's right."

If Billy Ray Wilson had been raised differently and had not lived such a sheltered life, he would have realized that at twelve going on thirteen years of age, he was twice as big as any of the three boys confronting him. He could more than hold his own in a fight with any of them, but he didn't see himself that way. Inside he felt small and scared and wished he were home eating a Popsicle. All he could offer in his defense was a desperate, empty threat.

"I'll tell my daddy if you don't leave me alone."

As if on cue, Big M, Little M, and Jimmy Simpkins began laughing. Aiming his air rifle at Billy Ray's feet, Big M fired off a round and shouted, "Dance Billy Boy dance." And Billy Ray tried to do just that, but he really didn't know how. A second and third shot from Big M's Daisy kicked up little puffs of sand. The fourth shot hit Billy Ray in the left foot, stinging him through his black and white Converse tennis shoes. Then he wet his pants and began to cry. More laughter and taunts of "Cry Baby" erupted from his three tormentors.

Suddenly, Billy Ray surprised everyone by jumping into the waist-deep creek where water moccasins had been spotted on more than one occasion and a mythical alligator was rumored to have eaten Arthur Johansen's poodle. He half-waded and dog paddled to the other side. Soaking wet, Billy Ray sloshed furiously through the blackberry bushes and brambles as fast as he could, running through the woods toward the safety of home.

"Let's catch him when he cuts through old Lady Fowler's back yard," shouted Big M as the three BB gun-toting marauders scrambled for their Schwinns.

Billy Ray ran hard and breathed harder, his water-logged sneakers squished their way toward First Street, while the predators pursued him in a cloud of summer dust. All four boys were sweating profusely—one from fear and the others from the thrill of the hunt.

Everything in life depends on one's perspective. Leona Fowler and her friend Myrtle observed the chase on their way to the Shoe Mart's semi-annual sale in Newberry. The two women shook their heads with a certain disdain as they drove by in Myrtle's Ford Fairlane.

Myrtle pursed her lips, "Leona, would you look at that? Those Jones boys and the Simpkins' son are chasing another boy."

Leona Fowler, a widow of ten years, had viewed similar incidents from her kitchen window and had dutifully reported each one in detail to her friends through extended party-line, telephone conversations.

With a disapproving tone, she replied "Doesn't surprise me a bit. Those second street hellions are always up to no good. I should know. They've trampled and torn up my flower beds more than once. The boy they're after is Billy Ray Wilson. His father is a professional man."

To Leona and Myrtle, the event was a minor intrusion into their morning shopping spree, nothing more than a childish prank. To Big M, Little M, Jimmy and Billy Ray it was an epic struggle. As far as Billy Ray Wilson was concerned, he was literally running for his life. He remembered the booger-eating incident all too well, not to mention the BB gun induced dancing that comprised his most recent humiliation.

Billy Ray was a settler who had foolishly ventured too far from the safety of the fort and had been caught in a surprise attack with no means of defense. As he pushed his body to its physical limits, he promised himself that next time, he would pay more attention to his surroundings—if there was a next time.

To someone like Leona Fowler, Big M, Little M, and Jimmy were "hellions." To Billy Ray, they were worse than that; they were more like the devil incarnate. The three boys, however, saw themselves as heroes, protecting their homesteads from the carpet-bagging likes of Billy Ray Wilson and other First Street land barons.

Billy Ray almost made it, but not quite. Jimmy, the fastest rider of the three, cut off his escape route while Big M and Little M surrounded him. Billy Ray, panting from the heat of a blistering hot Georgia sun, found refuge in Leona Fowler's metal utility building. He hunkered down in a back corner of the shed. The late Mr. Fowler's yard tiller and self-propelled lawn mower was all that stood between him and Armageddon. All he could do was clutch a broken-handled yard rake and shout over and over, "You better leave me alone!"

Meanwhile, Big M showed Little M and Jimmy how to aim their air rifles at an angle so the BB's would ricochet off the walls and ceiling of the metal building. When one of the stinging projectiles found its mark, a yelp of pain from Billy Ray was their reward for persistence. After inflicting a barrage of BB gunfire, the three boys eventually became bored. Big M concocted a variation of their torturous game. Several times they rode down the alley, pretending to leave only to circle back and hide behind a nearby hedgerow. As soon as Billy Ray tried to emerge from the utility building, he would be met by a hailstorm of BB's from his well-concealed attackers, sending him back in full retreat to the rear of the building. Each time they pretended to leave he would wait longer before trying to make his get-away. Each time he was fooled and sent scurrying back into the building. The torment continued for almost two hours with no relief in sight when a miracle happened. Big M and Little M heard Miss Emma ring the dinner bell.

Even families on the back side of middle class could afford maids in the 1950s. Low wages and no benefits aside, even bad jobs were scarce for black women. The dinner bell rang a second and a third time. Big M and Little M looked at each other and smacked their lips. That sound could mean only one thing—chicken pot pies and maybe a little left-over peach cobbler for dessert. Chicken pot pies, four for a dollar at the local Winn-Dixie, were the hardtack and field rations of the fighting boys of Second Street.

Big M left Jimmy on sentry duty with strict orders: "Keep Billy Ray cornered until we return from lunch. Fire a few rounds ever so often to keep him trapped." No excuses would be accepted. Jimmy's reward for following orders would be that he would escape Big M's wrath and would be treated to some of Miss Emma's peach cobbler after they had completed their mission.

As always, Miss Emma's pot pies were superb. However, the peach cobbler was not to be. It had been requisitioned by the boys' father as dessert for his and their mother's evening meal. Big M and Little M would have to settle for a graham cracker to go with the last of their milk.

Wiping the cracker crumbs from his Batman tee shirt, Big M was none too happy about missing out on the peach cobbler. And as far as he was concerned, in a few minutes, Billy Ray Wilson was going to pay the price for that disappointment.

Full of chicken pie, graham crackers, and milk, Big M and Little M felt refreshed and re-energized. Mounting their trusty Schwinns, they were ready to return to battle. Little M carefully wrapped two graham crackers in a paper napkin and stuffed them in his tee-shirt. It wasn't the peach cobbler he had promised Jimmy, but it was better than nothing.

As Big M and Little M turned the corner toward Old Lady Fowler's yard, it was eerily silent. There were no sounds of BBs ricocheting off metal walls or taunts, or screams of pain—only a couple of blue-jays squawking and a dog barking in the distance.

"I don't like the sound of this," Big M grumbled, cocking his Daisy, "I don't like it one bit!"

"Where's Jimmy?" Little M whispered as he and his older brother surveyed their most recent battlefield, later referred to in various historical renditions as "Old Lady Fowler's building" or just the "Fight at Fowler's Place."

Their search first led them to the building itself, where there was no sign of Billy Ray or Jimmy. Their calls for Jimmy initially went unanswered. They found him sprawled on the ground, moaning and holding his bruised head, a casualty of a desperate counter attack.

Apparently Billy Ray Wilson had finally come to his senses. As confused and frightened as he was, he came to the conclusion that his chances, unarmed or not, were better against one than against three. His body, pumped up on adrenaline was more than ready for a dash to freedom. He was still afraid, but he sensed intuitively that his best chance for survival was to make his move.

At first he tried negotiating.

"Hey Jimmy, why don't you let me go?"

"No way," came the terse reply, followed by several quick rounds from Jimmy's air rifle.

The clock was ticking. It wouldn't be long before Big M and Little M returned and the torture resumed.

"Hey Jimmy, I'll give you my original Mickey Mantle baseball card if you'll let me go."

Billy Ray had upped his ante. He had gotten Jimmy's attention. The only thing Jimmy Simpkins liked as much as riding and shooting was playing baseball and collecting baseball cards.

Jimmy didn't answer right away. He was thinking the proposition over. Bribing one's guard to escape punishment is as old as history. Of course, Billy Ray Wilson had no intention of giving Jimmy his Topps Mickey Mantle card, but Jimmy didn't know that. He was considering whether or not such a rare treasure was worth Big M's wrath. Billy Ray was lying to Jimmy and Jimmy was wondering if he could tell a convincing lie to Big M. Absorbed with several possible scenarios, Jimmy laid his BB gun on the ground and began to rub his chin with his right hand, a nervous habit that signaled the rare occasion when he was trying to use his mind.

The distraction was enough.

When Billy Ray Wilson saw Jimmy drop his Daisy, every cell in his large body came alive in a spurt of self-preservation. From some former gene pool deep inside him emerged a blood-curdling rebel yell as he charged his tormentor. Eyes wide open with surprise, Jimmy reached for his Daisy and thinking better of it turned to run. Too late. Billy Ray lunged at him, half on purpose and half because he tripped over his size eleven tennis shoes. Whatever his intention was, the end result was that Billy Ray did a full belly-flop on Jimmy Simpkins. When they hit the ground, you could hear the air go out of Jimmy like a punctured birthday party balloon. Jimmy Simpkins lay in a crumpled heap on the ground, his right leg trembling uncontrollably. He wanted to cry, but first he had to get his breath. Realizing his advantage, Billy Ray picked up the air rifle. Holding the barrel with both hands, he pretended he was chopping wood on Jimmy's head. While Jimmy clutched his head and wailed in pain, Billy Ray took one last arching swing against a yellow pine, breaking the Daisy in two pieces.

Yelling "Home Run", Billy Ray Wilson ran victoriously toward the safety of First Street. His final action only increased Jimmy's agony, "You broke my gun, you broke my gun," he groaned between sobs.

Of course, the story Jimmy Simpkins told Big M when he arrived ten minutes later was slightly different. There was no mention of the Mickey Mantle baseball card or of Jimmy's inclination to abandon his post when Billy Ray charged him. As memory served him best, he stood his ground and after throwing several devastating punches was finally overwhelmed by Billy Ray's superior size. As best he could tell, he must have gotten knocked unconscious when Billy Ray hit him over the head with his air rifle.

To be fair, when Billy discussed the day's events with his chiropractor father, his memory proved to be selective as well. Forgotten were the dancing and wet pants or the crying and begging for mercy, and most certainly the attempted bribe. Instead, there was one against three—good versus evil. It was high noon and Billy Ray was Gary Cooper. All he had were his fists against three punks with air rifles. Sure he got hit with several BB shots as his mother listened in horror. But then, no pain, no gain. He knew somehow he had to get to the ring leader of the Second Street terrorists. It wasn't Jimmy Simpkins that he disarmed and beat over the head with the assailant's own weapon. No, it was Big M himself.

"Big M!" his little sister exclaimed in awe.

Of course, it was Big M. After that, the other two fled for their lives.

As evening drew near, Big M, Little M and Jimmy Simpkins said their goodbyes before turning their bicycles homeward.

"Billy Ray Wilson better watch out," Big M imparted to his fellow marauders, "Tomorrow will be payback time."

Of course, everyday was payback time for somebody as far as Big M was concerned. And Billy Ray said pretty much the same thing as he finished his version of the day's battle. Rising from the dinner table with his father giving him a "that's my boy" smile, his mother still looking horrified, and his little sister beaming with a pride that could only come from having a big brother who had whipped the notorious Big M, Billy Ray's final words were: "All I can say is Big M and his two sidekicks better watch out if they cross my path again."

It should be noted that although both boys said pretty much the same thing, there was a certain distinction regarding the meaning of their comments.

Big M meant what he said and Billy Ray Wilson did not.

Discussion Questions

1. How do children reflect the values of their parents, culture and neighborhood?
2. In William Golding's classic novel, "Lord of the Flies," he examines how a group of young boys who find themselves alone on an island can end up resorting to intimidation and violence. How does this story reflect those qualities?
3. What impact can things like bicycles and BB guns have on young boys' attitudes and behavior?
4. Some people feel they are in a more preferred class and status than others—working class, wealthy class, etc. What are some ways this story reflect class bias and resentment?

2

SARAH SALVATION

Like a cockroach seduced by a bug light, Francis Quiet Moon shuffled to the edge of an unmarked street corner and stared into the flickering pulse of a streetlamp. A frayed, mustard-yellow knit cap nearly swallowed his head and his tired frame ached from behind the stained, gas-station-attendant's shirt he was wearing. A tattered American flag was tied around his waist—some of the stars had been filled in by different colored crayons, courtesy of his two sons who lived with their mother. His feet were decorated by red and green bowling shoes two sizes too big.

With the remains of his existence stuffed into his Vietnam issue duffel bag, Francis had hitchhiked, but mostly walked, his way through the last 100 miles of hill country, traveling the cracked back of a stubborn two-lane that twisted and curled around the Carolina mountains like a serpent. When he walked, the dog tags around his neck clinked like the teeth of a chattering skull. The sound made Francis uncomfortable and he thought about how something as insignificant as two pieces of metal hitting each other could bring back so many bad memories—before and after the war. At one time, Francis had built wind chimes in the cramped basement of the garage apartment he rented with his wife. He couldn't stand the sound of them anymore. They made his head hurt and his heart ache. At night, he would try to force those memories away, make them set with the sun. But every morning they would rise again, burning into his back as he walked, never letting him forget.

He had been losing his grip on sobriety since dawn and had to concentrate just to keep his balance. Francis cringed as the sounds of a honky-tonk version of Sinatra's "My Way" crackled from a nearby convenience store. Picking at the loose threads of his toboggan, he retrieved a near-empty bottle of "Cisco" brand liquor from beneath the remnants of Old Glory. He would often, as he described it, "Disco with Cisco," referring to the bottle as his faithful friend, "Fran-Cisco." The bottle spilled the truth to Francis in a numbing language he could understand. It never cheated on him, never lied to him, or blamed him for a failed marriage. It never confronted him with his past or promised him a future. Although "Fran-Cisco" had been his best friend since a rehab stint after the war, the relationship was stormy. But at least it was his. At least, he could depend on it.

He closed his eyes, took two quick, punishing gulps and gritted his teeth. Peeling open his left eye to squint, Francis could barely make out the lettering of a neon-crimson sign that spelled *Crystal Grape Diner.* Lured by the aroma of food, he slowly gathered up his road-weary carcass and stumbled across the intersection.

Francis stepped inside the diner and slid into a tattered, lime green booth patched by gray duct tape. Sounds from a Crosby, Stills, Nash & Young forty-five wafted from an elaborate jukebox squatting in a smoky corner of the diner like some kind of mechanized Sumo wrestler. Francis' hollow eyes scanned the surroundings for signs of activity while his fingers fumbled with a half-empty pack of Marlboro Lights. He thought about how he used to never smoke. His wife hated it.

Settling on a smoke that seemed dry enough to ignite, Francis lit up. Inhaling deeply, he ran his hands through his hair and observed the other examples of aimless humanity around him. An elderly man in a wheelchair, hooked up to an oxygen tank and dressed in a threadbare tuxedo, played solitaire at one booth. He would light a fresh cigarette every few minutes and let it burn on the edge of an ashtray; never smoking it, just letting it burn.

Francis' eyes followed a succession of Elvis paintings to the other side of the room where a small ruckus was erupting. He extinguished his cigarette on a small tin ashtray and peered through the smoke. A young woman, dressed in a checkered apron and combat boots, was juggling steak sauce bottles, three and four at a time to the cackling delight of four elderly, drunken La-Z-Boy warriors. After finishing her performance, the waitress took a modest bow, laid the party's check on the table and disappeared into the kitchen.

The old men applauded her and were still snorting with laughter as they began to eat their food.

Francis was about to light up another Marlboro when he caught the scent of a pleasant fragrance. A smudged menu slid gently across his knuckles as he lit the cigarette and looked up. Smiling lips asked to take his order. Francis looked above the lips, into eyes warm and dark—shimmering as if fireflies were trapped inside. The tag artfully stitched onto her shirt said "Sarah." She glanced at his duffel bag while fumbling in her pocket for a pen.

"Where ya headed?" she inquired.

"Home," Francis replied in a raspy voice brought on by the late autumn cold.

"Where's home?"

"Don't know yet," he answered, grinning and rubbing his head.

She smiled to herself and nodded while pulling out her pad and pencil to take his order.

"What are your specials tonight?" Francis mumbled.

"Honey, everything I make is special."

Francis drew deeply from his cigarette and grinned so wide his face hurt.

"Well, how about a special cheeseburger and some special fries?"

The woman chuckled while taking down his order.

"You're pretty good with those bottles," he added, putting out another cigarette.

"Oh, yeah," she said, laughing. "Well, the way I see it, everybody has a special talent and I guess juggling Heinz 57 bottles for the enjoyment of my red-eyed regulars is mine."

"Aren't you afraid of dropping one of those bottles on someone's head or something?" Francis inquired, rubbing his chapped nose. "You know, with all the lawsuits these days, and what not?"

She smiled and took the menu from his trembling fingers.

"Sometimes you gotta do something risky to make sure you're still alive," she whispered. "Something special, coming up."

She smiled at Francis and clomped off in her combat boots toward the kitchen.

Francis laughed to himself and shook his head in amazement. Taking a last draw from his cigarette, he looked out the window and watched a couple of young boys in the shadows across the street, kicking an old cardboard box around. He wondered what their names were. His head began to hurt.

He wondered what his own boys were doing, what they had for dinner, what they dreamed about. Francis wondered if they wondered about him. Lighting another cigarette, he thought about how his boys used to always be in his dreams. These visions were like mirrors stitched on his heart, reflecting a time long since past. The last dream he had was like something out of a movie. It involved a big spread of blue sky that looked like a movie screen in the middle of a dark space. One arm, with the palm open, came in from one side of the sky and another arm, a boy's, came reaching across from the other side of the sky. Both arms were wrapped in barbed wire and reached for each other. That was all Francis could remember. He didn't know what it meant and hesitated to think about it too much, but it haunted him.

* * *

Francis finished his meal, laid a few wrinkled bills on the table, and hauled himself and his bag back out into the cold. A crushed velvet night covered him and he stared into its million eyes—"God's peepholes," as his grandmother once called them. The frigid night air filled his lungs and he turned toward the *Crystal Grape,* lighting another cigarette.

The half-lit neon sign whirred and popped, making the little shambled building stand out in the shadows like a kind of beacon. A faded "Help Wanted" sign rattled against a storm window.

"Sometimes you have to do something risky to make sure you're still alive." Sarah's words rolled around in what was left of Francis' pinball mind. He stood in the quiet moonlight and looked down the desolate stretch of road that brought him to this place. Putting out his cigarette, Francis turned his head and walked back inside.

Discussion Questions

1. War affects people in different ways. As a Vietnam veteran and a Native American, what are some of the internal and external conflicts Francis Quiet Moon faces? How do you think you would feel as a Native American and Vietnam veteran?

2. Although we don't know the reasons, Francis is divorced and misses his two sons who he hasn't seen for a long time. His drinking problem may be the result or in some measure the cause of his family's breakup. Could his war experiences also contribute to his family and drinking difficulties? How does alcoholism in general affect anyone's family?

3. What does Sarah, the waitress, represent to Francis and the other customers at the Crystal Grape? How does she express compassion and care to them?

4. In a more existential sense, what does the "Help Wanted" sign offer Francis?

3

BLACK AND BLUE

Mike buckled the heavy utility belt, stealing a look in the bathroom mirror. He couldn't help it. He was still secretly thrilled at the sight of himself in the police uniform. Although he'd admit it to no one, perhaps not even to himself, he couldn't resist surreptitious looks in store windows and side mirrors—anywhere his image in the uniform appeared as he went about business in his first days as a police officer. He looked good! Tall and handsome, he looked like a recruiting poster for law enforcement. And he would have posed for one. He believed in the motto, "To Serve and Protect" as much as he believed in anything. Raised on a diet of television cop shows, he had never wanted to be anything else. Cops were the modern day sheriffs or marshals; the closest one could get to being a hero in real life. He joined the Law Enforcement Explorers club in junior high and majored in criminal justice in college. And now here he was, hired, trained and in glorious uniform.

"Mike, honey, are you going to be late tonight," his girlfriend, Sally, asked. She stuck her head in the bedroom door, yawning while bringing in his cup of coffee.

"Don't think so. If I am, I'll call."

He gulped the coffee down as he finished dressing and kissed her as he left the apartment.

This is what it's like to be a grown up ... the silly thought flashed through his mind as he headed to work.

It had been only a week since he had graduated from the academy and hit the street. His F.T.O. (Field Training Officer) was a good guy. Jack Henderson was a 15-year veteran of the department. He was the proverbial gruff cop; didn't say more than 10 words to Mike the first morning and by lunch Mike was beginning to wonder how he had managed to already piss him off. Turned out Henderson was always like that when he met someone. Took his own sweet time checking a person out and seeing how they acted before he wasted his breath. After Mike had handled a few calls and didn't screw up too bad, Henderson deigned to make a few suggestions, like get the cars off the street in minor fender benders so that the backed up traffic wouldn't cuss him out as they slowly inched by. He also finally told Mike to stop rushing into the call before taking a minute to check out the situation.

As the days went by, Mike lost the little quiver in his voice that he hoped no one noticed and he learned how to get out of the squad car quickly without getting tangled up in his seatbelt. He quickly picked up the little things that "boots" (new recruits) had to learn, like how to keep it short when on the radio, how to work the radio, computer and drive all at the same time, and how to take control of a situation even though he didn't know what the hell was going on. He even managed to not blush when women came on to him in a traffic stop, despite Henderson's smirking countenance in the background.

* * *

Mike balanced his coffee and a bagel on his clipboard as he lowered himself into his seat. He acknowledged the officers around him with nods and hellos.

"Alright, listen up guys."

Lt. Wilcox shuffled papers and someone offered an earsplitting whistle that cut through the morning chatter, hushing the room as the dayshift settled in for the morning roll call. His announcements were routine—beat assignments, active B.O.L.O.'s (be on the lookout for's), a procedural change in how sick leave was accumulated and a short report of greater gang activity in the south sector. A normal day.

"One last thing, someone backed into Danforth's car yesterday in the back lot."

Hoots of laughter erupted from the back row as the Captain scowled at the room.

"The person didn't leave a note or acknowledge the accident. If anyone knows anything about this, they better come forward."

He looked at the officers. The back lot was for the officers' private vehicles and no one could enter except another officer. That meant that an officer had to be the one who committed the misdemeanor. The laughter that rippled through the room had a malicious edge. Danforth was not well liked. He was rigid and without a sense of humor. A year earlier, he had stopped a well-respected Sergeant for drunken driving. The cop was right at the legal limit and Danforth brought him in for booking. The arrest of a fellow officer, especially one as well liked as the Sergeant, broke the unwritten rule of the department that such a transgression would be dealt with informally by taking the officer home. As long as no one had been hurt and there was only one vehicle involved, the general feeling was that everyone deserved a break once in awhile. Trouble was, Danforth didn't know or didn't care to know how to give one.

The casual disdain shown to Danforth hardened into hostility and he endured six months of "incidents." Only after Danforth made noises that he was going to sue the department, and the administration made it clear they were serious in their threats to fully investigate and charge any offending officer, did the campaign of slashed tires, threats and dirty tricks slow to a trickle. This may have been an innocent accident or, then again, maybe it wasn't.

* * *

"Ma'am, if you'll just sit down over here. MA'AM, please sit down!" Mike's patience snapped. They had caught the call of a disturbance and arrived to find a family in the middle of a brawl. Mom was screaming at Dad, Dad was yelling at Son and Son was yelling at them both. Neighbors were gathering and, given that no love was lost between the residents and cops, it threatened to turn into a real problem. Mike was trying to de-escalate, as he'd learned in the academy, by separating the combatants and getting them to sit down. Angry people erupt into violence, but sitting down tends to lower the emotional level as well as thwart any physical acts they might think of. However, what wasn't fully clear to him until now was that angry people don't want to sit down. And, despite the communication course he'd been through, it was damn hard to keep your voice level and calm when an angry woman's spit is hitting you in the face and she is yelling and pushing and shoving her way past you into an assault charge.

"I SAID SIT DOWN!" He grabbed the big woman's shoulders and forced her backward down onto the couch where she landed with an expelled whoosh, her rolls of fat rippling. Although she outweighed Mike by probably 60 pounds, he had the benefit of surprise. She looked up at him, momentarily distracted from her boozy attack on her husband, a "good-for-nothing louse, who never cared about them and always hated their son who was the best thing that ever happened in her life and he better not forget it."

Henderson, in the meantime, was between Dad and Son. Son was doing a little dance back and forth behind the officer, taunting and baiting his father as one might an enraged bear. Drunkenly swaying back and forth trying to get past Henderson, Dad's unfocused eyes were mere slits. Indeed, he brought to mind the image of a bear. It was clear why most people run from bears.

Henderson was struggling to keep them apart and the son didn't help because he continued to excite the man by yelling endearments like "You're a worthless piece of shit, Dad, you know that? You don't scare me! You can hit me all you want, you always have, but you don't scare me. I'm going to kick your ass and see how you like it!"

Of course the comic-tragedy could take a serious turn. The young man was directly behind Henderson making him vulnerable to who knew what and he couldn't turn his back on the father either. Mike would have been over there to help in a heartbeat except that the woman was obviously just as aggressive as either of them and could easily hurt someone or get hurt if things turned violent. Even now she was straining to push herself off the sofa and rejoin the melee. To make matters worse, crowds of neighbors had come to watch and were clustered on the front porch peering in the door and windows.

Into the breach the second squad car arrived like the cavalry. Sirens wailing, it pulled up and two officers jumped out, scattering the crowd with epithets and commands to get off the porch and clear the area. Barreling into the room, they instantly sized up the situation and one took the young man's arm and hustled him out the front door and the other moved to help Henderson. Each took an arm and "escorted" the giant man into the bedroom where they forced him down on the bed.

"What are they doing to him? Don't hurt my husband you bastards! Leave him alone!"

The woman evidently had forgotten that only a moment before she had wanted him dead. Mike, with great difficulty, pushed her back down and told her if she didn't sit still he'd arrest her for assaulting a police officer. She sputtered and swore, but when no screams of tortured agony were heard from the bedroom, she evidently decided that maybe her husband wasn't being beaten after all.

Curt Lewis, the officer who had taken the son outside had evidently convinced him that those who run away live to fight another day (or get yet another $50 from Mom, which was what he really wanted). Dad had deflated like a burst balloon after the target of his anger had been removed from his sight and sat on the edge of the bed with his head in his hands. Perhaps he was wondering how life had degenerated into this series of alcohol-fueled rages, or maybe he was just starting to feel the incipient hangover. In any event, the drama was over.

Later they met Lewis and his partner Harry Ansley for coffee. Mike took their good-natured ribbing in stride and had to admit that he must have looked pretty silly practicing "academy-speak" in real life.

"Now Ma'am, please have a seat," Henderson mimicked in a falsetto voice, hamming it up and exaggerating Mike's delivery in his recital of the events that led up to the time the others arrived.

"Damn, Mike, if she had a knife were you going to ask her to pretty please give it to you?" Ansley laughed.

He was 35 with dark curly hair and brown eyes that (if rumors were to be believed) several women besides his wife found very attractive. His partner, Lewis, was as fair as Harry was dark. Frick and Frack they were called in jest. They had been partners for years, fishing and bowling together on their days off. They and their wives formed a foursome that often threw parties. Sometimes a dozen or more officers and their families would congregate in Ansley's backyard, bringing food and helping him grill the burgers and hotdogs to feed everyone. It was easier to socialize with other cops because you didn't have to put up with the snide jokes about needing to hide the drugs, or the prurient interest of others over whether you'd seen any dead bodies, or the inevitable jerk in the group who pontificated about how all cops were racist louts who liked nothing better than to find someone to beat up. With other cops, you could just be yourself and not be on the defensive.

Mike liked the two. He didn't even mind their kidding. It felt like he belonged.

"Can you believe that thing about Danforth's car?" Ansley shifted the conversation away from Mike.

"Yeah, right, like anyone would rat out somebody for Danforth," Lewis agreed, shaking his head. "If I'd have done it, I'd have made sure it wasn't just his back end that was dented."

"Danforth deserves what he gets," Ansley stated, standing up and finished his last swig of coffee. "If he thinks he's so perfect, the self righteous little prick should have been a priest instead of a cop."

"Why, does he like little boys?" Henderson deadpanned. They all laughed as they left the diner together.

* * *

"Officer Taylor, isn't it?"

Mike was returning the squad car to the police lot while Henderson finished filing their reports. The speaker was Danforth and he was standing there expectantly as Mike emerged from the car.

"Yeah, and you're Steve Danforth, right?"

Mike had heard all the stories, but tried to keep an open mind. He knew that the academy instructors would have agreed that Danforth did the right thing—publicly at least. But some things weren't for public consumption and he had a hard time understanding how Danforth could have arrested a fellow cop. He shook hands with Danforth who was evidently going to use the unit on his next shift.

"You know regulations say that you need to fill up the unit for the next shift," Danforth commented as he leaned into the car and spied the gas gauge.

"Oh, yeah, I forgot, but hey, it's got almost three quarters. We were stuck in court most of the afternoon."

"It doesn't matter, the point is that the next rotation doesn't have time to fill up," he emerged from the car holding some candy wrappers. "And I'd appreciate it if you guys would pick up your trash. Every night I have to clean out candy wrappers and burger sacks."

He shoved the wrappers at Mike.

"You might read the regs again concerning how squad cars are to be checked out and checked in. I'm going to note in my report the gas gauge was not on full."

Sheeeyat. Mike thought. What an asshole. No wonder he's got a reputation. He told Henderson about the incident later over a beer.

"The trouble with that guy is that he doesn't know what's important," Henderson said, waving the bartender over for refills.

"If an officer was really dirty, like using drugs or diddling little girls, of course you'd have to turn him over. But he pays as much attention to a broken rule as a homicide and treats them the same. All of us make mistakes. We're human and this is a tough job. If you can't depend on each other to cover for you on some things, who the hell can you trust?"

It was the longest speech he had ever heard coming from his F.T.O. and it made a lot of sense. He knew that he had already felt the blessed relief of being able to depend on other officers to come to his assistance and knew that he could trust Henderson with his very life. That's just the way it was. Henderson was a good F.T.O. He never let Mike get into too much trouble, but he never demeaned him in front of the public. If he needed to tell Mike he was screwing up, he acted like they needed to get something in the unit and set him straight in the privacy of the squad car. He trusted Henderson's judgment and knew that he was right.

* * *

"So what did you learn at that college of yours that you've actually used on the street?"

Henderson was driving while Mike was finishing his lunch. They had exhausted the weather, the playoffs, and now Henderson was going to go into the "forget all that crap" speech that he'd already heard from others. Mike finished his burger and wadded the paper into the bag.

"Well …"

BEEP. BEEP. BEEP.

The computerized tone came from the radio and Mike and Henderson instantly went on alert.

"We have officers in trouble. 600 Block of Whitney. Code 3."

The calm tone of the dispatcher was in direct contrast to the effect the announcement had on all the squad cars in the vicinity. Henderson immediately flipped on the siren and floored the accelerator. There was no need to inform dispatch that they were en route. It was understood that all units in the area would respond.

Henderson was navigating a residential street at close to 55 M.P.H., weaving his way around those who pulled their cars aside and adding his horn to the siren for the jerks that didn't seem to remember that sirens meant to pull over. Several times as they sped through an intersection oncoming cars almost broadsided them and the drivers screeched to a stop seconds before they hit. Mike caught glimpses of their horrified expressions as the squad car miraculously avoided catastrophe.

They were getting closer. Mike could hear a stereo siren effect as other units approached from different directions. His adrenaline pumping, Mike was thinking, "this is it, this is it." It was the first Code 3 that he'd run since he hit the streets. He didn't know if he was more scared than excited or the other way around.

Ahead of them was Frick and Frack's squad car halfway pulled up on the sidewalk. Whitney Street was on the "wrong side" of town. Dotted with boarded up businesses and derelict houses, it was a haven for prostitutes plying their trade on the corners, and crack dealers who set up house in abandoned buildings, playing hopscotch with the raid teams. Mike saw that the few residents up and down the block were coming out to find out what was going on.

As they screeched to a stop, he saw Ansley on top of a prostrate young black guy, swinging his baton at the guy's head. Over and over the baton came down thudding sickeningly at flesh and bone. The suspect was on his stomach with his hands over his head in a futile attempt to protect himself from the blows. Lewis had another guy bent over the unit with his hands behind his back. He was just snapping the handcuffs as Henderson and Mike came running. Lewis and Henderson both reached Ansley at the same time and pulled him off the prone suspect as Mike knelt down and cuffed him.

Ansley was a mess. His ear was bleeding profusely and his shirt was ripped from the shoulder down the front. He struggled against the restraining arms of Henderson and Lewis with a glazed, wild look—his eyes still focused on the target of his assault.

"Sonofabitch bit me," he sputtered. "Sonofabitch bit me—the little shit bit me, tried to take my gun...."

They pushed and pulled him away from the guy over to the squad car where they all struggled to catch their breath. Others had already arrived. Mike had been only dimly aware of the other units pulling up but in a few seconds the area had become a sea of blue uniforms. Mike let himself be pushed aside by others who roughly examined the prone figure, called for an ambulance, kept the crowd from approaching and hustled the other suspect into a squad car which went screaming away, sirens still blaring. The ambulance's arrival was blessedly swift and in short order all that was left at the scene was a slowly spreading pool of blood where the man's head had been.

The Sergeant and Lieutenant arrived, and then the Deputy Chief, indicating the seriousness of the situation. There had always been strained relations between the minority community and the police department and this was not going to help. It bore all the markings of a major media circus. Already the camera crews were setting up and the reporters were interviewing citizens. Some were yelling for a statement from the brass across the hastily set up barriers.

Lieutenant Wilcox ordered all involved officers to go to the station immediately and fill out their reports. Mike had been standing aside, somewhat dazed by all the activity. He felt someone looking at him and while glancing around, connected with the penetrating gray eyes of Lieutenant Wilcox. Wilcox's slight nod indicated he hadn't imagined the scrutiny.

"Let's go."

Henderson touched Mike's shoulder and they retrieved their squad car. Other units would stay and disperse the crowd and the crime scene guys were already starting to take their pictures and do their measurements and collect evidence. Before he started the car, Henderson stared intently at two guys in plainclothes who had gotten out of an unmarked unit.

"Bloodsuckers," Henderson muttered under his breath.

The ride to the station was unnaturally quiet. Henderson, Mike noted, was white under his tan, and seemed uncharacteristically shaken.

"It's going to turn to shit," Henderson finally uttered his pronouncement as they pulled into a spot behind the stationhouse. "Mike, this is going to turn to shit, you got to be ready. Ansley's going to be eaten alive by the sharks, sure as shit. Those two guys at the scene were Internal Affairs. We need to get it straight what happened."

Mike knew that in an incident like this one, procedures called for each officer involved to write his own report. What wasn't supposed to happen was officers talking to each other and agreeing on a version that would then be gospel. Of course that's usually exactly what did happen. He knew what he had seen. Ansley was out of control and swung that baton over and over again as they were pulling up. He was using unlawful, excessive force. That's what Mike saw. Didn't he?

They saw Lewis in the squad room. Ansley was heading down the hallway. He looked awful. Paramedics had taped his ear but the blood was seeping through the bandage. Bruises were emerging around his eye and his torn shirt hung in shreds.

"Thanks." Ansley stared meaningfully at Henderson who gruffly cuffed him on the shoulder.

"I.A." Ansley jabbed his thumb upwards as he glumly waited for the elevator.

There Ansley would wait for his Police Association lawyer and give his statement. They silently watched him as the elevator closed and he was carried upstairs to his fate. They went back to find Lewis.

"Alright. Let's get this shit over with. The perp was offering resistance, you were subduing. End of story." Henderson's tone indicated that he wasn't asking, he was stating a fact.

"We had a B.O.L.O. on a black guy with a hooded sweatshirt. Pulled up and they started giving us a line of b.s. One was a real smartass, got in our face, asking us where the hell was our probable cause, and all that shit. He started pushing Harry and next thing happens is they're in the middle of it. My guy starts to run; I'm wrestling with him ..." Lewis' words tumbled out.

"Are your reports ready?" the Lieutenant's booming voice cut off Lewis' rush of words.

"No sir," They all mumbled like schoolboys, aware they shouldn't even be speaking to each other.

"Well I want them on my desk in 10 minutes. Get to it!"

He stared at them until they each broke away and went to a computer terminal. Mike looked up to see Danforth, Smith and Jackson enter. Silently, each went to a terminal. With a jolt, Mike realized that Danforth had been one of the officers who arrived seconds after he and Henderson had. As he sat at the computer screen he pondered the implication of the situation. Their reports would be forwarded to Internal Affairs. Any inconsistencies would mean that they would all be pulled in for heavy questioning by I.A. Investigators.

Steeling himself, he began typing. "Officer Henderson and I responded to Code 401. We arrived on the scene and observed Officer Lewis cuffing Suspect A by the patrol car. Officer Ansley was subduing Suspect B on the sidewalk. We arrived and provided assistance to Officer Ansley. I handcuffed Suspect B...." He doggedly typed on, completed his report and, without looking at Henderson or the others left the stationhouse. They all had been relieved of duty for the rest of the day.

* * *

Mike felt the caffeine eating at his stomach lining making him nauseous. He hadn't slept last night. At 4:00 a.m., he made a pot of coffee. Drinking cup after cup at the kitchen table, he waited for 8 a.m. to roll around so he could go in and get it over with. Sally had tried to talk to him, but he didn't know how to explain the situation to her. She wouldn't understand. She couldn't understand.

Now he was sitting in the hallway outside Lt. Wilcox's office waiting his turn. He knew that Danforth's report conflicted with the others. He knew that the witnesses reported seeing an officer beating a helpless young man who was lying on the street trying to stop the blows by covering his head. He knew the guy was in the hospital with several head fractures and 8 broken fingers. He knew that the guy turned out to be a college kid who had a smart mouth

and a temper, but no record. He knew all these things. He just
didn't know what he was going to tell the Lieutenant.

Discussion Questions

1. What do you suppose are Danforth's motivations for not covering
   for other officers? What do you think his report will be?
2. What are the motivations of Henderson? Why would he tell
   the other officers what to write on their report?
3. What might happen to Ansley?
4. What are the choices open to Mike and what are the
   consequences of each choice?
5. What should he do when asked whether or not Ansley kept
   hitting after the suspect offered no more resistance?

4

A DIFFICULT CHOICE

"But I don't know why you won't just consider it," Sam argued as Susan packed the sandwich in Aaron's lunch box. The first grader, sensing the tension in the room, looked at his parents uneasily as he ate his cheerios.

"We've talked about this Sam. You knew how much I wanted to be a cop. I don't want to work for your Dad. I don't want to wear a dress every day and sit in an office. I want to do what I'm doing."

"But it's dangerous! I think you should be thinking of your son. Of me! What could happen …"

Susan held up her hand in warning with a nod toward Aaron who now looked at them with concern. It was a rule they had established that they didn't talk about Susan's job in front of Aaron, not wanting the young boy to worry about his mother.

She glared at Sam and he glared back, tossing the rest of his coffee down the sink. He pulled the dishwasher door open and angrily threw the cup in the top rack, slamming the dishwasher shut again. There was an uneasy silence in the kitchen as the trio finished the morning routine. Susan kissed Aaron goodbye as Sam backed the car out of the garage. She couldn't take him to school because she was pulling the graveyard shift and her "day" was just ending. She would close the blackout curtains and try and sleep during the day amidst the neighborhood lawn-mowing, trucks speeding, and toddlers screaming from the daycare next door. Aaron would get picked up from school by Sam's mother and arrive home just as she was getting up. She would have a few precious hours with him before heading down to the station.

The argument with Sam this morning was an old one, starting when they made their plans for the wedding. Susan had discussed her desire to apply for a police officer job and, at first, he had laughed it off, thinking she wasn't serious. She insisted though that her goal was to be a police officer. But then she got pregnant with Aaron. They rushed the wedding a bit and Susan stayed home with her baby as Sam's job at his family's grocery store chain amply provided for their needs. She did an associate's degree online and kept busy with other activities, but once Aaron began school, the dormant idea of applying to be a cop took hold again and last year she did it. She sailed through the application process and the academy and had now been on the street for a little over a year. She usually loved the job—she was energized by the variety of each day, and enjoyed solving people's problems, comforting them when they were upset or scared. She didn't even mind the mouthy teenagers or young adults who felt they had to act like a jerk toward any cop they came in contact with. Their "I don't have to do what you tell me to do" never pushed her buttons as it did some other officers. She grew up in a large family of seven siblings so verbal conflict was something she was comfortable with. Even-tempered and personable, she received positive evaluations from her FTOs for her calm and decisive approach to calls. She didn't even mind the public drunk calls although, truth be told, dealing with someone covered in vomit and piss wasn't on her favorites list. Still, she had a bit of sympathy for all kinds of people and knew that the worst, most pathetic drunk probably had some family member somewhere who might be worried about him or her. It helped her keep everything in perspective when she thought about the fact that this person she was rousting from a doorway or park bench was someone's father or uncle or brother or son.

Most of police work though, she told people, was being a "social worker with a gun." She had talked suicidals out of taking their own lives, convinced crazies that the voices in their head were not aliens (at least for the short time it took to get them an emergency detainment so that psychologists could get them the meds they needed to quiet the voices), and counseled dysfunctional parents as to what their duties were regarding their own children; more specifically, that they couldn't let their three-year-old wander up and down the street dressed in nothing but a dirty pair of underpants while they drank and partied inside. One of the most memorable nights of her short career was a call to a run-down apartment building. Dispatch had little information other than a family disturbance, but once she was there at the apartment, a crying mother led her to a bedroom where a distraught young boy cowered on the floor in a corner, holding a knife to his own throat, screaming and crying that he was going to kill himself. Susan "took a knee" meaning that she got down to his level; not necessarily protocol or the smartest thing to do with a weapon involved, but she instinctively knew that a show of force may push the boy over the edge. She talked softly to him, saying, "My name is Susan. What's your name?"

"Joseph. You can't stop me! I'm going to do it!"

"OK Joseph. Let's just slow down for a minute, ok? I'm not going to come closer, but you need to put down the knife before we can talk, would you just do that for me if I promise not to come any closer?"

The boy looked at her suspiciously but lowered the knife. With a bit more coaxing, he placed the knife on the floor by his side. Still not ideal, but Susan felt that the situation was secure enough so she could take the time to talk to him and see if she could find out what the problem was. She eventually got his story. He had been hassled and bullied on the way to school every day and on that particular day the little psychopaths who tortured him pulled down his pants, held him down, and attempted to sodomize him with a stick. Luckily, they were interrupted in their sadism by a motorist who had been driving by and saw the assault. As was typical in this neighborhood, Joseph didn't tell anyone and never even considered reporting the crime to the police. He couldn't stand the thought of going back to school though and his solution was to end his suffering by ending his life. She finally convinced Joseph to push the knife over to her and he collapsed in large sobs, crying in Susan's arms as she radioed for an ambulance to come and take him to the local hospital. He wasn't physically injured, but every suicide call required an evaluation by the county medical unit. Afterwards she was shaky and amped up as she told Chuck was happened. Even though back-up officers were in the apartment dealing with Joseph's family while she was in the bedroom with the boy, she felt that she alone had averted a tragedy, and she was right. On the other hand, she didn't know what she could do about his long-term problem. Joseph and his parents were adamant that they would not pursue the case. "We have to live here!" Joseph's mother argued, explaining that formal action would make them pariahs in the neighborhood.

Susan did find out who the other boys were and paid them a visit in their homes, explaining to them and their parents that even if no formal charges would be filed, she was watching them and if anything ever happened to Joseph she would be back. They didn't look scared though. That, in a nutshell, was police work she mused. Every once in a while, the feeling that you were involved in life and death situations, but, most often, an overriding feeling of powerlessness over people and events that seemed unsolvable and never-ending.

* * *

"What's cooking, cookie?" The goofy smile on Chuck's face and silly greeting was his standard comment every night as they met each other in the hallway before the night watch commander's briefing. Patrolling separately, she and Chuck usually met for dinner halfway through their shift, or more accurately, breakfast, but cops on graveyard did maintain a semblance of normal routine in their dinner meal even if it occurred at 3:00 am. They had gone through the academy together and had each other's backs during the hazing that characterized the social world of the cohort where alpha-dogs jockeyed for position. Neither she nor Chuck tried to stand out, but they did in the sense that their scores were always the highest and instructors seemed to depend on them for demonstrations when needed.

"What's happening with you?" She smiled.

"Same old. Same old. Looking for love in all the wrong places." Chuck was on a perpetual search for the perfect woman, a creature Susan always told him did not exist.

Before she could respond, their commander's voice brought everyone in the room to attention. "There's been a shooting over on the east side. Gang related probably but news is sketchy. Second shift officers are still on the scene. Sector 2 and 3 officers will need to check out reserve vehicles and get over there to assist with traffic and crowd control. Sector 4 patrol will cover dispatched calls for 2 and 3 sectors except for the area around Third and Vine streets. Pay attention out there, things look like they are heating up between the Crips and the 4th Street Bandits. There may be some retaliation action tonight."

Susan race-walked to the garage to get her unit as did Chuck and the other two officers assigned to Sector 2 and 3. They knew that the sooner they got there, the better it was for those officers now on overtime who were controlling the scene while the medical examiner and crime scene guys did their jobs. Citizens didn't understand why bodies lay in the street while evidence was collected and became increasingly upset as the hours ticked by. The best thing they could do was keep the crowds as far away from the crime scene as possible—something difficult to do in a residential area. She knew that it was going to be a long night.

* * *

"Ma'am, you have to move on. There's nothing for you to do here."

Susan coaxed the distraught woman to let go of the yellow crime tape. The middle-aged woman had tried to rip it and push through to see the body that still lay in the street. The crowd was growing increasingly vocal toward police officers who tried to keep them away. The shooting victim was an eight-year-old girl. The child's mother was in the back of an ambulance where EMTs were giving her something to quiet her screaming. Despite the numbers of people on the street, as always, no one saw anything.

Susan heard the detectives speculate that the girl had been caught in a crossfire between a drive-by shooter and his target on the street. It happened too often.

"Why don't you cops do something?" yelled a young woman who was openly crying as she watched the young victim being lifted finally onto a stretcher to be taken to the morgue. "How many of our babies are going to die while you cops just drive around in your cars, treating us like dirt?"

Relations between the police department and this minority community were strained to say the least. A shooting of a black motorist last year raised tensions in an atmosphere that wasn't good to begin with and things just seemed to be getting worse. When Susan stopped anyone, there was an attitude that she was only stopping the person because he or she was black. Since it was a black neighborhood, it didn't take a rocket scientist to figure out that most of the drivers she stopped were going to be black. She dealt with their anger as best she could, reminding the driver of the stop sign, speeding, or lack of signaling. Many times, if they didn't argue with her and admitted what they did, she would give a warning instead.

She did understand how people might get the wrong idea about cops though. She was often dispatched to back-up another officer who had pulled someone over and then searched the vehicle after supposedly smelling marijuana. The driver would be sitting on the curb, softly swearing at the officers while the car was searched. Most often nothing was found or maybe a small baggie of pot—nothing Susan thought was in the category of serious crime and nothing that balanced out the antipathy she saw on the faces of the driver and residents who passed by glaring at the officers. All too often young black men were treated like criminals even if they weren't. Susan understood their anger at being treated like that, but she also understood the zeal of officers who wanted to get the gangbangers and bad guys off the streets so eight-year-old girls wouldn't be shot while they were playing outside on a warm summer night.

"Why don't y'all do something about these shootings!" The older man had been standing quietly watching and now addressed Susan.

"We do what we can, sir. It's difficult when there never seem to be any witnesses. If we don't know or can't prove who did it, what can we do?"

"Even when you know who did it, you don't do nuthin!" A young woman joined the conversation shaking her finger in Susan's face.

"What do you mean?"

"My grandpa was killed last year. Right down the block from here. We knew who did it. You guys did too. We told you where Roscoe was—he had ran off to Georgia after he killed my paw-paw. Now he's back, struttin his stuff, acting like he's such a big shot because nothin happened to him."

"Did you tell the detectives all that?" Susan couldn't believe that a case would not be cleared if they had witnesses who were willing to testify.

"Of course we did! They didn't want to know. My momma went down there every day to talk to that detective—Sawyer or something like that—and he couldn't care less. He told her he had 10 murders he was investigating and he didn't have time to chase someone down in Georgia. How do you expect us to trust you and tell you things, when we do and you don't do anything!"

Susan knew she was getting above her pay grade here, but she couldn't leave the conversation without getting the woman's name and the name of her grandfather. Not promising anything other than to check into the case, she hoped she didn't raise the woman's hopes up since she figured something was preventing the detectives from pursuing the case.

* * *

"Did you work that shooting over on Vine last night?" Sam asked her as she got ready to grab a few hours of sleep. It was Saturday morning and Sam was home today and would later take Aaron out to the park or someplace so the house would be quiet.

"Yeah. Horrible case—little girl." Susan didn't want to talk about it. The vision of the lifeless body was burned into her memory as was the pool of blood on the sidewalk when she was gone. Nothing was worse than a child-victim.

"There's been a lot of murders this year, haven't there? It seems like it's a lot more."

"Yeah, we're up by 50%. No one knows why. Maybe it's parolees coming out after being sent away in the 1990s. Gang activity is up."

"I worry about you Susan." Sam began the old argument again. "What would Aaron and I do without you?"

Susan couldn't get angry at that question. She just couldn't. She hugged Sam and kissed him instead of answering. She really had no answer and she knew that the question wasn't going to go away.

* * *

"Who are you again?" The detective moved the toothpick in his mouth and looked lazily at Susan who stood in the doorway of the detectives' bullpen. He leaned the office chair back and slowly looked her up and down, lingering on her chest. She felt less like an officer with a gun at her side than a call girl being considered for purchase.

She had tracked down Detective Sawyer who had the case of LeRoy Johnson, the grandfather who had been shot the year before.

"I'm Officer Susan Staples. Sector 4. I am trying to find out about the murder of LeRoy Johnson and where you are with the case."

"Where I am with the case?" The detective grinned a little as he looked to his fellow detectives to see what sort of audience he had. "And what's it to you *Officer* Staples?" placing a sarcastic emphasis on "officer" to make it clear how much lower her status was than his.

"I have been in contact with the granddaughter and she says that they told you Roscoe Hamilton did the shooting. I told her I would check into it."

Seeing that no-one else in the room was paying any attention to the exchange, Sawyer lost interest in Susan and abruptly brought his chair down to make contact on all four wheels, swiveling as he did so away from Susan.

"I don't recall the case and don't have time to chit-chat with you. Fuck off."

She was shocked that he dismissed her with such rudeness, and incensed.

"Excuse me, Detective Sawyer, but if you could just let me see the file of the investigation, I'll check it out myself."

"It's an ongoing case and you have no reason to see the file so get your ass back in your patrol car where you belong and leave the detecting to the detectives."

* * *

"He's a lazy SOB." Chuck commiserated with her during their evening meal as she told him about the encounter. "I've heard he's got the worst clearance rate in the precinct and no one can do anything because he's the brother-in-law of the chief of d's."

"Chuck, that doesn't make me feel any better, what do you suggest I do?" Susan asked.

"Forget about it. What difference does one murder make in this city? This Roscoe guy will probably get his eventually anyway."

"That's the point!" Susan argued. "We always complain about no one wanting to be a witness, but then when they do and nothing is done, what does that tell them? It's no wonder there are retaliatory shootings if they don't feel like we will follow through when they do tell us!"

Susan steamed all shift. She knew that the bureaucracy was such that she would get nowhere if she tried to go above Sawyer's head. She knew that her paygrade was too low to try and pursue the case herself—even if she bumped into Roscoe in the local diner, she couldn't do anything about it. If she ran into Chantel, LeRoy Johnson's granddaughter, on the street, she knew she could do nothing in the face of accusing looks and scornful "I told you so's." That night when Sam began again about the dangers of the job and how he didn't see how she could put the job ahead of her son's happiness, the doubt that had been a very tiny flame in her heart began to grow.

What was she doing anyway? She wasn't changing the world. She couldn't help Chantel. She couldn't help Joseph. She couldn't do much of anything except respond to dispatched calls—band-aids instead of cures. Should she say, "Enough!" and go get a nice 8 to 5 where she was home at night to make dinner and help with homework? Why not?

Discussion Questions

1. What's the ethical duty of a police officer in a case like Joseph where the family refuses to press charges?
2. Is there anything one can do in an organization when those above your rank don't seem to be doing their job?
3. What steps could be taken in this fictional city, or some of the real cities such as Chicago and Baltimore, where race relations are seemingly at an all-time low?
4. How can police departments encourage citizens to come forward and testify against fellow residents and neighbors who have broken the law? Is there danger in doing this?
5. How do police officers prevent burn-out when they feel powerless in their jobs?

5

ROSY

Before he decided he wanted to be a border agent, Chris didn't know Spanish at all. When it looked like he was going to be hired, he took a conversational course at the local community college and, upon entry he tested pretty high on the agency's aptitude test. That led to his placement in an immersion course.

Now here he was: pulling up to a small wooden shack in the border town of Juarez. The Mexican family was supposed to speak to him only in Spanish which worked out pretty well since they didn't know any English. He was supposed to figure out what they were saying and, according to plan, pick up the language quicker than sitting in a classroom. Great plan; but, like all great plans, the devil was in the implementation. He guessed he would be playing lots of charades.

"Buenos días. ¿Cómo era su viaje?"

"Uh, buenos días señor," Chris responded. "Muy bueno … buen. ¿Y tú?" Whoops, he had just asked the man how his journey was, Chris thought, probably not a particularly relevant question unless the guy had come home just before Chris arrived, which he doubted since the only vehicle in the driveway was an old donkey that grazed placidly in the straggling weeds that grew out of the dirt driveway. Now the wife came out smiling and bowing and saying something so fast that Chris gave up trying to understand so he just bowed and shook his head yes, and smiled as well, hoping that she wasn't asking him if he was a serial killer or something. This was not going to be easy.

"Gracias por compartir su hogar. Aquí está un símbolo de mi gratitud."

Chris recited the prepared speech that thanked him for his hospitality and offered Señor Hermosa a box containing fancy jellies, cheeses and nuts. He had decided that a bottle of whisky might be more to the man's liking, but not exactly appropriate coming from a representative of the U.S. government.

"Aquí está mi hija Rosy."

Señor Hermosa motioned for a young woman to come out of the doorway where she had been hovering.

"Estoy satisfecho satisfacerle Rosy."

Chris shook her hand and had to stop himself from grinning like an idiot. Rosy was about 20 and had black, shiny hair and a shy smile. If Chris had met Rosy in a bar, he'd have been asking her out; as it was, he realized that any thoughts along those lines would have to be strictly ignored. It wouldn't help his career at all if his supervisor received a complaint from Señor Hermosa that Chris was harassing his daughter.

Over the next several weeks Chris accompanied Señor Hermosa on his daily rounds to sell the trinkets that he and his wife made. He sold to the shops and vendors that targeted American tourists. On the streets of the small town, there were as many gringos as Mexicans—tanned Texans from Dallas, wrinkled Minnesotans who had traded in their homes for an RV that followed the sun, and heavyset Midwesterners whose trip to cowboy country included a mandatory jaunt across the border. Norteamericanos filled the sidewalks and bargained with vendors for pottery, leather and other trinkets they would bear home proudly, bragging about how well they bargained. Tourists crossed the border in search of cheap tequila, cheap merchandise and cheap sex.

Chris struggled to understand the rapid fire exchanges that went on between Señor Hermosa and the vendors; at first, he could only make out words here and there and picked up what was happening more by instinct and context than translation. Gradually, however, he understood whole exchanges and fairly quickly he was able to make rudimentary conversation.

A big incentive to his growing language skills was Rosy, the pretty girl that smiled at him the first day. He was drawn to her gentleness and shyness and found himself struggling to find something to say in Spanish. She actually spoke a few words of English that she had picked up serving tourists in a gift shop downtown. Initially, their conversation was simple.

"¿Cuál es su color preferido?"

"Mi color preferido es azul."

"¿Cuál es su día de fiesta preferido?"

"Mi día de fiesta preferido es Navidad."

Gradually, though, they spoke of their favorite music and eventually he was able to ask her more detailed questions as to what her plans were and did she have a boyfriend. As to the latter question, she did not, despite a couple young men from the town who pestered her for dates. Chris observed the exchanges between her and these men in the front yard as she came home from work, and often felt the urge to step in but his language skills were not sufficient to enter the conversation and, besides, Rosy looked like she was handling them herself anyway.

As to the first question, her answers provided a glimpse into a life very different from the one Chris had lived. Rosy had dropped out of school in the 11th grade to help her parents by working and earning money. She shyly expressed the desire to finish school one day and her "secret dream" was to design clothes, but she had no idea how to do that, nor did she have the time to do anything about it after a long day in the store and evenings at home helping with the chores. She sadly explained that her duty to her parents came before any individual plans she might have, and then she added that she would probably end up marrying a man like her father and continue to live the life of her parents, and her children would perhaps be able to do something different.

He didn't know what to say to that. Although Chris' family were not rich by any means, there was never a time in his life that he worried about his parents or felt that he had to help them economically. In fact, if he was completely honest, he'd have to admit that he was a little spoiled. He assumed it was their job to pay for college and when he decided to become a border agent instead of an accountant, as planned when he majored in business, it never occurred to him that they'd be anything but supportive. In fact, they offered to pay for his apartment for 6 months while he was in training so he'd have some place to come back to. He had, in fact, never actually known anyone who was so poor that they worried about paying the bills. While he could tell her to work for her dreams, it seemed to him that it was unrealistic since he saw first hand how hard she did work every day.

One night there was a festival in the small town and Chris asked Rosy, "Would you like to go dancing?"

She replied enthusiastically, "Amo el bailar!"

At the dance she taught him the steps to the traditional dance that everyone was doing and they laughed together at his clumsiness. He was amazed at how much fun he had at such a simple event and they walked back to the Hermosa home slowly, talking about the stars. As they approached the front door, Chris fought back an overwhelming desire to kiss Rosy. The shy smile as they said goodnight let Chris know that she knew what he was feeling.

All too soon, it was time to go. His Spanish had improved tremendously and he was anxious to continue his training at the federal training headquarters in Artesia, Texas, but he was very sorry to say goodbye to the Hermosas, and especially Rosy. Even with their language difficulties, he felt more comfortable with her than with any woman before. Over the past several weeks they had forged a bond that was warm and comfortable. He felt that she understood him—sometimes he didn't even need to say much and it was like she could read his thoughts. He was going to miss her smile and their conversations. As he said goodbye, he asked her if it would be ok to call her to help him practice his Spanish. Her eyes lit up and she replied enthusiastically that she would very much like that and so, their bi-weekly phone calls began.

Training was tough—it was a combination of physical and classroom training and the dry, barren landscape of west Texas provided no solace. The men and women who were chosen for border patrol came from a variety of backgrounds, many were ex-military, some had college degrees, but many did not. They came from all over the country, and there were a variety of motivations for their desire to be border patrol agents. Some saw a federal job as a guaranteed income for life without the worry of dot-com layoffs. Some had been municipal police officers and were looking for what they saw as a step-up in status and pay. Some saw the job as a form of domestic military service with "protecting the borders" of the country as their mission and patriotism their motivation.

Chris' frequent phone calls to Rosy did not go unnoticed. Even though he tried to call when no one was around, it didn't always work. His classmates soon realized that he was talking Spanish to a Mexican girl and he endured a range of ribbing from good-natured to barely veiled criticism.

"La Señoooooreeeeetttta, pooooor favoooor kiiisss mee!" wailed Jesse Carina, a loudmouth from New Jersey who was always giving Chris a hard time about his Texas upbringing.

"Shut up Jesse. We're just friends."

"Oh sure, Tex, you're on the phone all the time—just practicing Spanish, huh? Your little señorita would probably like nothing more than a gringo boyfriend. You better watch out or she will be asking you to look the other way while 12 of her relatives sneak across the border."

Chris was appalled by the innuendos and accusations that he was somehow being disloyal by talking to a Mexican. After all, as he complained to Sam, the one classmate he felt understood, it wasn't like we were in a war with Mexico.

"Good grief, it was the agency who put me down there with the family! I didn't ask to become friends with them!"

Sam explained that most of the talk was just showing off—nervous young men and women who wanted to appear tougher than they felt inside. But the comments made it very hard to remember what it was like to be sitting next to Rosy on a clear, dark night looking at the thousands of stars that were spread like diamonds across the sky.

The trainees often argued about what the best solution was for illegal border crossings. The most vocal argued that "shooting the bastards" was the only way to "teach them a lesson." All pretty much scoffed at the idea of a fence. That the idea was promoted by the ladder manufacturers was the running joke. What Chris came to realize though was that to be a border agent meant that you were instantly suspicious of anyone with brown skin. Chris could see it happening on the rare occasions when he went with his classmates to Carlsbad or someplace that actually could be called a town within driving distance of Artesia. The group would pass by a group of Latinos on the street and conversation would slow to a stop. A few of the loudmouths made motions of swimming as they continued down the sidewalk to the muffled sniggers of others.

* * *

Chris turned to the wall and cupped his hand around the phone to create a cocoon of privacy in the crowded dayroom.

"Está sí. The heat is unbearable ... El calor es unberable aunque funcionamos por la mañana temprana. No, I don't know when I'll call ... No, no sé cuándo puedo llamar otra vez. Maybe next week.... La semana quizá próxima alguna vez. Es justo que estamos tan ocupados."

Chris cut the conversation short. He had tests to study for and graduation was coming. Turned out he was being assigned to Laredo and Rosy thought that meant he could come and visit. She didn't understand.

* * *

Chris didn't think he would ever get used to the heat of south Texas even though he had been working out of the Laredo office for over a year. Heat rose from the desert sand in undulating waves. This was the type of heat that could kill. And had. Border patrol agents and local sheriffs routinely came upon parched bones or the bloated and stinking bodies of illegals that were left behind. The steady stream of desperate poor who traveled northward for the chance to make money left backpacks, clothing, body waste and dead relatives behind as they slowly made their way through the Texas scrubland to meeting places where they would be picked up by "coyotes," entrepreneurs who helped them for a fee, for the next stage of the journey. If they were not betrayed by ruthless "coyotes" who took their money and left them stranded in the desert; if they could escape the federales in Mexico who would demand payment or shoot them or both; if they could avoid the U.S. border agents who used increasingly sophisticated technology to track and capture them; and, if they survived the perilous journey and didn't succumb to starvation, heat, parasites or disease, they might earn the chance to beg for work. The meager wages that they were likely to make in the U.S. would still be a king's ransom compared to what they had to look forward to in the rural countryside of Honduras, Ecuador, Bolivia, Mexico or any other of the poor nations whose people were so desperate that a 1400 mile journey on foot was seen as a feasible alternative to a lifetime of economic despair.

Chris and his partner bumped and bounced over the dry, parched ground until they saw the lights of the deputy's jeep ahead. They pulled up and joined the deputy who was looking down at the body of a young woman. Her long journey was all too clearly written on her bleeding feet and parched lips. Exhaustion, heat, lack of water or all of the above had probably sapped her of energy and forced her to stay behind while her compadres moved on. Then she died under a lone mesquite tree, providing a stingy shade by its narrow shadow.

"That makes it an even dozen this year," the deputy announced as he turned away to speak into his radio.

"Damn idiots—why do they keep coming?"

Chris looked at John, his partner, who, after blurting out his question, turned away from the body and was stomping back to the jeep.

"I suppose they dream of a better life."

"Yea, well, they ought to dream at home. There's nothing for them up here."

He and John had heard all the arguments. They had had run-ins with the organized groups that had men from other states coming down to protect the borders by driving around in open jeeps and shooting their guns and mouths off in the border counties of Texas. They didn't approve of these tactics, although they were sympathetic with the frustration that created them. They knew ranchers that set out traps for the unwary, tired of them cutting fences and looting stock. However, they also knew ranchers who laid out water and supplies where the desperately tired and thirsty might find them and be saved from the fate of the dead girl. It seemed at times as if everyone was right and everyone was wrong.

He looked back at the young woman in the dirt … her black hair splayed across her face. He wondered what her name was and what her dreams were. He thought about another black haired girl whose dream was to be a fashion designer and hoped she was doing okay. He wondered how long she waited for his call that never came. He wondered if he would ever meet a girl that he felt as comfortable with as he did with Rosy.

Discussion Questions

1. Why did Chris stop seeing Rosy?
2. Why do people risk their life to come across the border illegally?
3. What is the solution to the illegal immigration issue?
4. Do you think Chris will call Rosy again? Why or why not?

6

AMNESIA OF THE HEART

"All these fru-fru snacks—sesame sticks, snow peas and pine nuts. How about some old-fashioned, all-American snacks? Have they passed a law against serving plain old salted peanuts?" Jack Hamilton said more to himself than anyone else as he sat nursing his second bourbon and water at the bar in the Holiday Inn just off the I-85 exit near Greenville.

The green, silk floor plants and artfully placed strands of white Christmas lights framed the "Generations" Bistro and Bar. The bartender positioned herself as far away as possible from Jack Hamilton, pretending to dry wine glasses that were already dry. She had seen his kind before—retired, lonely men who felt entitled to rerun their Nick-at-Night life stories for the price of several bourbons. The Christmas season brought them out in full force. Separated from her husband after one year of marriage and facing a psychology final in the morning was enough stress for Sylvia. She would keep him supplied with bourbon and "fru-fru" snacks as he put it, but nothing else.

A cold rush of December burst into the tiny bar as a middle-aged, heavy-set man made his way to the counter and removed his parka.

"How 'bout a Bud Lite, Ma'am?"

"Coming right up," Sylvia replied as she reached into the cooler. "You want some party mix?"

"Yeah, sure. Why not?"

The sound of dulcimer inspired Christmas music wafted into the bar from the restaurant. Jack turned toward the stranger. "How's the traffic?"

"Busy."

The two men drank in silence, serenaded by dulcimers and the sounds of interstate traffic as Sylvia hid behind a newspaper.

Jack turned again to the stranger.

"Let me buy you a drink."

"Sure, why not," the man answered, extending his hand in appreciation. "Thanks."

"How bout a Bud Lite for my friend and another Jimmy Beam and water for me, Missy?"

"Coming right up. Would you like some more 'fru-fru'—I mean party mix?" Sylvia offered, her face turning slightly crimson.

Jack's brow crinkled slightly in amusement. "Yeah. And you had it right the first time. Give us another helping of 'fru-fru.'"

The two men tipped their glasses to each other and continued drinking while Sylvia placed their glasses in the dishwasher, grateful that the new customer had taken the pressure off her for conversation. From dulcimers to Zamfir's pan flute, the Christmas music continued to make its way from the restaurant in muted and muffled tones.

"Where you headed?" Jack inquired as he searched his dish for an elusive peanut.

"I'm going south for Christmas. Down to 'Hotlanta.' How about you?"

"Guess I'll stay around here. Got a condo not too far from here."

The stranger seemed to be warming up to his libation benefactor much to the relief of Sylvia.

"Don't much like to be alone at Christmas. Going to my brother's and his family. Me and my wife split up last year. Been married ten years when she up and ran off with the plumber. Always thought jokes about wives and plumbers were pretty funny 'til my wife ran off with one."

"Sorry to hear about that," Jack replied, taking a long pull from his bourbon and water.

"Yeah, me too. Whole thing caught me by surprise. My job took me on the road a lot. Every time I came home, there'd be another plumbing problem that needed fixin'. Never suspected a thing. The house was two years old. That's what we always worked toward— to have a new house of our own. That's what I wanted—a new house. I got the house and the plumber got my wife. Guess I got the best damn plumbing in my neighborhood. How stupid is that?"

Jack lit a cigarette. "We all got plenty of stupid in us. Here I am sitting in a bar, drinking and eating 'fru-fru' party mix two days before Christmas while my daughter wonders why I won't spend Christmas with her, my two granddaughters, Susie and Edie, and her husband, Ed."

"Ed must be a jerk."

"No, Ed's okay. He's been a good husband and provider. I couldn't ask for a better son-in-law."

"I don't get it," the stranger said, reaching for the party mix. "What about your wife? Maybe she and Ed don't get along too well. Hope he's not a plumber."

Jack chuckled softly. "No Ed's no plumber. He's in insurance. Fact is, my wife died six years ago of cancer."

Jack's drinking companion stopped eating.

"Sorry to hear that."

"That's alright. It was hard to lose her, but when you see someone suffer like she did...."

Jack looked away and cleared his throat.

Returning to his drink, he looked at Sylvia, still hiding behind the newspaper.

"Missy, how bout another round for me and...."

"Name's Tom McElroy," the stranger interrupted, extending his hand. "I'll buy the next round."

"Well, thank you kindly, Tom," Jack replied, extending his own. "I'm Jack Hamilton."

The drinks arrived with more party mix.

"Don't mean to pry Jack, but for the life of me, I can't figure out why you're not with your daughter and her family eating turkey and dressing instead of drinking Jim Beam and eating party mix with me. I mean, I wish I had a daughter like that. Me and my wife never had kids. I love my brother and his family, but being an Uncle ain't like being a Daddy."

"You got a point Tom. It's my own fault. Strange as it sounds, I just don't feel that comfortable at my daughter's."

With the confidence that three Bud Lites can bring, Tom pressed Jack a bit.

"Why don't you feel comfortable? Sounds pretty comfortable to me."

Jack took another swallow of his bourbon.

"Truth is, I don't know my daughter all that well. I retired from the FBI ten years ago. My wife pretty much raised her. I put my work first. Thought I was doing it for my family, but that was only partly true. I was as married to the Bureau as I was to Jill and Hope."

Jack swirled his drink with a swizzle stick and continued.

"Hope was a beautiful baby. I remember when I brought her and her mother home from the hospital. What a day it was. I remember Jill and me taking her to her first day of school. Got to attend one or two dance recitals, but missed most of them due to work. I was on assignment in D.C. when she went to her first prom, but the pictures turned out great. Likewise, her high school graduation. Me and Jill did make it to her college graduation, but work kept me from a lot of the stuff in between. Then she and Ed got married. She was some beautiful bride. I cried like a baby when I gave her away. I was glad none of my bureau buddies saw me … none of them could make the wedding. Then she and Ed had Susie and little Edie."

Jack looked away again and rubbed his left eye as Tom looked down at the party mix dish.

"Every year since Jill died, Hope asks me to come up for Thanksgiving and stay through Christmas. And every year, I promise to do it … and I mean to. After a few days I always end up leaving and coming home. I start feeling out-of-place a day or two after Thanksgiving. I love my daughter, but in a way, I don't know her. I've got some good memories, but in between those memories are gaps—a lifetime of empty spaces. She and Ed still invite me each year, but I can hear it in their voices. They know I won't stay. I feel guilty about the whole thing. I made my bed and I guess I'll have to lie in it."

Jack grew silent, lost in his spent opportunities. Even Sylvia, peeking from behind her newspaper found herself drawn into Jack's predicament. Tom said nothing as he chewed on a toothpick and stared at a snow pea laying on the counter.

Taking the toothpick from his mouth, Tom looked at his newfound acquaintance.

"Jack, you know a person can change beds. My wife sure did. She didn't give me a chance to make up the gaps—or if she did, I was too dumb to notice. Can't do nothing 'bout the gaps of the past, but you also got some good memories to build on. Ain't like your daughter's holding those gaps against you. I know it ain't easy, but none of us got forever to make things right. And maybe you can't even if you try. Question is, are you running from your chances or toward 'em?"

Jack felt his neck stiffen up. He didn't particularly like what he heard, but if thirty years at the Bureau taught him one thing, it was to listen—to pay attention before he reacted.

"You got a point, Tom, but it's two days before Christmas. They wouldn't be expecting me. They probably have other plans."

Jack chuckled, "They'd probably have a heart attack if I showed up on their doorstep Christmas Eve."

"Maybe that's the kind of heart attack they're wishing for this Christmas," Tom replied, smiling as he got up from the bar and placed a five-dollar tip on the counter. "I got to be getting on to 'Hotlanta.' My folks'll be expecting me."

"I need to get going too," Jack responded, rising from his stool. "Merry Christmas, Missy."

"Merry Christmas, fellows. You both drive safe now," Sylvia replied as she scooped the tip money into her apron.

The two men shook hands outside the bar and wished each other a happy holiday.

"Tom, if you ever get this way again, look me up. I'm in the phone book."

"I might just take you up on that," Tom replied. "You gonna call her?"

Jack looked at Tom and smiled. "Don't know. Maybe."

With a wave of his hand, Tom was gone. Jack watched his tail lights disappear into the cold, December night. It was beginning to snow as Jack zipped his parka all the way up to his chin.

Climbing into his Ford pick-up, Jack lit a cigarette and looked at the cell phone lying on the seat next to him. He cranked up the truck and exhaling a plume of smoke, whispered, "Reach out and touch someone."

Discussion Questions

1. Is law enforcement the only occupation that may take a parent away from important childhood and family events? What are some others?
2. In what other ways do careers in criminal justice affect family relationships?
3. What effect do you think her father's behavior has on Hope and her family?
4. What does Jack need to do to attempt to resolve his dilemma with his daughter and her family?
5. How does a parent find a meaningful point of balance between work and family?

7

STRAY DOGS

With a grace and sureness of step that belied her considerable size, Minnie Cook briskly climbed the Cook's Dimestore Dream stock-ladder, stretched one desperate arm above a stockpile of tin Raggedy Andy lunchboxes and flicked at the store radio's volume dial, transforming Bing Crosby's swelling croon to a hush. The Dream's old wood floorboards creaked as she backed her heft down each rung, and three wood bracelets—green, red, green—on her left arm click-clacked with each brisk movement.

Heights made Minnie nervous, and her role was usually relegated to operating and protecting the store's cash register, but on this day in which a brick suddenly found itself lodged—dead center—in the store's primary display window, emergency maneuvers were warranted.

The nervous corner of Minnie's mouth twitched as she peered above the origami reindeer mounted atop the cash register and watched her husband, Simpsey, standing eyes closed and motionless inside the storefront's display window, which was now a cracked pane of glass on the verge of collapse.

Simpsey could feel the warmth of the setting December sun on his face, and a soft breeze found its way through the window's cracks, which fanned out like a spider web from the brick's impact point. He slowly opened his eyes and made a soft-boned attempt to calm the escalating anger rising from his boots. The breeze continued to blow through the hole, past the brick, past Simpsey, through the aisles of Cook's Dimestore Dream, dislodging a stack of cheap plastic Halloween masks that had been sleeping beneath a blanket of dust in the bargain bin for months. The crisp December burst sent them skittering, a half-dozen or so Donnie & Marie Osmond faces, across the floor.

Bing's voice on the radio was barely a hush now, interrupted by the periodic tinkle of glass shards falling to the floor.

Simpsey reached out with his left hand to graze the tip of the brick, its jagged point an angry finger jutting back at him. His right hand, growing blood red, grasped the blunt wood hull of a brushless broom handle, which he kept as a constant companion to help defend his struggling business from what he considered to be "the stray dog scourge." Etched on the stick's chipped wood shaft were the words The Educator, and as an unfortunate handful of bruised and knotted young men could testify to, The Educator bore hard, painful lessons. Hijacking a fistful of Chick 'O Sticks could cost you a broken finger or two. A failed attempt to swipe a soda from the Tastee-Pop cooler would be heartily rewarded with swift strokes to the back, the groin, the head. Didn't matter. Simpsey wielded The Educator like a butcher worked a meat cleave. And for any off-colored comments directed at Simpsey's wife, Minnie?

Few, if any, had even hatched the thought.

Still motionless, Simpsey caressed The Educator's hull with fingers oily from assembling a Christmas order of Schwinn bicycles. Across three reddening knuckles were scrawled the words "ho! ho! ho!", a home-cooked deterrent/physical threat for any member of "stray dog scourge" in search of an unwarranted Christmas discount.

Looking through his shambling window, Simpsey could make out the thin silhouette of a boy, standing with his back to a red Georgia sun, and tossing back and forth what looked to be the other half of the brick that had, moments ago, taken up residency in his storefront window pane.

Laney Mack, swaddled in a weathered leather jacket once owned by his brother, playfully tossed the other half of the brick back and forth, from one hand to the other. His dark brown hair was greased back into a sort-of pompadour. A makeshift necklace of ceramic Christmas lights (courtesy of a strand that had lined the awning over Simpsey's store entrance) kept his neck company.

With deep red bells ringing in his head and his blood pressure barometer beginning to crack like the glass in his storefront window,

Simpsey curled his tongue around a swarm of profanities and launched them toward Laney Mack. Though they would burrow into the ears of the occasional passerby and become the spark for the following morning's barber and beauty shop gossip, the words, with all their fangs and fury, would not stir Laney, whose ears had heard much worse in his 16 years, from men with sharper tongues and harder fists.

"Son, you throw that, and the only lights you gonna see this Christmas are the spinning blue kind," Simpsey said, shifting his weight, his thick fingers rhythmically tapping The Educator's hull.

"Seen 'em before, mister," Laney said, scratching his hip. "Seen 'em plenty. I'll be right here, waitin'."

Laney sat down on the curb, he could feel his tailbone ache, still sore from a childhood incident. He rolled his left jean leg up to match his right and looked across the street. A young dog—its coat, a patchwork of frayed fur and bare skin—stared back at him with eyes of two different colors, one a blue tint, the other black as pitch. The dog quivered and paused once aware of Laney's presence, and his starving skin was drawn over ribs that pushed through the sides of his body, bending, bowing out like prison bars made of bone.

Simpsey could feel the anger, scaly and swelling, turning over inside, again and again. He took a firm hold of The Educator and pointed it toward Laney through the hole in his window.

"Do you want me to come out there and show you what I do to dogs like that—dogs like *you*—that come around here and stir up a fuss," he shouted.

Minnie placed her hand on Simpsey's and grazed it with her thumb. She gently removed The Educator from his hand and replaced it with a telephone receiver.

"No need for you two to be sharing the backseat of Hallis' cruiser," she said.

Unblinking and still, Laney scanned the fractured storefront window, the gold "Joy To The World" banner draped beneath the "Bicentennial Christmas Blowout" sign, the fake snowy setting with the rosy-cheeked wax figurine family of carolers on display. He quickly turned his attention to the face of Simpsey Cook, pulpy and enraged, his lips in a snarl, barbed words continuing to fire out of his mouth from behind the cracked glass.

But Laney heard nothing, not a sound. He only saw, in those fractured shards, the reflection of Simpsey Cook, and the faces of other men he had known—men of hard hands and hurtful words.

Tears began to well up in Laney's eyes, and in one swift movement, he scooped up the half brick resting at his feet, and with every ounce of energy in his slight sixteen-year-old frame, hurled it at what was left of Simpsey Cook's storefront window.

$S \quad M \quad A \quad S \quad H \quad ! \quad !$

Laney wiped his throwing hand on his jeans and picked a broken flower off the curb. He looked at it for a moment, grazed the delicate, white velvet texture of its remaining petal with his finger and sat down on the curb cross-legged. As a crop of flashing blue lights grew closer on the horizon, Laney closed his eyes and exhaled in a long, deep sigh beneath the sunset's dying glow.

* * *

The gold trim on Sergeant Hallis Rivers' nametag flashed like a lightbulb in the late evening sun. He carefully slipped a set of handcuffs around Laney's slim wrists, and noticed the ghosts of bruises and burns decorating his young forearms.

Rivers' sigh went undetected by Laney's ears as the young man slid his spindly frame into the backseat of the cruiser. A police radio crackled and popped. A series of anonymous voices blurting out random numbers and street names.

The cruiser's engine wheezed to life, and the sound of a dying fanbelt introduced itself.

"Buckle up young'n," Rivers asked, doing his best to suppress a chronic cough that had haunted him since late autumn. "S'cuse me, got a midget in my throat."

Laney reached for the belt buckle, its metal casing scalding to the touch. Something was etched on the chrome siding of the buckle, but Laney couldn't make out the words.

Rivers adjusted the rearview mirror, ceremonially tapped twice the Jesus air freshener wrapped around the radio dial and glanced at

Laney, whose pale blue eyes dammed up a sadness and suffering shared by a hundred other boys before him who had warmed that seat.

"Not much of a way for a young man to spend Christmas, huh?" Rivers said, adjusting the rearview again. "How old are you?"

"Sixteen," Laney answered in a voice small and quiet, "and spare change."

"Well I take it that spreading holiday cheer wasn't exactly your motivation for throwing a brick through Mr. Cook's window," Rivers said, again trying to keep his nagging cough in check.

"I just wanted a place to stay," Laney said, placing his hand on the belt buckle, which was much cooler now. "Figured jail would be safe, warm. Quiet."

Rivers pulled up to a stoplight and threw the cruiser in park.

"C'mere, you don't need those," he said, motioning for Laney's handcuffs.

Laney rubbed his freed wrists and looked out the window as the light turned green. A little girl wearing a red Rudolph the Red Nosed Reindeer bulb on her nose waved at him from the passenger side window of a pink Mary Kay Cosmetics car, her windy hair all braids and bows. He waved back.

Laney listened to Rivers warble official speak into a walkie talkie, and recognized a few random words: boy, lost, vandalism, grass stains.

Rivers hung up the receiver and looked at the rearview mirror.

"I'm gonna take you into the station for the evening until we get some things squared away, alright?" he directed in a calm tone. "We'll have a cot for you to sleep on, and a couple of roommates for the evening—Henry Bells—don't even get me *started* on that boy; and Reverend Sugars Mandrell, who always volunteers to keep watch over the flock on Christmas Eve. It ain't the Beverly Hills Deluxe, but it'll do. And my wife Evangeline sends in some fine tastin' grub every year, so maybe you'll get a plate full. Sound okay?"

Laney nodded and held his hand up to his nose; he could still smell the flower's fragrant scent.

Rivers looked at the boy briefly once more in the rearview mirror. A part of him wondered how many more like him he'd see in the coming years. Another part wondered how much longer he'd be able to take it.

* * *

Inside the Lunsford County Jail, a tabletop Christmas tree, draped in silver tinsel, blinked blue, red, green and purple, and cozied up to a pot of coffee, the steam still rising from its lid like ghosts. A woman's slow molasses croon crackled from a small red radio perched atop the warden's desk and drifted down a warmly lit hallway, its walls decorated with children's Christmas drawings.

Laney's hands were wrapped around two cell bars, and he looked between them to see the drawings—some colored in, others not. One in particular showed a boy with his arms wrapped around members of his family. An orange sun flowered behind them. The image would not shake loose of him.

"I used to draw like that."

Laney turned to track down where the words were coming from.

An old black man, dressed in a black pinstripe suit adorned with a yellow flower pin, smiled at him.

"Except I drew them on automobile hoods, water towers, bathroom stalls," he continued. "I was about your age, too. Just as scrawny."

The holding room's other resident, splayed out on his cot with one boot-covered foot and one bare, remained still, the rising and falling of his chest indicating a state of temporary hibernation.

The old man smiled at Laney, removed his hat and began tapping his red leather shoes on the floor.

"Where you from Little King?" he asked in Laney's direction.

Laney paused and hesitantly shook his head, not knowing to whom the old man was referring.

"You know who Elvis is?"

Laney nodded.

"You kinda look like him," the old man said, picking at the frayed interior of his hat, "so I'ma call you Li'l King."

"I once saw Elvis shoppin' for a Burmese killifish at Jonah Stu's pet store downtown," the other man, now slowly waking, chimed in, stretching his arms toward the ceiling and slipping his Uni-Oil '76 cap snug over his head. "Never liked Elvis, though. More of a Stones man."

The cap's bill was pulled down over the man's brow, so Laney couldn't see his eyes, but he noticed that he had no front teeth.

"So why you in here, King?" the old man continued. "Your momma know where you are?"

Laney glanced between the bars again and looked at the drawings on the wall.

"My momma's gone."

The old man slowly nodded, tapped his foot again to some mystery rhythm playing in his head.

"Your Daddy gone too?"

Laney hesitated a moment before answering.

"Might as well be," he said, running his hand through his makeshift pompadour.

"I see," the old man softly trailed off. "So why you here?"

"I needed a place to stay," Laney answered, slowly slipping off his leather jacket. "To sleep."

The napping man with the Uni-Oil hat flicked up the bill on his cap, revealing a look of disbelief.

Sugars Mandrell leaned out of the dark corner, stretching his long gaunt frame until he was almost face to face with Laney. He tapped his red leather shoes on the floor three times.

"Young man, I'm lookin' at you, and I'm hearin' the words tiptoe out of your mouth, and I'm *knowin'* you're looking for more than just a place to stay and sleep."

Laney could see his own reflection in the old man's eyes. They were fathomless but comforting.

"I see a stray dog in you son," Sugars continued. "It's in every man standing in this room—you, me, even Henry Bells over there. The thing about a stray is this: they always movin' from one doorstep to the next—*always* movin', *always* in search of … but always *hungry*."

Sugars moved his face closer to Laney, his eyes growing wider.

"I know you're scared, Little King, and I know you're hungry, but sooner or later you got to be still and *eat*."

Henry Bells sat up from his former reclining position and rested his chin on his knee.

"What'd you do to get yourself in this predicament?" he asked.

"I threw a brick through a store window," Laney answered.

"Which store?"

"Cook's Dimestore Dream."

Sugars shook his head and slipped his hat back on while Henry exploded in laughter.

"They ought to give you the key to the city, son," Henry said through hoarse waves of laughter, wiping his brow with his forearm. "As far as I'm concerned, you've already done your community service."

Laney removed his leather jacket and looked at Henry.

"How'd you get in here?"

Henry slipped off his cap and ran his hands through his thinning, black hair. Two lambchop-sized sideburns crept down the sides of his face and connected to a handlebar mustache prematurely peppered with flecks of gray.

"Well, I realize this ain't exactly the appropriate yuletide tale for this evening," he said, "but I woke up early this morning in the middle of that unpaved access road that intersects Cynthiana. I was messed up, to be honest. Just tore up. The headache, the bruises from a couple of unfriendly dalliances from the evening prior— the whole bit. I was on my back and opened my right hand; there was a note all scrunched up; it read "look in your back left jeans pocket for a Christmas surprise." The knuckles on my left hand were still busted, but I shoved it into my back left pocket and pulled out a little ziplock bag—with two of my front teeth inside.

Henry flashed a huge gap-toothed grin. Sugars and Laney both laughed.

"That's my story young man. Public intoxication was my ticket to these deluxe accommodations I share with you tonight."

Sugars shook his head.

"What did you do with your teeth," Laney asked, his smile unable to come undone.

"I sent 'em to my stepfather, wrapped up in a bow all nice and pretty. Slipped a note inside that read '*Somebody else got to me before you did—Merry Christmas.*'"

The sound of Hallis Rivers' 1964 Udelia High class ring repeatedly tick-tacking against one of the cell bars interrupted another round of laughter.

"Alright gentlemen," he said, slipping three paper boxes through a slot in the cell door, "Evangeline wanted to make sure all 'overnight residents' went to bed this Christmas Eve on a full stomach, so here are the goods: ham sandwiches, homemade biscuits, chocolate chip and pecan cookies. Got a quart of sweet tea to wash it down, too."

A chorus of thank you's chimed out to meet the Warden's generosity.

"What's this, the third Christmas Eve in a row Henry?" Hallis asked, cocking an eyebrow. "We gonna have to officially christen this the Henry Bells Holding Tank #3?"

"It's Evangeline's fault, son," he answered, smiling. "Her cooking's too damn good—drive a man to a life of crime."

After Rivers wished all a Merry Christmas, and continued his mission toward a half-empty coffee pot, Sugars poured three even cups of sweet tea and asked if Henry and Laney would stand with him to say a prayer before dinner.

As the three men stood together, arms interlocked and heads bowed, Laney opened one eye and looked again, through the cell bars, to the drawing of the family on the wall, their faces smiling, their arms wrapped around each other.

He felt a squeeze from Sugar's hand.

"Lord, may these stray sons finally find their way, be at peace—and eat," he said, finishing up his prayer. "Though I am here tonight as a shepherd, I am also one of the flock. Amen."

Sugars kneeled down, removed the yellow flower from his coat and pinned it on Laney's leather jacket.

"Every stray dog needs a place to be still and belong," the old man said. "Tonight, Little King, you among family."

A smile slid across Laney's face, and his eyes shifted focus from the welcoming embrace of the old man's eyes to the Christmas drawing, posted on the wall outside the jail cell—the same one that had caught his attention upon his arrival.

Looking at the drawing—a crude, crayon image of what looked like a boy wrapping his arms around his family—gave Laney a strange feeling, like when a thunderstorm sometimes cracks the sky open on a sunny summer day.

Biting into one of Evangeline's biscuits, Laney squinted his eyes in an effort to read the words inscribed on the bottom of the drawing. He squinted harder, his eyes reaching out like hands from between the bars. He squinted until his head hurt, but the words were just out of reach.

Discussion Questions

1. Why did Laney throw the brick through Simpsey Cook's storefront window?
2. Simpsey named his "disciplinary tool" The Educator. How does that reflect his attitude toward young patrons? Toward humanity in general?
3. Why do some people, who by nature are nonviolent, commit violent acts?
4. Why do you think Officer Hallis Rivers did not take Laney to task more than he did during the ride to jail?
5. What, ultimately, was Laney searching for?
6. Why do you think the story was named Stray Dogs?

8

THE END IS NEAR

From a pigeon's vantage point high atop the Mercantile Bank, the mass of people scurrying along the avenue below looked like the tide of some great ocean. There is a certain rhythm and symmetry to the movement of people going to work.

The early morning cadence was quicker and more stiff-legged than the evening quitting time promenade.

Why did they walk that way?

Perhaps their slightly desperate gait was motivated by a fear of being late and the heavy-lidded glances of disapproval that would be sure to follow. Other travelers in the urgent parade may have had a driving desire to be the early bird that gets the worm or at least hold onto the part of the worm they had. The edge they pursued was driven by a caffeine fortified staccato march toward the challenges that lay before them.

In the midst of this swirl of humanity stood an old man with a sign. The cardboard attached to a broom handle stated the message in large red letters: *Repent! The End is Near!*

The sign bearer was tall and gaunt with a long, meticulously groomed white beard. He wore a faded red plaid flannel shirt, blue jeans that had seen better days and white patent leather loafers. Perched on his head was a greasy baseball cap with an American flag pinned one side and a silver cross pinned on the other. His angular face framed deep-set clear blue eyes and wore a somber expression.

The current of men and women swept past him without so much as a glance.

Across the street, three well-dressed men in their thirties sat in a café and sipped the remnants of their Starbucks and observed the old man.

The first man said, "He's got to be crazy—standing in the middle of the business district with that goofy sign. Somebody ought to call the police."

The second man replied, "He may be a little off, but I doubt he's dangerous. He probably just wants some attention."

The third man said nothing and continued to sip his coffee.

The first man turned to him.

"Bill, what do think? Is the old man crazy-dangerous or crazy-harmless?"

"Maybe neither."

"Neither," the second man queried. "What kind of answer is that?"

Bill drained the last of his coffee and tossed his cup in the trash can.

"Maybe he knows something we don't."

All three men chuckled at the thought of it.

"Maybe, I'll go ask him."

"You've got to be kidding. That old man may pull a knife on you. You know how unpredictable those kind of people are."

The second man chimed in, "He may even hit you with his sign."

The first and second man laughed, but stopped when they realized Bill was serious.

Bill turned to his two companions. "Did you notice the first word on his sign?"

"You mean 'repent'?" The second man replied.

Bill took a sip of his coffee. "That's the word."

"So what?" interjected the first man.

Bill put his coffee cup down and looked at the two men sitting across from him. "I've been thinking a lot lately about what it is that we do for a living—what it means to work for a hedge fund on Wall Street. We've made a ton of money. Our investors haven't been so fortunate. They've lost a lot of their money—some have lost everything."

The second man looked at the first, then back at Bill. "Welcome to the world of finance. You place your bets and take your chances. You know as well as me that derivatives are a complex and sophisticated financial instrument. Sometimes it can be hard …"

"Cut the bullshit," Bill interrupted. "No matter how you dress it up, it still boils down to the fact that we sold bad debt to good clients whose only mistake was to trust us."

"We did nothing illegal," the first man chimed in. "So what if we made a lot of money. The guys at the top made a lot more. We explained the terms and risks to our clients. We put it all in writing."

"Explained it my ass," Bill replied. He could feel his face turning red. "How can we explain something we don't even understand. Hell, Albert Einstein couldn't decipher the fine print in our client's contracts."

The second man shifted uncomfortably in his chair. "Bill, what's gotten into you? We all got record bonuses last year. It's not our fault that the investments went south. We followed the lead of the firm's senior partners. If anyone did, they were the ones that dropped the ball."

Bill drained the last of his coffee and placed his cup on the table. "I'll tell you what's gotten into me. For the most part, it's extinct on Wall Street—it's called a conscience. When I look at that old man's sign across the street, it's easy enough to believe that we have plenty to repent of."

The second man turned to Bill. "Speak for yourself, I'm just doing my job and supporting my family—all legal and above board."

"Maybe legal, but hardly above board," Bill replied with more than a hint of sarcasm.

Bill's companions slid their chairs back and stood up. "Come on Bill, we'll be late for work. It's Friday, you'll feel better after a long weekend."

As the two men crossed the street, they realized Bill had turned toward the old man with the sign.

"Pardon me, Mister."

The old man turned to the sound of Bill's voice.

"I'd like to know why you are standing here with that sign?"

"What's your name, son?"

"Bill."

"Well my name's Henry. Nice to meet you Bill."

"To answer your question, I'm fishing for souls."

"Fishing for souls? What kind of answer is that?"

"It's the only answer I've got. I'm fishing for souls and this here sign is my bait."

Bill rubbed his chin.

"So you don't really believe what your sign says is true?"

"Young friend, I don't believe it to be true, I *know* it to be true."

"How can you know something like that."

"I just do."

"Sounds like a crock to me."

The old man said nothing.

"The sign says repent."

"That's right."

"What am I supposed to repent of?"

"Whatever you need to repent of."

"That's not much of an answer."

The old man pulled a toothpick out of his shirt pocket and placed in the corner of his mouth.

"I agree, it's not much of an answer, but it's enough."

"Enough for what?"

"Enough to get you moving to where you need to go."

"Well, Henry, my friends were wrong about you. You're not crazy, but I must say you don't make much sense."

"I'm not here to make sense."

Bill turned to leave, then stopped and looked into the old man's eyes.

"What's the point of repenting if the end is near—if it's all over anyway. What difference does it make?"

"Question is my young friend, what difference does it make to you?"

Bill looked at Henry then at a flock of pigeons swooping toward a high perch across the street. "I guess I'm not sure."

Henry pulled a pack of chewing gum from his shirt pocket and handed a stick to Bill. "Try a piece of 'Juicy Fruit.' It'll put a touch of sweet on the bad taste you're feeling inside you."

Bill popped the gum in his mouth.

Henry reached out and placed a hand on Bill's shoulder. "What's troubling you, son? What sorrow's got hold of you?"

Bill stared down at the sidewalk. "I got a big decision to make—maybe the biggest of my life."

He looked up. "I don't know why I'm telling you—I shouldn't."

Henry gently gave Bill's shoulder a gentle squeeze. "That's your call. Little choices along the path lead each of us to a place where a big decision is headed our way."

"I know," Bill replied, the strain clearly showing in his face. "I've made a lot of money with the firm I work for—some of it questionable. I mean, it's legal and all according to our corporate attorney, but our investors have gotten hurt—some even ruined—by the products we sold them."

Bill paused, pondering if he should say anything else.

Henry waved at a passerby and turned back to Bill. "Legal don't necessarily make something right. Sometimes it does. Other times, legal covers a lot of darkness and hurt, makes folks feel better about something they should feel bad about."

Bill pulled out a handkerchief and blew his nose. "Yeah, it seems like what's left of my conscience has finally caught up with me. A fellow from the Justice Department wants me to testify against one of our senior partners. They aren't after me, or so they say, but apparently have something on him. They want me to help them—do the right thing. The right thing will cost me my job, an income my wife and daughter depend on. That's a hell of a price to pay."

"True enough," Henry replied. "That said, you don't seem too happy with the price you been paying."

"Paying for what?"

Henry flipped his toothpick into the trash can he was leaning on. "Sounds to me like you been paying a right heavy price for your self-respect. What price is that worth—or your soul for that matter? You reckon your family would rather have all of you or just the part you been showing them?"

Bill ran his hand through his hair. "Good question. Good question with a hard answer. That's what I noticed about your sign. If I repent and testify, the end is near. It will be over for me. We will have to make some hard changes—put a lot behind us—friends, standard of living and God knows what else."

Henry looked at Bill. "You know what you need to do and God knows what else. Like I said before, it's your call."

Bill offered his hand to Henry. "I thank you for your time. I've got an appointment to keep. My life's about to end as I've known it." Bill turned to walk away.

"There's one more thing, Bill," Henry shouted.

"What's that?" Bill replied, looking back over his shoulder.

Henry's blue eyes danced and the corner of his mouth formed the hint of a smile. "The end is near, but so is the beginning."

Discussion Questions

1. Instances of Wall Street corruption and financial crimes in general, are well-documented. In a number of cases, the actions of offenders are deemed unethical and immoral even when they are not charged with crimes. What motivates people like Bill and his colleagues? What are some ways financial institutions like Wall Street may undermine one's personal values and ethics?

2. Why do you think Bill's "conscience" is troubling him and not his companions?

3. What does the character of Henry represent in the story? In what ways does Henry help Bill resolve his inner ethical conflicts?

4. Sometimes doing the right thing incurs substantial personal costs and sacrifice. In what ways do you think Bill's life will change if he testifies against his firm?

PART THREE

DUTIES TO
SELF AND OTHERS

In this section we examine the social context. Kant argued that we all have duties—we have duties as parents, sons or daughters, as citizens, and in addition, duties and responsibilities come with our chosen professions. A perfect world would be one where everyone did their duty. Unfortunately, sometimes our duty is not that clear. On other occasions, one duty may conflict with another.

There are also supererogations. These are moral acts that go beyond duties. While it may be a moral duty to care for one's children, it is a supererogatory act to care for a stranger. It is a moral duty to not hurt an innocent person, but supererogatory to go out of one's way to help someone who does not deserve or expect it. Yet, random acts of kindness make both giver and receiver feel good and even more alive and contribute in essential ways to what it means to be a moral person.

In these stories we explore duties and supererogatories. How we do our jobs, how we treat each person we come in contact with, and how we live our lives, for better or worse creates the mosaic of our existence, piece by piece.

Invisible Boy focuses on the relationship of a police detective and a neglected young man from his neighborhood. It comes to his attention that the young man has been arrested for drugs and prostitution. Could the detective have done more to help him when he was a boy? Is it too late to help him now?

Special of the Week explores the choice a used car salesman has to make regarding helping or not helping someone in need. A homeless woman with two small children is in need of a car. The salesman who waits on her is touched by her plight, but will he help her?

Rasheed's Ticket tells the story of a troubled youth in a juvenile corrections institution who is about to graduate first in his class and wants his mother to attend. He approaches a counselor and the Chaplain for help in getting a bus ticket for his mother. Instead, the help he receives comes from the last place he would expect.

Crazy Times looks at the contemporary challenges surrounding police shootings of civilians. A black female police officer shot an elderly wheel-chair-bound man who pointed what she thought was a gun at her. Political influence, the media and protestors are all contributing to increased tensions in the community. The police chief and a retired Sergeant discuss the dilemma facing them as well as what the best way to respond might be.

The Big Picture tells the story of a lawyer on the edge of burnout who tries to find meaning in a seemingly endless cycle of defending guilty and often unappreciative clients. She tries to remember the idealism she felt when she first started practicing law.

Short-cut examines the relationship between an elderly inmate who has been a career criminal and a prison psychologist. The inmate is aware of the bad choices he has made and that he has become in-stitutionalized, but at the same time, seems to have few regrets.

In *It's Too Bad about Tommy,* two politicians succumb to self-deception and rationalization as they try to reconcile political ex-pediency and compromise with a casualty of war experienced by one of their colleagues.

Truth Teller is about a man on the fast-track to success who watches as his life spirals out of control when he begins to tell the truth. This story examines the potential costs and sacrifice associated with trying to be an honest and caring person who possesses integrity.

9

INVISIBLE BOY

Although wavy blond hair and clear blue eyes gave Teddy a strange sort of handsome, "five foot two, eyes of blue" was not a description that lived up to a teenage boy's testosterone dreams. To make matters worse, Teddy was not a particularly good name for a fifteen-year-old boy of slight build trying to prove his mettle in a one-street, blue-collar subdivision. And if his name and physique weren't enough of a handicap, his family's well-worn singlewide trailer stood out like a sore thumb in the sea of split-foyer, ranch and two-story stick built houses.

While the adults in the neighborhood weren't about to roll out the red carpet for the trailer family perched on a kind of no-man's land in a cornfield just on edge of the subdivision's boundary, they had just enough decency to accommodate to some extent, the family's lonely son.

Teddy's story was originally told to Little Jack, the neighborhood renegade and closest thing to a friend Teddy would ever have. His story filtered its way from Little Jack's parents to the Smiths then the Johnsons and on to the Bartholomews until everyone in the neighborhood had heard it at least twice, everyone except old man Murphy who stayed to himself in a vinyl-clad split-foyer ever since his wife Norma died.

Of course, as Teddy's story made its way through the various families, it took on a number of twists and turns, exaggerations both added and subtracted. The gist of it is as follows: When Teddy was eight years old, his Daddy drank whiskey and beat and abused his mother while he and his younger sister were forced to watch. When in a drunken state, his father was fond of threatening to do his mother, sister and himself in with his good friends, Smith and

Wesson. Weary of his relentless abuse, Teddy's mother decided to turn his father's friends against him.

Three times these friends spoke his name and three times stunned, he watched the red, concentric holes appear on his mid-section. He only uttered one word during the entire ordeal and he only said it once. After the first shot rang out, he shouted, "Teddy!"

Teddy and his sister looked on in silence as their father fell against the living room wall and slid down it, clutching what was left of his Bud-Lite and watching its contents mingle with the blood pouring from his belly onto the shag carpet.

Two years later, Teddy's mother married his current stepfather and two years after that they moved onto no-man's land.

Although Teddy and his mother had never spoken of the killing, and as much as he believed in his own mind that his father deserved what he got, one thing had always bothered him about the incident. He didn't like the way his dying father spoke to him. He didn't like being called by name as if he were some kind of official witness— as if he could have done something about the shooting. If Teddy hadn't been called out by his dying Daddy, he could have remained invisible. Of course, to the parents in the neighborhood, he was still for the most part invisible, but not so much that they wouldn't invite him in when he knocked on their front doors looking for refuge and a prospective playmate.

Still, the welcome mats, one after another, were eventually withdrawn because Teddy—like anyone dying of an unquenchable thirst—couldn't stop drinking from any sign of friendship and kindness that was offered, no matter how small or fragile. So on he went, from one house and playmate to another. As he searched for the next sign of hospitality, what he left behind looked like a clear-cut forest. Whatever his circumstance, no matter how many doors were closed to him and how few were open, there was always one place Teddy was accepted or at least tolerated—the basketball court at the end of the street.

In the cul-de-sac on Muskgrove Lane, a portable basketball goal and backboard stood guard like a silent sentinel and waited. Around three-thirty each fall afternoon, Monday through Friday, you could hear it coming before you saw it. An ancient yellow school bus slowly belched its way down the single curved road of Muskgrove Lane and expelled its prisoners, free until 6:45 the following morning.

They came out of that bus like rats leaving a sinking ship—first grade through high school. The youth of the neighborhood sauntered and ran toward the houses that beckoned them with the promise of snacks and juice. Thirty minutes later, the rhythmic thumping of basketballs sounded like a war chant and signaled that the games were about to begin.

Younger boys watched older ones dribble basketballs between their legs, make fancy lay-up shots and attempt the occasional but rarely successful, dunk. Boys and the several girls who braved the hallowed court raised their hands and voices, begging to be picked. But their cries to be chosen fell on deaf ears. To the older boys of Muskgrove Lane, they had been designated the Peanut Gallery, spectators one and all—spectators not players. Nothing more needed to be said. The best the members of the Peanut Gallery could hope for Monday through Friday was the brief window of opportunity that presented itself between games. Their reward for being loyal and appreciative spectators was the possibility of five minutes of wild abandon on the court while the real players took a water break at the end of each game. The brief melee only faintly resembled the game of basketball.

Although Teddy was old enough to qualify as a real player, he wasn't chosen—partly because of his questionable athletic skills, but most importantly because of his penchant for combing his hair when he was supposed to be guarding a player from the opposing team. Every few minutes, Teddy would reach for the comb protruding from his back pocket. It was like a personal hygiene compulsion. Teddy would raise his left hand in defense while he carefully manicured his blond tresses with his right hand.

It is no secret that one-armed basketball defenders don't fare well when their opponent dribbles past them while they are in mid-stroke for an easy lay-up. And no amount of laughter and derision from the older boys seemed to deter Teddy from his compulsion. So he was exiled Monday through Friday to the Peanut Gallery where he could comb in peace.

There was also one other more subtle, unspoken reason why Teddy wasn't picked to play in the real games. Technically, he wasn't a member of Muskgrove Lane and since it was important to many of the adults in Muskgrove Lane that Teddy and his family knew their place, it was also important to their children. The one exception was Little Jack. As the neighborhood rebel, he stood on more than one occasion as Teddy's sole defender. Although he was smaller in stature than Teddy, he was a fierce competitor on the Court and was known for starting fights that he knew he couldn't win.

Most of the boys in Muskgrove Lane, younger and older, were not inclined to rile up Little Jack because of his volatile nature, but even Little Jack couldn't get Teddy out of the Peanut Gallery. His one vote simply wasn't enough and besides, he didn't really want Teddy playing on his team. On Monday through Friday Teddy couldn't play, he could only watch, but on Saturday, things were different.

On Saturday, Detective Burns played. He was the only father in the neighborhood that was a Saturday regular. While the other fathers cut their grass, fished and golfed, Lloyd Burns played basketball with a bunch of kids. In fact, his wife, Myrtle, on more than one occasion indicated to the Detective that he was nothing more than a big kid himself. Of course, her comments went in one ear and out the other. While Lloyd loved his wife dearly, as far as sports were concerned, Myrtle definitely belonged in the Peanut Gallery.

All the kids and teenagers of Muskgrove Lane referred to Detective Lloyd Burns as "Sarge" in deference to his slight limp, the result of a wound he received in Vietnam and for which he received a Purple Heart. In truth, Sarge was admired not so much because he had received a combat medal or was a Police Detective, but because he could dunk the basketball with either hand whenever he felt like it. He designated his trademark dunk as the "Muskgrove Megadunk" or "M and M" for short.

Although he was judicious in its use, he always demonstrated the "M and M" once or twice each Saturday to the squeals and delight of the "Peanut Gallery." On Saturdays, Sarge was also the Team Captain and Referee. More importantly, he always made sure everyone got to play. His authority and skill were unquestioned.

Sometimes Sarge's team would win and sometimes it wouldn't, but to the bewilderment of the older, more talented players, Sarge always chose the same person first to be on his team. He always chose Teddy. The Monday through Friday spectator was always the first one chosen on Saturday by the neighborhood Superstar.

Sarge's only requirement was that Teddy hand over his comb for the duration of the morning's activities. The older boys looked at each other and shook their heads in disgust as Teddy proudly took his place beside Sarge at Center Court. No one ever knew why Sarge always chose Teddy first. Teddy imagined that Sarge saw some hidden talent in him that wasn't apparent to the others, but then Teddy had always had a vivid and overactive imagination.

Sarge was every bit the Field General on Saturday mornings, preferring to pass the ball and set picks for his younger teammates from the Peanut Gallery. And the Monday through Friday All-Stars knew if they got too rambunctious or aggressive with Sarge's teammates, they would end up eating one of his "M and M's." Sarge would bark orders to his charges as if they were on a do or die combat mission.

"Teddy, guard your flank! PJ's moving to your right!"

"Hands up, Joey!"

"Defense team, Defense!"

"Shoot, Susie, Shoot!"

On Saturdays, the bonds of oppression were cut loose and the spirits of the weekday underclass soared. They imagined they were also players. When the lucky shot was rewarded with the swoosh of the net, they could count on a smile and a wink from Sarge.

"Money in the bank," Sarge would reply, giving the one who scored a "high-five."

On Saturdays, Teddy most of all, came alive for a few hours. On that day, he stood in the light and heard the applause and was called by his name. Unfortunately, Saturday only came once a week. There were six other days in between.

Then one Saturday, Teddy began to change.

Everyone had headed toward home except Sarge, Teddy and Little Jack. Sarge decided that the two of them needed some extra help with their free-throw shooting.

"Hey Sarge, Teddy says he's gonna become a Ninja," Little Jack commented as he threw up another errant free-throw.

"That so?"

Sarge gathered up the rebound and passed the ball to Teddy.

"Yeah," chortled Little Jack. "Teddy's done ordered his uniform."

Teddy bounced the basketball two times, and then swished it through the net.

"That so, Teddy?" Sarge queried, throwing the basketball to Little Jack.

Teddy pulled his comb out of his back pocket and began to run it through his hair.

"Yes Sir, Sarge. I'm gonna earn my black belt in Ninja."

Sarge leaned back against the pole that held up the backboard.

"Teddy, how you gonna do that—become a Ninja?"

Teddy's eyes lit up in a way Sarge had never seen before. His enthusiasm drew in Little Jack as well. It was like Teddy had found something important that he had been looking for and had eluded him until now.

"I ordered me a Ninja black belt training course from the International Ninja Training Academy for two hundred dollars. It took all my savings, but it'll be worth it. And they included the uniform for free!"

"That so?" Sarge grunted.

"Yes Sir."

"After I complete six lessons and send them in to Master Nu, he'll send me my Black Belt and official Certificate of Graduation."

Although Sarge showed little hint of his approval or disapproval of Teddy's venture, his eyes smiled ever so slightly in response to Teddy's excitement.

"Teddy, why do you want to become a Ninja?"

Without hesitation, Teddy revealed his plan.

"The thing about being a Ninja is that they teach you how to be invisible—you know—in a good way. You can sneak around and even though people won't know you're there, you can be on the look-out."

"Look out for what?" Sarge asked.

"Look out for any danger that might come their way so you can rescue them," Teddy replied somewhat impatiently.

"Your identity stays a secret. It's like you're a secret hero helping out people in trouble. Nobody might ever know the good you do, but at least you'll know. I'm gonna be like the invisible protector of Muskgrove Lane."

Sarge looked at Teddy and gave him a smile.

"Well Teddy, all I can tell you is that I'm glad there'll be a Ninja looking out for me in Muskgrove Lane."

That said, he picked up his basketball and began to walk toward home.

Looking over his shoulder, he shouted, "See you boys next Saturday."

* * *

As the years passed, Muskgrove Lane, like all neighborhoods, endured the usual timeworn transformations marked by the end of some things and the beginning of others. Seasons changed places, hairlines receded, and graduations brushed shoulders with first birthday celebrations. Even Jack shed the "Little" from his childhood moniker. On his fifteenth birthday, Little Jack made it clear that henceforth he would be addressed as "Jack." Anyone who referred to him as Little Jack would do so at his or her own peril, which translated into the teenage code of Muskgrove Lane as an "ass whipping." Occasionally adults slipped up and addressed him as Little Jack. When they did, he met their response with a cold stare and a stony silence. Only Teddy who had always been oblivious to neighborhood etiquette and traditions seemed able to get away with calling Jack, "Little Jack."

On a cool autumn afternoon, Sarge spotted Teddy walking in the rain on the shoulder of Highway 87.

Sarge eased his Jeep Cherokee off the highway, rolled down the passenger side window and waited for Teddy. Within several minutes, Teddy peered in through the open window.

"Hi, Sarge."

"Hi, Teddy. How 'bout a ride home?"

"Okay. Thanks," Teddy replied easing himself into the back seat.

Lloyd looked at him in the rearview mirror.

"How's things going?"

Teddy didn't respond right away.

"Me and my stepfather ain't getting along too good. Never really have. He don't understand me. Guess it's hard to understand someone you don't much like."

Teddy's eyes met Lloyd's in the rearview mirror, then he looked out into the rain.

"I don't know what's gonna happen."

The Jeep Cherokee came to a stop where the gravel road began that led to the house trailer.

Lloyd put the gearshift lever in park and turned to Teddy.

"Teddy, whatever happens, I want you to remember something."

"Remember what, Sarge?"

"That you're a good boy."

"You really think so?"

"I know so, Teddy," Lloyd replied.

The corners of Teddy's mouth curved in the hint of a weary smile. He didn't quite believe what Sarge said, but appreciated the gesture nonetheless.

Getting out of the Jeep, Teddy closed the door and peered through the passenger window.

"Thanks for the ride, Sarge."

"Anytime, Teddy."

Lloyd listened to the gravel crunch grinding beneath his wheels as he pulled away from Teddy. He turned his head to look back. He could, just for a moment, barely make out Teddy, climbing his driveway with the heavy uncertain feet of an old man.

* * *

Time moved on. Like most people, the residents of Muskgrove Lane were preoccupied with the busyness of their lives—births, funerals, weddings, graduations and everything that went on in between. Jack and the others graduated from high school and then went off to college, work or wherever else their dreams and fears led them. The basketball court in the cul-de-sac looked lonely, having to settle for sporadic contests of "Horse" or "21." The glory days were gone and like all holiday seasons, Detective Lloyd Burns was overworked and underpaid.

Staring out of his office window and finishing the last of his stale, lukewarm cup of coffee, Lloyd watched the snowflakes float by in the dusk of evening. For police officers and detectives, Christmas wasn't particularly merry. When the phone rang at the precinct station, it wasn't to announce that Santa was passing out gifts, but more likely that he was passed out in an alleyway downtown. For the men and women of Precinct 44, Christmas was a time of drunken domestic squabbles, traffic accidents initiated by harried, preoccupied last-minute shoppers and barroom brawls where patrons, not reindeer, sported red noses. Lloyd chuckled softly to himself.

"'Tis the season to be jolly."

"Hey, Lloyd, Officer Klein wants to see you down at Intake," bellowed McGillicutty, the burly Desk Sergeant.

"What does she want?"

McGillicutty looked up from the mound of paperwork on his desk and scowled.

"Hell if I know. What do I look like, a damn encyclopedia!"

Lloyd Burns looked at the clock. Ten minutes to quitting time. He grabbed his briefcase and ambled down the hall to the Intake room where he found Patrol Officer Susan Klein thumbing through a dog-eared card file.

"Susan, what can I do for you this fine evening?"

"Probably nothing. I thought I'd give you a head's up on a young guy we just picked up on a solicitation and drug possession charge down in the 'fresh meat' district. Said he knew you."

Lloyd's heart sank.

"What's his name?"

Officer Klein flipped through the paperwork on her desk

"Let's see—here it is. He goes by the name Teddy Runion."

Lloyd took a deep breath.

"Yeah, I know him. What's the deal on him?"

Scrutinizing her report, Officer Klein talked as she read.

"Looks like it's his third arrest. Twice for prostitution and once for drugs. He's currently on probation which more than likely will be revoked, and since he's just turned eighteen, he may buy some time."

Rubbing his chin, Lloyd stared at Officer Klein.

"How 'bout diversion programs? Teddy was a good kid. Grew up in my neighborhood. He had a tough life—not many breaks."

"Yeah, didn't they all," Klein said as she neatly stacked the arrest reports.

"You might try Chris Smith's half-way house over in Chillicowee. He runs a good program. Better than most. A lot of his kids seem to make it."

"Thanks, Klein. I'll check it out. And thanks for the heads up."

"Don't mention it."

Lloyd called his wife as he had done so often before and begged off the Christmas party at her sister's. Having been a police officer's wife for twenty years she understood, but still found it difficult to mask her disappointment. Although he wasn't sure why, Lloyd didn't tell her about Teddy. There would be time enough for that later.

Lloyd spent the next two and a half hours making calls. Two programs turned him down and a third put Teddy's name on a waiting list. Finally, Chris Smith returned his call. Mustering up the last of his day's energy and stopping just short of begging, Lloyd gave Chris his best shot.

There was a long pause on the other end of the line.

"Okay, Detective. It must be the Christmas spirit. I'll find a way to make room for him. Bring him by tomorrow morning."

"Thanks, Chris. I owe you."

"Yes, you do Detective. Yes, you do."

The good news seemed to refresh Lloyd as he sauntered back down to Intake. He allowed himself a small smile and imagined that this could be the life-changing break that Teddy needed.

Lloyd looked through the interview window at Teddy. He had changed. His blond hair was still meticulously combed, but his face had a drawn, gaunt look to it. His left arm sported a tattoo of an angel.

Lloyd opened the door and walked inside.

"Sarge!" Teddy exclaimed, standing up and extending his hand.

"Hi, Teddy. Long time no see."

Teddy rubbed one eye and kept the other fixated on the badge clinging to Lloyd's coat pocket. "It really has been," he said, nodding to intensify his delivery. "Been a long while. How you doing?"

Teddy stopped rubbing his eye and smiled.

"I've had better days—worse ones too."

Lloyd nodded to an invisible beat and tapped on his coffee cup, his mind scrambling for words.

"Teddy, you know you don't have to live like this. I have friends who could find you a place at a half-way house. There are drug treatment center options, counseling—anything you need."

Teddy's face softened, his eyes a little less shaded.

"Sarge, I really appreciate you trying to help me," he said, "but the truth is, I don't want to change."

Lloyd leaned in closer.

"You sure? 'Cause I really want … I really do know some folks who can help you."

Teddy's face looked older, lines and creases sculpted by long walks up a gravel driveway.

"Yeah, Sarge," he said, "I'm sure."

Lloyd Burns tried, but couldn't hide his distress. He felt like he had been punctured with a giant pin and all the air had been sucked out of him. He tried to give Teddy a smile, but only partially succeeded so instead, he patted him on the shoulder and motioned to Officer Klein that he was through. As she led Teddy out of the office, he turned and looked at the Detective.

"Hey Sarge, you remember that time you gave me a ride home in the rain?"

Lloyd looked up and nodded his head.

"You said I was a good boy. I've never forgotten that."

Sitting in silence, Lloyd cradled his coffee cup in his palm and watched Teddy disappear down the hallway.

Discussion Questions

1. How do you feel you would have reacted if you had experienced what Teddy did?

2. Is there anything Sarge or the other neighbors could have done differently that might have improved Teddy's chances regarding

a more successful and adjustment and future? What are the ethical/moral implications of their actions?

3. To what extent do you feel Teddy is responsible for his situation? What are some other, more positive choices he could have made?

4. How could public institutions like the criminal justice system and education do a better job of not letting the Teddys of the world fall through the cracks?

Special of the Week

"It's cold as a witch's teat out there," Jimmy "Fastball" Burns exclaimed as he bustled through the main entrance of "Everybody Rides" used car lot, passing out cheeseburgers, fries and steaming cups of coffee.

"I ain't never seen a cold spell like this in the middle of December."

"You got that right!" Sam Jenkins, who was also known as Sam "Batboy" Jenkins, chimed in.

Buzz "Homerun" Renfro took a sip of coffee. "Why don't you two yahoos shut up and pass me some fries before they get cold."

J.J. "Coach" Moran, the Manager, looked at the three salesmen with mild disgust, the way a father would look at his rambunctious children. "Why don't all three of you quiet down so I can finish this here book on Joe DiMaggio, the greatest baseball player who ever lived."

"Everybody Rides" was actually the budget used car lot of the mega-dealership, "King of the Road Jaguar/Chrysler/Dodge/Kia/Daewoo." In automobile sales, this was the bottom of the barrel. The good used cars were on display in a paved lot adjoining the new car dealership. "Everybody Rides" was located two blocks from the other lots. "King of the Road" owner, Wild Bill Hancock, didn't want a car lot that proudly displayed in bright red letters under its name— NOTHING OVER $3995 and YOUR JOB IS YOUR CREDIT—to be too closely associated with the classier side of his business. As added punishment, "Everybody Rides" had to stay open until 10 p.m. each night while the rest of the dealership closed at 9:00 p.m.

If an outside observer were to come to the conclusion that Coach had a thing for baseball, he or she would be right on the money.

He had coached Little League baseball for over thirty years and never had a winning season, but to hear him tell it, he had always been one hit or pitch away from baseball glory.

The only sounds in the office that evening were the sounds of four men inhaling their supper as they chewed, gulped and belched their way down to the last french fry. Each man had his own story of what brought him to this place. Coach had successfully managed the upscale used car lot for ten years before he punched out an opposing Little League coach who happened to be the cousin of Wild Bill Hancock. The others were exiled to "Everybody Rides" for different reasons and in keeping with his passion for baseball, Coach had given each of his "players" a nickname.

Jimmy "Fastball" Burns had been the leading Dodge truck salesman for three years in a row. Nobody knew more about pickup trucks than he did and nobody could close a truck sale as quickly as he could. Unfortunately, "Fastball" decided to celebrate his third divorce by driving off in a brand new loaded Dodge Club Cab that he hadn't cleared with the manager. With a fifth of Jim Beam riding shotgun, he totaled the truck and his sales career.

Sam "Batboy" Jenkins was a wiry fellow with nervous eyes. Coach had named him "Batboy" because as he frequently reminded him: "Boy, you ain't even in the game. You can't score, if you don't get to the plate." Coach used to call Sam "Third String" Jenkins, but after three consecutive months at the bottom of the sales ladder, demoted him to "Batboy."

Sam was the only one of the four men who had never been married. In fact, he had allegedly only had two dates and one didn't count—the occasion of his senior prom when he paid his next-door neighbor, Debbie Ann Muskgrove twenty dollars to accompany him. Rumor had it that he offered to pay her another five dollars for a goodnight kiss.

The truth was that Debbie Ann told Sam that the only part of her he could kiss for five dollars was her ass.

Coach was married to his second wife; "Fastball" was, as he liked to put it, currently "playing the field"; and Buzz, also divorced, was heavily involved with Darlene, a former dancer with "Sand and Sun

Cruise Lines." She was presently employed as senior nail technician for "The New You Salon."

Buzz and Darlene had been going together for more than a year and although he had told no one, he was planning to pop the question on New Year's Eve.

Leaning back in an office chair with his feet propped up on his desk, Buzz fingered the gold-plated money clip in his left front pocket that secured the five $100 bills he had saved to buy Darlene's engagement ring. He smiled in anticipation of her excitement. No one could get as excited as Darlene. Buzz's daydream was abruptly interrupted by the grating voice of Jimmy "Fastball" Burns.

"Customer on the lot. It's your turn Renfro," he bellowed.

Buzz lit a Marlboro Light and peered out the office window into the cold, black December night. Who would be looking for a used car at 8:45 on a cold Saturday night? Blowing a spiral of smoke rings toward the ceiling, Buzz said, "Why don't we give them a few minutes to see if they are really serious."

Without taking his eyes off the page he was reading, Coach took charge of the situation: "Batter up Renfro. Get your ass out there and into scoring position. Batboy, you're in the on deck circle."

Batboy grinned at Buzz. "I done taken a peek Homerun. I can tell from here, she ain't much to look at and more'n likely she ain't got no money. Them two kids means she ain't got no man which means she ain't got no money which means you ain't gonna make no money. Comprendez, Amigo?"

Buzz blew another series of smoke rings toward the door. "Two things, Batboy: First, I'm not your Amigo and second, can you comprendez that?"

Zipping up his parka, Buzz ground out the remnants of his cigarette in the ashtray, closed the door behind him and stepped out into the cold night.

* * *

Agnes was cold and not just from the threadbare parka she was wearing, but cold deep inside, down in her bones. She felt like her heart was almost frozen shut—like it was barely beating. The only thing on this freezing December night that gave her any warmth was her son, Kenny, and her daughter, Sonja. And they gave her just enough to keep her going a while longer. Ten years seemed like a lifetime ago when she up and married their father, a truck driver twenty years her senior. They met at the small mountain top café where she had worked as a waitress. Harold had promised her the good life, but what he had given her was too many years of misery. He finally left her and the children two years ago with unpaid bills and no goodbyes.

Agnes wasn't a woman given to bitterness, she was just tired. Somehow, having Kenny and Sonja made the misery worth the trouble. At eight and six, they were still young enough to make up the difference between the poverty and hopelessness with a few well-practiced dreams, the most recent incarnation being what Santa Claus might bring them. At least it seemed to be so as far as Sonja was concerned. Agnes wasn't as sure about Kenny. He acted happy enough, but she had seen the sad, uncertain look in his eyes when he thought she wasn't paying attention.

Working two jobs, one at a nursing home and the other at Taco Bell didn't make for much of a life. They had been evicted from their apartment for unpaid rent three days after her truck had been repossessed. Agnes had no illusions about her chances of getting the salesman walking towards her to sell her a car for a fifty-dollar down payment, but fifty dollars was all she had.

* * *

"How do you do, Ma'am? You gotta a couple of fine looking children. Name's Buzz Renfro. What can I do for you?"

Agnes looked at the salesman for several moments before she spoke. "Mr. Renfro, my name's Agnes Davis and these here are my children, Kenny and Sonja. We are in great need of a reliable vehicle."

"Yes ma'am. Well, you've come to the right place because 'reliable' is our middle name. Every vehicle we sell has undergone a 21 point inspection."

"Mama," Sonja interrupted, "I'm hungry!"

"Hush Sonja, we'll get something to eat when we finish our business with Mr. Renfro."

Dropping her head at the tone of reprimand in Agnes's voice, Sonja buried her face in Kenny's jacket.

"Tell you what kids, how 'bout candy bars and cokes on me while your mother and I check out the cars," Buzz offered, pulling three one-dollar bills out of his pocket.

"I couldn't let you do that, Mr. Renfro," Agnes protested.

"I ain't hungry anyway," Kenny added, stuffing his hands in the pockets of his denim jacket.

"Well, I am," Sonja exclaimed, peering from behind the folds of her brother's jacket.

"Hey, I insist," Buzz responded. "Besides, you'll be warm inside. Ask for a Mr. Moran when you get inside. He'll show you where the goodies are."

Agnes relented and Kenny took the three dollars and Sonja by the hand and proceeded toward the office. Buzz lit another cigarette as he and Agnes stood watching the vapor trail of Kenny and Sonja's breathing as they made their way toward food and warmth.

"Now, Mrs. Davis, what would you like to look at? We only have about an hour until we close."

Agnes' eyes escorted her children into the office. "Mr. Renfro, I'm going to be honest with you. I'm in desperate need of a vehicle. I have two children, two jobs—if I can come up with transportation—nowhere to live, and fifty dollars in my right coat pocket."

Buzz took a deep draw from his cigarette before he spoke.

"Ma'am, please don't take this the wrong way, but sounds to me like you need a lot more help than just a vehicle—at least more help than I can give you. You need to get a hold of some area churches or the Human Services Department or something else like that. Besides, the cheapest vehicle on our lot requires a down payment of several hundred dollars. Maybe you ought to call your family."

Agnes turned her head slightly to compose herself. "No offense taken, Mr. Renfro. Don't have no family, but I'll figure something out."

She took a deep breath and extended her hand. "I want to thank you for the kindness you showed my children. I'll be fetchin' them now."

"Well, Ma'am, at least let me get you a hot cup of coffee."

"Thank you, but that won't be necessary," Agnes replied as she walked toward the office, leaving Buzz to ponder the crisp night air. "Hellfire," Buzz muttered to himself. "Why do I always have to get the hard-luck customers? Life's tough for *everybody*."

He could see Kenny's and Sonja's faces peering out of the office window as their mother approached them and thought to himself, Where will they go? What'll happen to them? What does it matter to me? It don't.

All Buzz had on his mind was the wad of cash in his pocket and Darlene. He popped a piece of chewing gum in his mouth and pretended to check the cars on the lot. He also pretended it would be less embarrassing for Agnes and her kids if he waited until they left.

Buzz watched as Agnes and her children made their way across the car lot toward the bus stop on the corner. As they started to cross the street, Sonja turned and waved to him and shouted, "Hey Mister! Thank you for the candy. I hope you have a Merry Christmas!"

It was at that precise moment that Buzz Renfro went temporarily insane.

He might as well have been hit by a meteor from outer space. The gold plated money clip in his pant's pocket seemed to turn white hot. He felt dizzy, his knees buckled slightly, and even with the chill of the night air, Buzz could feel a bead of sweat break out on his forehead.

Somewhere between Sonja's "Merry" and "Christmas," something—some great mystery—traveling faster than the speed of light, had penetrated Buzz Renfro and knocked him senseless. In that moment, the fake gold nugget ring on his right hand ceased to exist. Even the image of Darlene became little more than a dancing shadow. Buzz was pulled out of himself into a place he had never been before. It was as if he was having an out-of-body experience, observing himself running toward Agnes and her two children who were standing under the street light, waiting on the rest of their lives.

As he ran, his mind was saying stop, but his legs weren't listening.

When he caught up with them, Buzz bent over and grabbed his knees, breathing heavily.

"Mr. Renfro, are you all right?" Buzz took a deep breath, sucking the cold air into his lungs. "Yes ma'am, I believe I am. It just occurred to me that we might have a vehicle suitable to your needs."

"But I told you, I only have...."

Buzz interrupted her, "I forgot to tell you about the special of the week. If you could use a 1992 minivan, you could drive it away tonight for no down payment and one hundred and twenty-five dollars a month."

"I don't know what to say," Agnes' eyes widened.

"Say yes, Mama. Say yes!" Sonja exclaimed, jumping up and down as Kenny looked on silently.

"Yes," Agnes said, her face freed up the hint of a smile, the first she had felt in weeks.

Agnes with her coffee and Kenny and Sonja with their hot chocolate waited in the customer lounge while Buzz filled out the paper work.

Batboy shook his head. "I would've bet a month's pay that lady wouldn't have two cents to her name. Can't believe she's got the cash for the down payment."

"Well believe it," Buzz replied as he signed the last of the finance forms.

Draining the last of his coffee, Coach looked solemnly at Buzz and cleared his throat, "Well, Homerun, it wasn't one of our better units—certainly not of home-run caliber, but I will give you an infield hit."

Buzz handed Agnes the keys. Even Kenny seemed excited. Not like Sonja, but at least pleased. Looking at the keys in her hand, Agnes didn't say anything. Instead, she put her arms around Buzz and placed her head on his chest. He didn't know what else to do so he hugged her.

As the minivan left the lot of "Everybody Rides," all Buzz could see was the smiling face of Sonja pressed against the rear glass window. Her smile went right through him. His fingers grazed the empty money clip. It wasn't hot any more. And he knew Darlene probably wouldn't be coming down his chimney on Christmas Eve. Opening a fresh pack of cigarettes, Buzz looked up at the glittering stars and said to no one in particular, "Merry 'hotdamn' Christmas."

Discussion Questions

1. What would be your honest reaction if you were the salesperson on call when the homeless mother and her two children came looking for a vehicle on a frigid winter's night?
2. Why did Buzz risk his relationship with his girlfriend and use his money to help the family in need? Did anything about his personality suggest that he might take such an action?
3. Did Buzz's compassionate response mean that he had changed— that he would from now on, be more caring and considerate to those who were in need?
4. If you were Buzz, would you have any regrets?

11

RASHEED'S TICKET

The green vinyl sofa squeaked as Rasheed Smith shifted his weight in Mel Evans' office. Evans responded to the noise by casting an involuntary glance in the young man's direction, and then refocused his attention on the inmate's folder and written request.

As Evans studied Rasheed's file, Rasheed examined the details of the caseworker's office for the umpteenth time while a small oscillating fan did its best to dispel the humidity of a midwestern summer. An orange shag carpet, Jimi Hendrix poster, over-sized boom box and lava lamp were the predominant features of Mel Evans' work environment, or as he liked to refer to it, his "pad." Rasheed wondered to himself what the caseworker's real home must look like. Was it as funky as his office?

Two things were common knowledge among the brothers in the cellblock: first that Mr. Evans for one reason or another was lost in the sixties and seventies, and second, that he wanted to be accepted by black inmates. It was primarily the second reason that Rasheed had come to him with this particular request.

Mel Evans quietly folded the file and placed it upon the desk as Rasheed gazed absent-mindedly at the picture of Jimi Hendrix.

Evans smiled. "No one played guitar like Jimi. I'm convinced that 'All along the Watchtower' is the greatest rock song ever recorded."

Rasheed nodded. "Yes Sir, except that he didn't write it."

"What's that?"

"He didn't write it. Bob Dylan did."

"Had no idea. That's some Hendrix trivia lost on me."

"But you're right, though—he was something else with that guitar of his."

"Damn straight he was," Evans continued as he launched into his well known version of how black music, from slave-inspired spirituals to current rap and hip-hop, had shaped and enriched the musical landscape of American culture.

Rasheed sighed and did as countless other inmates of color had done, trying his best to appear interested in the caseworker's time-worn soliloquy.

Satisfied that he had duly impressed Rasheed with his empathy and understanding of minorities, Mel Evans folded his hands and placed them on his desktop.

"First, Rasheed let me say that I'm really impressed with your progress. Last year, you had six write-ups for fighting. This year you only had one. And here you are graduating at the top of your class. Out of 21 student residents, you have the highest grade point average. I can't tell you how proud I am of you."

"Thank you, Sir."

"While your request is out of the ordinary, I can certainly understand why you would want your Momma to share your graduation experience with you."

Rasheed broke into a smile.

"Yes Sir. She ain't never seen nothin' but trouble with me. This would show her another side. It would mean a lot to her and to me and…."

Caseworker Evans interrupted.

"I know it would. And I would love to help out. I really would. Trouble is I don't have any funds or resources to help you get her here for the ceremony. I'm really sorry I can't help."

"Not even for a bus ticket?" Rasheed countered. "She could stay with her sister in Lincoln. All she would need is a round-trip bus ticket."

Evans' silence accentuated Rasheed's disappointment.

"Tell you what; let me check with Chaplin Stinson. I know he has a small rainy day fund for special needs. Maybe he can help you and your Momma out. Why don't you make an appointment with him next week? I'll put in a good word for you."

A hint of hope returned as Rasheed shook hands with the caseworker.

* * *

Corporal Smitty Hudson scooped a fresh pinch of Skoal from the round tin and placed it under his tongue as he watched Rasheed close the caseworker's door behind him. He had never really liked the young man walking toward him. On more than one occasion, Rasheed had been a real pain in the ass. And besides he was black. Smitty's Granddaddy had believed in segregation. Even two generations removed, after a racial incident in his cell house, he would find himself reconsidering the wisdom of his Granddaddy's conviction.

"You ready to head back to your kitchen work assignment?"

"Yes Sir," Rasheed replied as he fell into step with the older man's slow walk.

"Evans still got that picture of that hippie guitar player on his wall and that orange rug?"

"Yes Sir."

Corporal Hudson chuckled to himself and spit a stream of tobacco juice into the styrofoam cup he carried in his right hand.

"That boy is a piece of work."

Talking to himself as much as to the Corporal, Rasheed responded, "That he is, Sir. That he is."

* * *

Chaplain Stinson was an earnest sort of man. A Methodist minister, he had pastored two small churches in Oklahoma before he was hired as Senior Chaplain for the State Prison. Although the title did appeal to him, he was well aware that he was not only the senior Chaplain, but also the only Chaplain serving over 2000 resident inmates in a prison originally built for 1200. He was grateful for the Catholic and Lutheran volunteer Chaplains and tolerant of the Muslim Cleric who held services once a month in the gym.

Chaplain Stinson's office was as calm and simple as Mel Evans' office was loud and gaudy. He personally found the institutional pale green color of his office and the chapel serene. A large bronze crucifix hung on the wall behind his desk. The Chaplain cared about the inmates in his charge in a serious, yet distant, sort of way. At the monthly meetings of the local ministerial association he was fond of referring to the inmate residents at the state prison as his "errant flock."

Other than a desk, an executive chair, and a computer hutch, the only other furniture was a single chair for visitors, positioned directly in front of his desk. Chaplain Stinson's office had a neat and austere look to it. There was in fact, a sense of order and authority. During last year's annual private retreat, Fred Stinson had experienced an epiphany. In the midst of the chaos of prison life and all the anguish and darkness the residents brought with them, his office and chapel was to be an oasis of clarity and certainty. While the authority of the criminal justice system had placed the residents in the State Prison, it was the higher authority—the Supreme Judge—that constituted his domain of concern. As he like to put it, he was not only concerned with correcting their misbehavior, but with their "eternal rehabilitation" as well.

* * *

Sipping the steaming cup of Earl Grey tea, Chaplain Stinson carefully perused Rasheed Smith's file and written request. The young man had certainly made progress. There was no doubt about that. From aggression in the cell house to aggressively pursuing his education—it was an excellent example of sublimation. The Chaplain smiled to himself. His continuing studies in psychoanalysis were bearing fruit. His personal reflections were interrupted by Jerry, his inmate assistant.

"Chaplain, your three o'clock is here."

"Excellent, Jerry, send him in."

After Rasheed had seated himself, the Chaplain quietly observed him for several moments before he spoke.

"I've read your request and reviewed your file, Rasheed. And I must say I am impressed with the progress you have made."

"Yes Sir. Thank you Sir," Rasheed responded with a mix of hope and consternation. "It's just that my Momma ain't never seen this side of me. She only seen what I was in the past—the bad part of me. She's scraped together all the money she can get her hands on and she can stay with her sister in Lincoln—so all she needs is fifty-five dollars to help pay for the bus ticket. Mr. Evans said you had a special fund that might be able to help my Momma to get to my graduation."

Chaplain Stinson folded his hands together and looked at Rasheed intently.

"It is true that I have access to a 'special needs' fund. Unfortunately, the balance of that account has been earmarked to handle expenses associated with the spring concert of the Singspirations. The men have been practicing all year and the townfolk always give a generous love offering at the end of the concert. Those donations are essential to our Chapel music program. So, as much as I would like to help you and your Mother, Rasheed, it wouldn't be fair to the choir members or townspeople. I'm truly sorry."

Rasheed said nothing. His disappointment was obvious. He could feel the anger of the "old" Rasheed boiling up in his belly as he rose to leave.

"Wait a minute, young man. Before you go, let's have a word of prayer. Tell you what, we will pray for a miracle. You know, God's in the miracle business!"

Rasheed bit his lip.

"That's alright Chaplain, I don't really feel…."

"I insist!" Chaplain Stinson interrupted.

The Chaplain waxed eloquent for a few moments about miracles and faith and such while Rasheed bowed his head and counted the tiny colored squares on the rug beneath his feet in an effort to keep his composure.

Like before, Corporal Hudson was waiting to escort Rasheed back to the kitchen. As they walked down the long corridor, the correctional officer leisurely worked the toothpick between his teeth.

"Those hamburgers at lunch had a lot of gristle in them."

Rasheed said nothing, counting the green floor tiles as the two of them proceeded toward their destination.

"Strike out again?"

"Struck out again," Rasheed whispered.

Hudson retrieved the toothpick from his mouth and pushed it into his shirt pocket for later use.

"Well, one thing's for sure. Getting a piece of paper with a high school diploma on it is a sight better than all the papers you got with write-ups on 'em. And I ought a know, cause I signed quite a few myself."

"Guess so," Rasheed murmured to no one in particular.

* * *

The keynote speaker for graduation day was the local high school principal who delivered an inspiring, if somewhat awkward "grand accomplishments/new horizons" kind of message. The 21 graduates and their family members sat in metal folding chairs in the educational annex for the duration of the ceremony. The day was hot and the participants sweated together in a sea of smiles and pride.

Dressed in cap and gown, Rasheed was grinning from ear to ear as he received a plaque and special medallion for graduating first in his class.

After the ceremony, the reception tables beckoned the graduates, family members and attending staff with sandwiches, cookies and punch, courtesy of the prison kitchen workers. There was even a special cake honoring one of their own, Rasheed, for his accomplishment.

As everyone circled around the tables, Rasheed insisted that his Momma help him cut the first piece of cake while her sister, Verona, took their picture. That photograph would become the most valued of personal artifacts belonging to Rasheed—a reminder of something positive to build his life around, a sign of possibilities, the hope of better times to come.

All the prison dignitaries were there. The Superintendent figured if he was going to show up and shake hands, so would every other professional who worked in the prison that he deemed relevant to such a high event. Caseworker Evans and Chaplain Stinson were among those professionals so identified. They stood among graduates and family members, smiling, sipping their punch and doing their duty.

Chaplain Stinson was especially pleased to see that Rasheed's Mother was able to attend her son's graduation.

As Rasheed prepared to refill his Momma's cup with punch, the Chaplain called out to him.

"Rasheed."

Rasheed turned to the approaching Chaplain.

"Congratulations, son. I am so pleased that your Mother was able to attend the ceremony."

"Yes Sir," Rasheed responded while refilling his Momma's cup.

"Remember our prayer that day in my office when everything looked so bleak? Events have a way of working out when we give God the credit and rely on his will. I believe your Mother's presence here today is proof of that. Miracles can still happen. With God, the impossible becomes possible."

Rasheed's smile disappeared. He quietly looked at Chaplain Stinson before he spoke.

"Can't say much about miracles or what God had to do with it, but I guess I'd have to give any credit that was due to Corporal Hudson."

"Corporal Hudson?"

"Yeah, it was the Corporal who sent my Momma the bus ticket. He never said nothin' to me 'bout it. 'Course I thanked him when my Momma wrote me."

The Chaplain was clearly surprised.

"I wonder why he did it? Of course, it's wonderful that he did."

"Don't know. Me and the Corporal never got along that well. Guess you'd have to ask him," Rasheed replied as he gathered up a chocolate chip cookie to go with the punch.

* * *

Smitty Hudson knocked on Chaplain Stinson's office door. He had come to retrieve a young inmate who had been placed on suicide watch.

The Chaplain opened the door and instructed the young inmate he had been counseling to wait in the reception area while he had a word with the Corporal.

Corporal Hudson closed the door behind him.

"What can I do for you Chaplain?"

"Smitty, I wanted to tell you how impressed I am regarding your gesture of generosity concerning Rasheed and his Mother last week."

"Nothing to be impressed about."

"I beg to differ," the Chaplain replied. "But I must confess to some curiosity as to why you helped out? As I recall, Rasheed gave you a great deal of trouble last year. I believe I remember that he even took a swing at you on an occasion when you were trying to break up a fight."

"Truth is he took two swings, not one. He missed with the first one, but I caught a black eye with the second."

Chaplain Stinson smiled, amazed.

"And yet, with all the trouble he caused you, you still helped him."

"Don't understand the fuss, Chaplain. Rasheed's done some bad things in his life. May do some more. But his schooling's a good thing that also took some doing."

"Still, the bus ticket for his Mother came out of your own pocket," the Chaplain said. "That's certainly going the extra mile. What was your inspiration for such an impressive act of generosity?"

Smitty Hudson looked at the Chaplain as though he was confused.

"Can't say as I'm getting your point. Like I said, the boy who was doing bad, done good. And his Momma deserved to see the good. Don't know about no extra mile or inspiration. What I do know—it's almost quittin' time and I got to get that inmate back to the medical section."

Smitty turned to retrieve his charge.

"See you later, Chaplain."

Discussion Questions

1. How important do you feel Rasheed's educational accomplishment is to his future? To his self-image and attitude?
2. Why would someone like Corporal Hudson who harbored some feelings of prejudice, help Rasheed's Mother attend his graduation? What ethical model might be reflected in his actions?
3. How might Corporal Hudson's efforts influence Rasheed's perception and attitude regarding corrections officers and criminal justice professionals in general?
4. What would be your recommendations to Caseworker Evans and Chaplain Stinson? What could they learn from Corporal Hudson's example?

12

CRAZY TIMES

The Midtown Diner was on the back-end of the lunch rush. Several booths still needed to be cleared and the once full counter now seated three retired regulars picking at the remains of their meatloaf Wednesday lunch specials. Two friends sat in the back booth, one wearing the uniform of the town's police chief and the other wearing the uniform of a retired police officer—a sweatshirt, jeans and a Mets baseball cap.

Retired Sergeant Sam Foster looked up at Verna, the waitress, and smiled. "I'll have the diet cheeseburger, a side of diet fries and coffee.

Verna laughed as she always did. "Diet burger and fries, coming right up."

"What will you have, Chief."

Chief Ed Green grimaced as if in pain. "I'll have the Greek salad with light Italian dressing and unsweetened tea."

Sam looked at his old friend and chuckled. "At least, you're losing some weight. If you are a good boy and eat all your salad, I'll save you a fry or two."

Ed Green shook his head. "Not funny. Doc says I've got to get my cholesterol and weight down if I want to keep kicking. And Madge—she's like a cross between Sherlock Holmes and a prison warden. I can't even sneak an oatmeal cookie in after supper."

"That's what a good wife does," Sam replied. "Beats living alone."

Ed's face softened. "I know you miss Nancy. How long has it been?"

Sam looked out the window. "Seven years … seems like yesterday."

Verna brought their food and refilled their drinks.

"Sam, I have to admit it—I miss your ugly face. More than that, I miss your counsel. You were always the one I could go to when I needed some common-sense advice and a straight answer. I guess you heard about the shooting in Bluestone where a black female officer shot a wheel-chair bound elderly African-American man who pointed what she thought was a gun at her."

Sam popped a french fry into his mouth. "Yeah I did. News said he told her he had a gun under his blanket on his lap except that it wasn't a gun, but the remote control to his television."

"That's right," the Chief replied. "He hadn't taken his medication and was apparently off his rocker."

Chief Green took a sip of iced tea. "The officer is catching hell from the community. Her daughter came home crying from her school after three girls slapped and taunted her."

"It's a damn shame," Sam said as he wiped his mouth with a napkin.

Ed forked a black olive and some lettuce into his mouth. "Bluestone's not that far away from Midtown. I'm hearing rumbling that there may be some kind of protest march there and here. Seems there's a group that calls themselves "Justice Now" that's made up mostly of a dozen or so college kids and a left-wing nut teacher—I think his name is Morrison—from the local college."

Sam Foster finished off what was left of his cheeseburger. "The fruits of higher learning?"

"To make matters worse," Chief Green continued. "Some redneck self-styled militia from Ogden county plans to protest their protest."

Sam picked at a half-eaten French fry. "I think I saw several of them at the Walmart last Saturday. They were driving old pick-up trucks with rebel flags painted on the hoods—not exactly high art."

"Sam, I need your input on what's happening. Maybe even get you back to work as a consultant for some strategic planning and officer training. The Mayor and City Council want me to do a 'show of strength' and make an example of whoever makes trouble. Haskell Simmons kept saying at the Council meeting last night that I need to 'nip it in the bud' by dressing the officers in full riot gear—even placing snipers in visible locations to intimidate protestors. What's your take on all this?"

Locking his hands behind his head, Sam leaned back in his seat. "Chief, the situation we find ourselves living in is what I call 'crazy times.'"

Chief Green rubbed his chin. "Crazy Times?"

"Yep," Sam replied draining the last of his coffee. "Fear sells. Politicians are selling it hard from the left and the right. They make little effort to work together—just get reelected, collect more money from lobbyists and keep their base happy—no cooperation or compromise, only conflict. Add to that, fear sells guns and makes folks edgy. Weak background checks and gun regulation. Hell, even people on 'The Terrorist Watch List' can still buy guns. They are too dangerous to allow on a plane, but not too dangerous to buy a military style gun with an extended magazine. It all adds up to 'crazy times.' More and more folks have concealed carry permits and while I understand their concerns, a one day training session with a 22 pistol doesn't prepare them for a live shooting situation police officers and soldiers are constantly trained for. I don't know if you know, but our state has the highest rate of accidental shooting deaths in the country. Like I said, 'crazy times.'"

Ed Green furrowed his brow with a look of concern. "Amen to that."

"Given all that craziness, police officers are skittish," Sam continued. "They know a lot of folks are carrying concealed weapons and they know there is the real possibility that they could be out-gunned like in the Dallas shootings that killed five officers."

"Not to mention the increase of law enforcement officers being ambushed," Chief Green interjected.

"That's right. And the cherry on top of that stress sundae are the increasing cuts in technology and training budgets. We can't even get the politicians to fund a decent national data base to help us track criminals and communicate efficiently with other law enforcement agencies."

Ed Green pounded the table. "Hell, we even had our in-service training budget cut by 40 percent. They tell us to do more with less funding. I don't see them cutting their pay on the state or federal level."

Sam Foster leaned forward. "Like I said, my friend, 'crazy times.'"

"Crazy times, indeed," Ed exhaled. "Troublemakers left and right. Local politicians who are 'Dirty Harry' wannabes advocating simple-minded get tough policies. And police officers who feel overwhelmed and unappreciated by too many of the people they protect and serve."

The two men sat in silence, lost in thought about their back and forth conversation.

Finally, Chief Green looked at his friend. "You know, Sam, there are some officers who are bad apples like in the Charleston shooting, but most of the men and women just want to do their jobs to the best of their abilities—protect and serve 'all' members of the community."

Ed Green stared off into space. "Even if they replace me—even if it costs me my badge, I'll be damned if I will declare war on the citizens of Midtown or the surrounding county. Protestors or not, I aim to use some of those crisis intervention and community relations skills we've been trained in before escalating any conflict. I expect my officers to protect themselves, but not unnecessarily provoke folks no matter who they are."

The Chief picked up the lunch check. "I still need your help. How about it?"

Sam Foster retrieved a toothpick from his jeans pocket and placed it in his mouth. "Under one condition."

"What's that?" Ed replied.

"I get all the diet cheeseburgers and fries I can eat."

Ed Green laughed as he rose from the table. "Done."

Discussion Questions

1. Was the female police officer's response correct? Did she have any other options? If you had been her, what would you have done?
2. What does Sam Foster mean when he talks with the Chief about "crazy times"? What role does politics—local and otherwise—play in how effective and ethical law enforcement is in a given community?
3. What do you think about the Chief's attitude and approach in how he plans to deal with what appears to be the coming protests?
4. Why does a "Dirty Harry" approach—the use of force—often appeal to citizens? What kinds of unintended consequences can be the result of such an approach?

13

THE BIG PICTURE

"You can't count that as a win."

"No conviction. That's a win. Six capitals, no death sentences. I'm on a roll." Stinson leaned back, swung his legs onto the table and crossed his ostrich boots. He laced his fingers behind his head and smirked.

Rachel Young couldn't tell if he was serious or kidding her. She was inclined to think the latter.

"Your client committed suicide in the jail. How do you count that as a win?"

"Hey, he didn't die in the electric chair. The prosecution didn't get a conviction. That's a win for our side," he argued.

She swept the remains of her lunch onto the tray and stood up. Kidding or not, this conversation was too weird for her and she took her leave of the small group of defense attorneys. Their table was in the corner of the courthouse cafeteria. Rarely did an interloper intrude. For one thing, someone from their informal ragtag group was usually there. There always seemed to be at least one or two of them drinking coffee in the morning waiting for a docket call, having an early lunch before heading back to the office, or taking an afternoon break from a trial.

She needed to get back to the office she shared with two other women. They both practiced family law and constantly encouraged her to switch over and drop her criminal practice. Truth be told, they didn't much care for her clientele and she could hardly blame them. Actually, she did most of her work in the courthouse hallways. Since she passed the bar, she had been building her practice by picking up court appointments. Supposedly all that was required was to put your name on the list with the judge's clerk. In reality, there was a little more to it than that. Since there was no rotation system and there were a lot of names on the list, it was necessary to help the judge in his or her decision-making process. She soon learned she needed to hang around the courtroom for those times when a judge needed a lawyer quickly, appear at the right social functions and even contribute to re-election campaigns. The amounts weren't huge, but they were enough to remind the judges that she was around. At first, she was appalled at the implicit graft; but she quickly became inured to the idea that she had to play the game in order to survive.

* * *

"Jack, you know this is not only a probation violation, it's going to be a new charge. The prosecutor is offering 5 years. With parole and time served you'll be out in less than three years. I think that's fair."

Rachel wearily argued with her client, a man in his 30s who believed in creative ways to get income. She was sitting across from him in the tiny closet that they called the attorney's conference room in the county jail. He smelled of sweat and the room was hot. She desperately wanted to open the door and get some air.

"That's bullshit! I know a guy who had 5 counts at the same time and he walked away with probation! You just want to get rid of my case and collect your paycheck!"

The pudgy redneck pushed aggressively against the table between them. He was trying to scare her. A year ago she had been very nervous about meetings in the jail. The surroundings and her clients were so foreign to her that she was easily intimidated. Gradually, however, she realized that most of them were bullies and blowhards. They barked, but they didn't usually bite—at least not on the very short leash that the county jail provided.

"Well, it's up to you. We can go to trial. But you'll be spending a long time in here before you even get to trial and if you're convicted, you may get a lot longer than five. The sentence is 5 to 99 years."

"Shit. If I could afford a real attorney, I'd be out of here. Instead I get a courthouse whore!"

"That's it!" Rachel had had enough. "Talk to the judge, get a new attorney if you can. If not, I'll help prepare the case for trial. It's all up to you. Let me know what you decide."

She had thrown her papers into the briefcase as she stood up and was walking out the door when her client tried to make amends.

"Well, sheesh, don't get your back up. What, are you on the rag or sumthin—talk to the prosecutor—I'll take two."

"Fine. I'll talk to him."

She knew that the prosecutor wasn't going to go for two. He had a 7-year suspended sentence from the probation and his new count carried a possible 99 year sentence. If he hadn't been so greedy, she might have made him a better deal. As it was, the truck he hijacked from the back of a Walmart loading dock contained $20,000 worth of merchandise. What he got for it on the street was another matter. It was a game to guys like Jack. They gambled with the possibility of getting caught. Then they bargained their punishment like they were in a Tijuana flea market. She had nothing to go to trial with. He was caught red-handed with the empty truck and a pocket full of cash. Damn fool hadn't even thought to get rid of it, just kept driving it around because he liked the feeling of being a trucker.

Wearily she thought about all the other clients she had in her active case files. Most were biding their time in jail while she struggled to find the time to check into their cases. Most of them proclaimed their innocence even though the police file had eyewitnesses and physical evidence. Not that eyewitness testimony was especially reliable. One of her first cases involved an assault outside a bar. Three people identified her client after police presented him in a photo array. He was well known as a drinker and brawler and the club was one of his favorite hang-outs. The physical description matched roughly so police showed his picture to the witnesses and the victim. They all agreed he was the guy. It was only pure luck that he had been in a police lock-up in another city on the night of the alleged assault. If he hadn't had an ironclad alibi, and if she hadn't believed him and gotten the booking records to show where he was, those three eyewitnesses would have convinced a jury of his guilt. So much for eyewitnesses. The unbelievable part was that, even after all that, she still had to go to trial because the prosecutor wouldn't drop the charges. In a new twist on "innocent until proven guilty" he joked that the guy was probably guilty of something and since they had a pretty good case, he was going to run with it and let the jury decide.

One of the things she hadn't fully realized in law school was that the legal profession was not a world of ideas, but rather it was a world of mundane details. Her mind was full of deadlines for hearings, filing subpoenas, motions to suppress and other motions. Her day was spent calling clients to remind them of court dates, tracking down witnesses and trying to talk to police officers who never returned her calls. She had been attracted to criminal law because of the enormity of what was at stake. Even though she knew it was naïve, she was thrilled to think that she would be involved in concepts like due process and civil liberties. On the law review, she wrote briefs on issues such as the legality of deception in interrogation, and the expansion of hearsay exceptions. She enjoyed the challenge of these legal arguments as well as the intellectual stimulation of understanding and utilizing Supreme Court decisions to present new arguments regarding legal issues. When she left law school, she had this crazy notion that she would be an advocate for justice. In her heart of hearts, she even hoped for a case that she could take to appellate courts, perhaps even the Supreme Court one day.

Well, so far that hadn't happened. Rachel felt washed over by a tide of humanity that seemed to be always guilty, always broke and often stupid. She had always believed herself to be a liberal but after countless defendants swore at her, berated her for not getting them a better deal or believed they should be exempt from any punishment, she felt flashes of pure conservativism flowing through her veins.

* * *

"So, why is it your job to tell the prosecutor that?" argued Clara, a young black lawyer who was known as "the crusader."

"In fact, your job is to further your client's interest and if you go to the judge or prosecutor, it will definitely NOT be in the client's best interest," she continued.

The issue being discussed at the defense attorney's table that day was the prosecutor in one of Rachel's cases. He had forgotten to subpoena the child-victim witness. Her client was a stepfather that was accused of molesting his 12-year-old stepdaughter. The stepdaughter didn't want to testify. The family didn't want her to testify. They wanted the stepfather to come home. It was Friday and trial was set for Monday. It would be easy to suggest to the girl and her family that it might be time to take a long summer vacation. The prosecutor would have a red face on Monday morning and, if the defendant was lucky, the judge would dismiss the case. Since a jury had already been seated, it would be a dismissal with prejudice meaning that double jeopardy would apply.

"The judge will know what I did. He could find me in contempt," Rachel argued.

"Well, how could he? You didn't do anything wrong."

Clara usually had a very absolutist view of what was right in defense work. Anything that could get the client off was okay by her. She saw the system as an evil giant octopus, reaching out its tentacles to destroy individuals and families. To her, the system was an organism with no conscience, but with the capacity to do enormous harm. She had never met a police officer she didn't think was a liar, or a prosecutor who she didn't feel was ready to lie, cheat, or manipulate the system to get a conviction. In return, she took first strike options. She was not a favorite among prosecutors or judges. She fought every case as if it were her only case. She did not get any court appointments and survived, evidently, only because she did "at counsel" work for the local N.A.A.C.P., as well as work a criminal caseload.

Stinson shook his head and added his two cents, "What you want to do is go to Andy and get something for this. After all, he'll owe you. Get a better plea agreement, get the physical thrown out, something—after all, he'd rather give you something than look like an idiot in front of the judge. Or hold it over his head and save a favor for later."

Stinson seemed to view the entire practice of law as a game. Winning was the object and everything was played with an eye to the angle. He prided himself on his win-loss record as if he was a football team of one. Even a certain number of penalties were usually calculated into his strategy for winning. The defendant was important only insofar as he or she presented a winnable case. He didn't take court appointments unless they had the potential to give him publicity. He once told her that "a cynic is someone who has been burned once too often." Rachel wondered if his zeal for the defense practice hadn't started out with different motives than merely winning for the sake of winning.

"You do that and your client doesn't walk which he might do if you keep your mouth shut and tell the kid to get outta town," Clara argued.

"But, Clara, he did it. I mean do you think he deserves to walk away scot-free after molesting a child?"

Clara shrugged. "There's lots a guilt in this world, girlfriend. It's not your job to be judge, jury and executioner. If you want that job, you're on the wrong side of the fence."

Rachel sighed. She could see both sides of the argument. Somehow she didn't feel right telling the girl to get out of town, nor did she feel it was appropriate to inform the prosecutor. She decided to do nothing at all and hope that the judge would be mad at Andy and not her on Monday morning.

* * *

"Is the prosecution ready to proceed?"

"Yes, your honor."

"Is the defense ready to proceed?"

"Yes, your honor."

Rachel looked around the courtroom. She did not see the girl with her family who were huddled immediately behind the defendant in the first row of the spectator section.

"Your honor, I would like to invoke the rule," Rachel said, which would mean that all those who were to testify must leave the courtroom.

"No objection," Andy added.

In general, both sides got this bit of business out of the way in a pro forma manner. Andy looked back at the courtroom gallery and Rachel thought she could see the exact moment when his brain snapped to the fact that his star witness was missing. As people shuffled out and rearranged themselves on the wooden rows, Andy became more concerned, looking down at his witness list and up again at those who were filing out. He whispered to his co-counsel and the young woman hurried out, no doubt to see where Esperanza was hiding.

Rachel was somewhat ashamed to realize that she was enjoying his discomfort. It was a nice situation to be on the right side of a screw-up for a change and, after all, he did bring it on himself. His carelessness was compounded by the fact that he hadn't even bothered to check that morning before the trial started to see if the girl was there. She knew why. Prosecutors got used to the idea that their witnesses would show up. Most victims do if a case goes to trial. Defense attorneys, on the other hand, always checked.

The trial began with opening statements. Rachel reserved her time for after the prosecution rested and she began her defense. She hoped that she may not have to give it at all. Although she didn't tell the family that they should send Esperanza out of town, she did tell them in response to their question that if Esperanza didn't get subpoenaed, she did not have a legal duty to be there.

The other prosecutor came back and, again, the two conferred in an agitated whisper.

"Well, Mr. Anderson, would you like to share whatever it is that's got you flustered with the rest of us?" Judge Sommerville taunted, pushing his glasses up on his forehead and leaning forward towards Andy who immediately stopped whispering and stood up.

"Judge, could we approach the bench?"

The judge waived both of them forward and Rachel and Andy came to stand before the judge.

"It seems that I am missing one of my witnesses. Esperanza Gonzales is the victim in the case and she's not here."

"Well, if they've ignored the subpoena, get an officer over there and pick her up!"

"Well, that's the thing, your Honor, uh, I guess there was some mix-up in my office and that subpoena didn't actually get filed." Andy's discomfort was palpable.

Judge Sommerville had a fierce reputation, embarrassing prosecutors and defense attorneys alike with no favor. Rachel had tried a few cases in his court and held her own, but she was always tense and anxious. He was like the teacher who delighted in finding fault.

Right now he was fixing Andy with a stare that could have peeled the paint off the wall of the courtroom.

"Is that right? Well, Mr. Anderson, do you plan to try this case without the testimony of the victim?"

"No sir, I would like to request a continuance in order for us to get the subpoena signed and enforced."

"Miss Young, what do you have to say?"

"Your honor, I would like to move for a dismissal." She could have hammered home the idea that she had every right to ask for a dismissal and that it would be an injustice to make the defendant wait after the prosecutor had stated his readiness for trial. She didn't expound on any of this, but, even so, Andy shot her an angry look.

"Well, I'm inclined to agree." He looked from one to the other and Rachel held her breath. She was truly conflicted about whether or not she wanted the judge to dismiss the case. Legally, it could go either way. Ethically, she could have done no less than ask for the dismissal. Personally, she thought that Alberto ought to learn that he couldn't touch little girls. It wouldn't hurt her feelings to lose and see him sent away to prison.

"However, this is what we'll do. Mr. Anderson, get your associate to process that subpoena pronto and hope to hell that Miss Young here hasn't given her a one-way ticket to Disneyland."

The judge fixed Rachel with an appraising look and she gazed back innocently.

"You will start with your other witnesses and if the young lady is brought here by the time you finish your other witnesses, the trial will continue. If not, I plan to dismiss. O.K., step back."

* * *

Rachel was bone tired. She had finished the Gonzales trial yesterday. He had ended up with a 10-year probation sentence instead of prison, which to the defense bar, was considered a win because juries were notoriously unsympathetic to child molesters—unless they were middle class white men. To Andy Anderson's relief, the girl had been in school, was brought to the courthouse in the afternoon and the trial proceeded. She would have dearly loved to take a few days off but she had a docket call this morning, several defendants in jail that she had to meet with and a bond hearing in the afternoon. She was sitting in the back of Judge Wasserman's courtroom going over some case files when she became aware of someone standing next to her. She looked up to see a twenty something young man with washed out blond hair in a ponytail and a bit of peach fuzz around his jaw line that evidently passed as a beard. He was definitely not someone you'd have much confidence in if he was on your side in a brawl.

"Can I help you?" she asked, hoping he just wanted directions to the men's washroom.

"Miss, I hate to bother you, but I've been trying to talk to the prosecutor over there...."

He pointed over at Andy Anderson who seemed to pick up his name even across the noisy room and looked over at them, nodding almost imperceptibly to Rachel, and then turning back to his conversation with a police officer.

"He said he couldn't talk to me, but maybe you could help. I've been charged with theft by fraud through insufficient funds. I don't understand why. I've been trying to talk to him..." he gestured again towards Andy.

"I have been trying to tell him that I had my driver's license and checkbook stolen in June. I guess whoever stole them wrote a bunch of checks, but I didn't do it. I got pulled over for speeding two weeks ago and they arrested me!"

It is always a shock to law-abiding people when they get caught up in the machinery of the system. They can never quite believe that the police and prosecutors and judges don't just let them go when they tell them that a mistake has been made. They are truly surprised when the system's machinery begins grinding away, the process moving inextricably, unbelievably toward changing one's life forever. The best that an innocent person can hope for is to regain his freedom and lose his bank account. Lawyers' fees are not cheap and they are not refundable upon acquittal.

"Are you asking me to be your lawyer?" Rachel held up her hand to stop the flood of explanation.

"Well, I don't know, I don't have any money. I mean I had to borrow money from my stepdad to make bail and I don't have a job. He's not too happy about it and I need to pay him back. I had a job, but then when I spent a couple days in jail, they said they didn't want me anymore. I'm living with my girlfriend right now but I need to get a job and help her with the rent. So I don't know what a lawyer costs or anything."

Rachel sighed. At least court appointments came with checks that could actually be cashed for real money. She rummaged in the pocket of her briefcase and brought out a standard contract for services.

"O.K., look at this contract; we can settle up later and you can make payments or something."

He signed the contract and they moved into the hallway. Luckily the docket call that was supposed to have started at 9:00 a.m. was late for some reason so Rachel actually had a few minutes to spend with him. She discovered that he not only had a police report for the theft of his wallet, but that he had also taken the initiative to go to several of the store clerks who had accepted the forged checks and they had all written letters indicating he wasn't the one who cashed the checks and that they would testify to that. What she needed to do was line up those witnesses, investigate the theft report and gather the evidence showing his innocence. All that unfortunately would cost time and money: his money and her time. Or, more likely, her time and money because he wouldn't or couldn't pay. She should ask for all the money upfront instead of the token amount that established the contract, and she knew that most defense attorneys would. They had to in order to survive. She sighed again.

"Well, give me a minute and let me talk to the prosecutor." She told the guy to sit tight and she'd be right back. Running a few steps to catch up with Andy, she fell in step beside him.

"Hey, can we talk a minute about this theft by check case?"

"What's the name?"

He stopped walking and propped his stack of files on his knee while he thumbed through the stack, looking for the name she gave him. Finding the right one, he put the rest down and scanned it quickly.

"So what's the deal?"

"No deal. The guy is innocent. He's got a theft report that states his driver's license and checkbook were stolen back in June. We can get testimony from the clerks that he wasn't the one cashing the checks. Maybe video cameras."

He looked up at her with raised eyebrows. They both knew that now, months later, it was highly likely those tapes had been used over and over again.

"Look, Andy, the guy is innocent. I bet you have a clean record in there somewhere."

She peered over his shoulder to get a peek at the case file.

"So, he's never been arrested before, doesn't prove he didn't deserve this one."

But he lacked conviction in his voice as he scanned the case file and she seized on his hesitation.

"Look, let's cut the guy a break. He doesn't have any money. He's going to have a world of problems with his credit that he's going to have to untangle anyway. I'll be able to prove he's innocent of the criminal charge and all it will do is use up time and money that none of us have. How about just dismissing it?"

He looked at her and over at the guy who was pacing nervously and biting his fingernails. Prosecutors had the power to dismiss a case that was without merit. It was a power that they didn't use as often as they should as far as Rachel was concerned. It could all be over for the young man with a stroke of Andy Anderson's pen, or it could be a long drawn out process that would end up costing him, at the very least, thousands of dollars. He faced this only because he had the misfortune of having his wallet stolen. Unfortunately, the system worked best for those who were guilty, not for those who were innocent. She realized she wanted very much to end this ordeal for the young man.

"O.K." he said.

Discussion Questions

1. Describe the different motivations of Rachel, Stinson and Clara. Who has the more "ethical" viewpoint?
2. What was Rachel's ethical duty regarding the presence of the victim-witness in the molestation case?

3. Why did Rachel care whether or not the young man's case was dismissed?
4. Why would a prosecutor pursue a case in a situation where the defendant obviously was not guilty (as in the assault case)?
5. Why do you think that Andy Anderson cooperated with Rachel in the theft by check case?
6. "A liberal is a conservative that has been falsely accused of a crime." Discuss.

14

SHORT-CUT

His face looked like a road-map of missed opportunities and wrong turns. Woodrow "Short-cut" Evans didn't see it that way. In his mind's eye he was a player who on occasion, hustled too close to the edge and got burned. The criminal justice system saw him in a different light—a three-time loser and a career criminal with anti-social tendencies.

Short-cut had put his previous two stints in state prison to good use, earning an Associate's Degree in Sociology during his first bid and a Bachelor's Degree in Psychology in his second go-around. It was the sixties and seventies, a kind of rehabilitation renaissance in corrections where enlightened corrections officials believed education and counseling could change folks like Short-cut. From a career in crime to a career in sales or some other traditional vocation, the behavior of the Short-cuts of the world could be modified and transformed into law abiding, productive citizens.

R.J. Higgs poured a cup of coffee and handed it to Short-cut, then poured himself a cup and settled into his easy chair behind his desk.

"Much obliged, Doc. How long you been doing this—being a prison psychologist?"

"Long enough to know better," Higgs replied as he leaned back in his chair.

Both men laughed.

"Short-cut, you know you're eligible to go up for parole next month."

Short-cut smiled and sipped his coffee before answering. "I think I'll pass on my hearing. I'm coming up fast on 70 this spring. Been in the joint 40 of my last 50 years. There's nothing waiting for me outside. My life's here."

R.J. folded his arms across his chest. "I could get you transferred to 'The Farm' if you are interested. You would have an easier time of it there."

A shadow of alarm flickered in Short-cut's eyes. "Don't do that, Doc. Please don't do that. That place is for old farts who are disabled—on their last legs. I might be 70, but I'm a young 70. Besides, if I left, who would run the prison library and meet with you once a week for some stimulating conversation?"

Short-cut rose from his chair and reached for the coffee pot. "Here, Doc, let me pour you some more coffee."

"My coffee's okay," Higgs replied with a smile. "Don't worry about a transfer. I have to agree it wouldn't be the same around here without you."

Short-cut settled back into his chair. "Doc, I really do appreciate you seeing me every Tuesday. If I have any tension or burdens building up, you always seem to know what to say."

Higgs shook his head, "I would say you have as good or better way with words as I do. I have to admit, Short-cut, you are an enigma to me."

"An enigma?" Short-cut queried. "What do you mean?"

Higgs took a swallow of coffee. "I mean you have all the ability you need to have made something of yourself in the world. I've read your file and have seen your aptitude test scores. You are bright—earned two degrees. And yet, every time you get out for a few years, back you come. A scheme here, a hustle there, and next thing you know, you're back. Fact is, you could have been like your brother, Herman, two years younger ..."

"Harmon," Short-cut interrupted. "His name's Harmon."

"Harmon," Higgs continued, "went to medical school and became a physician."

"Internal Medicine," Short-cut interjected.

"Okay, internal medicine," Higgs replied. "Good parents raised the both of you. Herman—I mean Harmon goes to medical school and you go to prison. I just don't get it."

Short-cut rubbed his chin as he pondered the psychologist's words. "I have to agree with you Doc. In a way it doesn't make sense. My poor parents died wondering why and my brother retired wondering the same. Truth is Doc, I've always had a taste for walking on the edge of trouble. Like one of those thrill rides at a carnival, I got off on pulling something over on folks. Harmon wanted to make our parents proud and impress his peers. It's true enough I hated to see the hurt in my Mama's eyes when I got in trouble, but I didn't hate it enough to turn away. I guess you could say the pleasure of a successful con exceeded the risk of pain I might bring my Mother. My brother always wanted to earn his way into high society."

Short-cut smiled. "I always wanted to take what they had."

The intercom announced that the anger management group session had been postponed until next week.

Short-cut stared off into space. "My brother always believed that if you worked hard and did the right thing, you would be rewarded and treated fairly. Harmon figured most folks were good and decent—on the up and up."

"But not you," Higgs replied.

"No, not me."

"You see things differently," the psychologist continued.

"I do, indeed," Short-cut responded. "Harmon's been burned more than once. His office receptionist embezzled ten grand from him and the sap didn't press charges—let her pay it back. You need another example? His first wife picked out the most expensive house she could find, then left him for the real estate agent who sold them the house. My brother never learned that there's two types of people: the ones who take and the ones who get taken."

Higgs arched his eyebrow. "Yet, Harmon is playing golf in a retirement community in Florida and you are drinking prison coffee in Jackson."

Short-cut's face grew more serious. "Maybe so, Doc, but I can't say I have that many regrets. I'd be lying if I did. Harmon's not in the best of health and from my way of looking at things, playing golf everyday with a bunch of old farts in a retirement community is just another kind of prison. I would just as soon take the prison I'm used to."

"Besides," Short-cut added with a grin, "Prison ain't so bad. I remember 40 years ago at Mountain State Prison when we didn't have any education, counseling or recreation. And the food was none too good either. Yessir, our 'recreation' was bustin' rock all day in the stone quarry. The only 'counseling' we got besides a monthly visit from a holiness preacher was from the older convicts. Their advice was simple: Bust rocks, keep your mouth shut and do what the Captain says. Those who didn't follow their advice were 'educated' by the Captain and he was quite an educator—big and strong with a ten gallon cowboy hat perched on his head. Compared to those days, we're living the good life."

Higgs leaned back in his chair and folded his hands across his belly. "Fair enough point, Short-cut. It doesn't sound like the Captain was familiar with the possibilities of reform and rehabilitation."

"You can say that again, Doc," Short-cut laughed. "I will say one thing for him, though. He did have his own kind of fairness. If you did what you were told, he didn't give you much trouble. Truth is, he was open to a challenge."

"A challenge?" Higgs replied.

"That's right. Every morning when we lined up and marched off to the quarry to bust rocks, we had to say 'Mornin' Captain' when we passed by him. If he was gone somewhere, we still had to say 'Mornin' Captain' to his hat as we marched by.

"To his hat?"

"Yep, to his hat. Once and awhile, one of the convicts who thought he was a badass would tell the Captain he wanted to go out behind the barn. So that's what they would do—go out behind the barn and see who was the best man. The rest of us would wait to see who came out from behind the barn. Usually, it was the Captain. When that happened, he would send a couple of us to carry the loser up to the infirmary."

Short-cut chuckled. "Of course, every once and awhile, it wasn't the Captain who walked out from behind the barn. Now and then, it was one of the convicts who showed up, usually marked up and missing some teeth, but standing nonetheless."

R.J. Higgs shook his head. "What happened to him?"

"He got to wear the Captain's hat for the day while he busted rock," Short-cut replied with a gleam in his eye.

The psychologist looked at the clock on the wall, then at Short-cut. "Short-cut, Short-cut. What could have been—should have been."

"It could have been worse, Doc. I could have been one of those violent criminals instead of a con artist. I had my successes—a couple of big scores. Except for a bad break or two, I might have been a big-shot business man."

Short-cut smiled at Higgs. "But if that had happened, we wouldn't have had the pleasure of each other's company."

Short-cut rose and waved as he left Higgs' office. "Same time, next week?"

"I reckon so, Short-cut, I reckon so," Higgs replied, thinking to himself, "You can't help everybody."

Discussion Questions

1. Short-Cut clearly appears to be an "institutionalized" person, more suited to the regimentation of prison life than the decision-making responsibilities of the free world. In general, how should the we balance the legal responsibilities that require justice for crimes committed with the practical ethical concerns of reintegrating non-violent offenders back into society?
2. Two brothers, Short-Cut and Harmon, raised by the same parents in a law-abiding household by good parents. One turns to the practice of medicine and the other turns to the practice of crime. How do you think such a transition happens? What are some ways the same family values can impact siblings so differently?
3. Despite several stints in prison, Short-Cut appears to continue to be somewhat manipulative and even proud of his "criminal career" as well as his pro-crime values. Is traditional rehabilitation likely to prove successful for such offenders? What treatment approach should the prison psychologist utilize with an offender like Short-Cut?
4. Prison psychologists and correctional counselors cannot help everyone even if they want to. How can a treatment professional's personal values help them face and cope with inmates like Short-Cut?

15

IT'S TOO BAD
ABOUT TOMMY

Joe Smith was middle-aged-handsome in an offhanded sort of way. He listened to the rhythmic drumming of rain on the window panes of the old brownstone. It was a cold, blowing rain, the kind that people turned their backs against as they scurried along the sidewalks looking for shelter. Joe didn't like rain.

Turning from the window, he placed two Cuban cigars on the desktop and settled into an oversized leather chair. He watched his older colleague search for a bottle of twenty-year-old scotch in the bottom drawer of a massive antique desk.

Looking intently at the two tumblers he was pouring the whiskey into, Walter Jones, senior Senator from the great state of Alabama, chuckled to himself as much as to the man sitting across from him.

"How long have we been meeting for whiskey and cigars my fine young friend?"

Joe fingered the cigar cutter in his pants pocket.

"It's the third year of my second term in the Senate, so I guess it's been about seven years."

Walter handed Joe a glass of scotch and in return, Joe offered the senior Senator a fresh cut cigar.

The two men touched glasses and lit up. Neither spoke for a few moments, listening to the rain and enjoying the taste of rare whiskey and a fine cigar. Exhaling a plume of aromatic smoke, Walter winked at his junior colleague.

"Twenty-year-old scotch and a Cuban double corona is a hard combination to beat."

"True enough. And the fact that we've been doing it all these years."

Walter shifted in his chair and peered out into the wet evening's twilight.

"I'm sure some of our brethren from both sides of the aisle might not approve of our friendship, especially with all the mad-dog partisanship running rampant through the hallowed halls of Congress."

Joe held his glass out for a refill.

"It's all about the extreme these days. Extreme right and extreme left. Extreme never got a damn thing done right. Nothing goes or everything goes. No in-between. All or nothing."

Walter nodded in agreement as he topped off his own drink.

"Yeah, and it usually ends up being more nothing than something. Matter of fact, things seem to be getting worse. Not enough give-and-take—just take-all-you-can-while-you-can. Even you and I have to make sure our amens are heard when the party loudmouths start waving their war flags over this or that self-righteous cause."

Both men sipped their drinks in silence. It was beginning to rain harder.

Joe relit his cigar.

"It's tough being a closet moderate."

Walter chuckled once more.

"I've been doing it for more than twenty years. Sure, I've had some close calls, like that increased relief budget for African children's health care. To cover myself, I had to cosponsor that automatic weapons bill with that idiot, Billingsly, but I was pretty sure it wouldn't pass."

Joe shook his head.

"You were considerably more confident than I was. It came within five votes of passing as best I remember. I had nightmares of soccer moms driving Hummers with thirty caliber machine guns mounted on the hoods."

Both men laughed out loud.

"Joe, we both had some close calls. We also know from experience that it is only through the art of compromise that anything worthwhile gets done in this town."

"Damn straight," Joe responded, sitting upright in his chair. "I may be a Minnesota Democrat and you may be a Republican from Alabama, but we're just as patriotic as the true believers. These are tough times and difficult times that call for sacrifice and compromise."

Walter raised his glass to Joe in agreement and drained the last of his whiskey.

"Yeah, the point is not to go down with the ship, but to keep it afloat. Our economy's struggling and there's that war on the other side of the world. Just because it may be in our country's vital interest doesn't mean I don't lose sleep when I vote, however reluctantly, to send our young men and women to a foreign country and place them in harm's way. There's no such thing as a clean war. Everyone always ends up with plenty of blood on their hands. Like the old union General Sherman said, 'War is hell.'"

"Yeah, that was a tough vote for me too. I'm still not satisfied with our diplomatic efforts. But like we said, compromise is the oil that keeps the machine of state moving. I just wish it had gotten over as quickly as the drum-beaters had said it would."

Walter refilled his glass and absent-mindedly stirred his drink with his finger.

"It never does. It never ends as quickly as the experts say it will. True believers are always good at beating drums, making speeches and marching in parades. They just like for other folks to do their fighting and dying for them."

The two men grew silent. The smell of cigars and whiskey offered up the only evidence of their presence.

Joe broke the silence.

"It's too bad about Tommy."

"Terrible news," Walter added. "I just heard last week. It's really affected poor Tom. His wife, Nora, died last year and now his only son. Thirty years of service and Chair of the Armed Services Committee. And he's a moderate at heart like us. It'll be a great loss for us. Even more so for the country. McGillicutty from Utah is in line to be the next Chairperson. He's nothing more than a rubber stamp for the President. It's still hard for me to believe Tom's actually resigning the Senate."

Joe placed his empty whiskey glass on the small table next to his chair and looked past Walter into the rain-soaked evening.

"I remember when Tommy worked as an Intern two summers ago. He was a good kid, bright with plenty of promise. Supposed to start Yale law in the fall. Told me he wanted to expand that third world literacy program old Tom got funded last year."

Walter drummed his fingers on the desktop.

"Like I said, wars are a terrible thing."

Joe sighed, "They say his Humvee hit a land mine of some sort. Word has it that he was trying to divert fire away from troop transports. He lost his left leg, right foot and left arm below the elbow. His face and upper body was burned pretty bad too."

Walter folded his hands across his chest as he chewed on the remnants of his cigar.

"Good thing, Tommy's right handed."

Joe gave Walter a rare look of disapproval.

"No disrespect intended, Joe. It's just a good thing—him being right-handed and all. You know, with Tom quitting the Senate to take care of him, at least until he gets back on his feet."

Grinding the butt of his cigar in the ashtray, Walter looked at Joe with tired eyes.

"If history has taught us one thing, it's that the price of freedom doesn't come cheap."

Joe said as much to himself as to Walter, "Maybe we should have lobbied harder for diplomatic efforts. You know the Secretary of State …"

Walter interrupted him, "You know as well as I do, 'maybes' don't get the job done. The polls were clear. John Doe public supported the drumbeaters. You and I did what we could behind the scenes. Neither we nor our country can afford to look weak during these difficult times."

Silence overtook the room once more.

Finally, Joe rose to his feet and smoothed his trousers.

"Friday after next?"

Walter smiled.

"You bring the whiskey next time. Maybe a small batch Kentucky bourbon. I've got my eye on a couple of Honduran Churchills I've been wanting us to try."

Discussion Questions

1. What is the importance of ethics and moral behavior in politics? Can you think of positive and negative examples in contemporary life?
2. Senators Joe Smith and Walter Jones talked of having to make compromises. What role does compromise play in ethics?
3. Can "extreme" positions and beliefs result in injustice? Can you think of any modern day examples?
4. What role does Tommy play in the story? How does the sacrifice and changes in his life affect the characters' attitudes and ethical considerations?

16

TRUTH TELLER

Two years ago I saw the truth.

Two years and fifteen minutes ago I started speaking it.

My life hasn't been worth a damn since.

I always heard that the truth will make you free.

Free from what? I'll tell you what. In the span of two short years, I was freed from my career, my wife and daughter, and even from the lousy efficiency apartment I have been living in for the last two months.

Hell yes, I'm free.

Free to take my last three hundred bucks and hit the open road in a worn-out Ford Taurus, 160,000 miles young. Free from everything that made my life what it was—everything that I wanted and worked for.

Two short years ago on a cold Friday evening I was nursing my third Sam Adams and bullshitting with the regular end-of-the-week-upper-management-wannabees for the *City Daily News*.

I was at the top of the mid-level career food chain where I toiled for my living. A Master of Arts degree in journalism and ten years of busting my ass had brought me to the edge of greatness and to Buddy's Bar on what turned out to be a cold day in hell.

As a hard-working assistant editor in charge of the sports and features sections, I was just a skip and jump and some well-placed ass kissing away from one of the two prized associate executive editors' slots. Given the inevitability of Ed McMann's impending retirement, that soon-to-be-vacant office with its own bathroom and big picture window had my name written all over it.

I had another advantage over the beer and bourbon swizzling reprobates I drank with during our Friday evening rituals. They had their eye on the same elusive prize that I did, but unlike them,

I could actually write. Yeah, I was kicking ass and kissing ass—a lethal combination that pointed like a champion bird dog sitting on a covey of quail to the golden ring I was about to grab. A ring that would make me and mine proud and the envy of all the other yahoos at the *City Daily News*.

Trouble is, I drank one beer too many because it was during that third beer that fate stepped in and punctured my balloon of ambition, laying waste to life as I knew it.

During that third beer I overheard Geraldine Stevens talking to the bartender about her sorry-ass husband. Several black eyes, a neck brace, and her son's increased bed wetting had lit a fire under her that only fear and loneliness kept in check. Enough was enough. Geraldine was ready to leave the worthless son-of-a-bitch she was married to and return to her parents in South Alabama. Trouble was, she was broke. As soon as she could put her hands on enough cash for two bus tickets, she and her son were heading south to freedom. At least that's what she told the bored bartender who was practicing the time-worn bartender's art of pretending to give a damn.

That's what she was telling him. But I knew better. The king-size gimlet she was sucking on was doing the talking for her and her boy. My guess was that she was at least a broken arm or preteen suicide attempt away from speaking for herself and acting like the mother she was pretending to be.

Yeah, I could see right through her. It was like I had known her all my life. And I didn't like what I saw. So be it. A quick trip to the men's room to relieve myself and I would be on my way home to Natalie and Natasha, my wife and daughter, respectively.

I even remember the sound of zipping up my Dockers and feeling the cold blast of air that hit me in the face as I stepped out to hail a cab on that armpit of a February night.

As I waved my arms to no avail, none other than Geraldine, the gimlet swizzler, exited the bar and sidled up next to me.

She stood too close for comfort and I didn't like the way she looked at me. It was like she wanted something. I stamped my feet against the cold and she just stood there looking at me as if she wanted to speak but was waiting for permission. I was thinking that sometimes strangers are best left strangers when she spoke.

Unlike the I'll-tell-you-a-thing-or-two voice from inside the bar, she asked me in a child's uncertain whisper, "Will you help me get a cab?"

That's what she said, but what I heard through some strange cosmic filter of fate was, "Will you HELP ME?"

Not taking my eyes off her, I stepped back in shock and *spoke.* I never do that—speak what I see.

The conversations of truth as I see it, should stay where they belong—in one's head. But not this time. This time it spoke me.

Offering her the contents of my wallet, I said, "Geraldine, you need to leave that worthless bastard and go home to your parents before you lose yourself or worse—your son's life."

Geraldine's jaw dropped and she looked as if she were about to reply. Instead, she snatched the money out of my hand and hopped into the cab that had just pulled up as if on cue in some third-rate movie.

That's right. She took the money and got into the cab without so much as a thank you. Did she go home, retrieve her son, and take the next bus to Alabama?

Damned if I know.

All I recall is that for the first time I could remember, I spoke what I saw.

Holding my empty wallet, I walked home in the cold to the waiting warmth of Natalie's inquisition.

Although I stayed away from Buddy's Bar, it didn't seem to help calm my new-found affliction. The truth had me by the balls and every time it squeezed, I spoke. I wanted to keep my thoughts to myself, but possessed by a clarity of insight I never imagined and an inability to remain silent, I could feel myself sinking ever deeper into the quicksand of opportunity.

Two months after my encounter with Geraldine, I elicited the same dumbfounded look of incredulity from my boss, Ned Jasper who—rumor had it—was about to appoint me associate editor.

The words rushed out, dragging my reluctant voice with them.

"Ned, we've been friends a long time, but I've got to tell you, screwing that journalism intern isn't worth your twenty-year marriage to Marge, not to mention the respect of your children."

Ned's response was to the point.

"Get out!"

As it turned out, his retort foretold a wider arc of response than I ever would have anticipated.

"Get out" not only referred to the immediacy of that embarrassing moment in his office, but also came to include the newspaper itself. Needless to say, I didn't get the promotion and soon after found myself reassigned to the "eastern front" of newspaper work—reporting on city commission and board meetings.

The day I finally resigned, I tried to explain to Natalie that personal integrity was more important than a promotion or a particular kind of job. Her expression of disapproval fed the hidden part of me that agreed with her.

Six months and a series of unsuccessful interviews and substitute teaching assignments later, Natalie uttered what has become a refrain in my life. Between sips of orange juice, Natalie's mouth opened and Ned Jasper's voice seemed to speak through her early morning smoker's rasp.

"Get out!"

So I did.

I left it all behind, not willingly, but of necessity.

Even Natasha shed no visible tears the day I left with suitcase in hand. The last sound I heard was a good riddance bark from Bobo, the cocker spaniel.

In short order, I went from writing for the newspaper to delivering newspapers. My pre-dawn route combined with education's constant need for inner city substitute teachers, afforded me the luxury of a well-worn efficiency on 10th Avenue and evening forays to Buddy's, where Mike, the bartender, offered me the same courtesy he had given to Geraldine a year earlier.

My friend, Sam Adams, was too rich for my current financial fortunes so I mingled with his more budget-minded kin and attempted to sort out what had become of my existence. I surmised to Mike that at least I was reasonably confident that things couldn't get any worse.

I was wrong.

I struck up an ill-fated friendship with my landlord, Buck LePew. Buck apparently saw some semblance of the management potential in me that Ned and my former wife had given up on. In exchange for managing the eight-unit apartment house I resided in, I got to live rent-free.

A spark of my former self slowly began to re-emerge as I considered my future prospects in the field of residential management. As I became more familiar with Buck's enterprise, I soon realized that some rocks were best not overturned. A clear pattern emerged of compounding the misery of elderly tenants on fixed incomes by excessively raising their rent and ignoring their pleas for repairs and basic service. Forcing such undesirables out of their apartments allowed the vacated units to be rented to higher-paying young professionals.

Even as I tried to maintain control, I could feel that ugly entity known as a conscience beginning to awaken and take shape. It wouldn't be long before my tongue would begin to work its black magic.

I still remember the day Buck LePew, chewing nervously on a cigar stub, was held captive by the logic of truth's outpouring.

I had just finished an impressive oration that concluded by telling Buck that he was too good of a person to torture his elderly residents for nothing more than a little extra filthy lucre, not to mention that what he did to them, good or bad, would be returned to him ten-fold.

Buck LePew said two things in response to my well-intentioned query.

His first response was, "Who the hell do you think you are, some crazy-ass prophet?

Then he uttered those dreaded, oft-told words.

"Get Out!"

I still remember the last moments I spent at Buck's establishment. My bag was packed and positioned next to the door, and I stood in the bathroom, looking out the window. I was lost in my thoughts. Not just in my thoughts, it was me that was lost. I had nowhere to go. I had nothing. I was nothing.

I peered out the frost-encrusted window and all I could see was a barren bush with a single branch reaching toward me. On the end of it was a single bud.

My wet face pressed against the glass.
It was a beautiful thing.

Discussion Questions

1. What is the up and down-side of seeing and telling the truth?
    Why is it important to be truthful even when great sacrifice is
    required?
2. When the main character in the story kept acting ethically and
    doing the right thing, he seemed to experience negative con-
    sequences. "Get out!" became a common refrain. Why?
3. What was the significance of the story's ending? Why did he
    think the branch with the bud on its end was a "beautiful
    thing"?

PART FOUR

JUSTICE AND REDEMPTION

In this section, we examine the "justice process." The pursuit of justice is a necessary and fundamental element of a civilized society. Given this pursuit or quest, compassion, restoration, and redemption are important qualities which contribute to personal, professional and spiritual fulfillment. It is important to understand that mercy and forgiveness are transformative—for the one who forgives and for the one who is forgiven.

An evil act doesn't necessarily mean the person who committed it is evil. We all have the potential to do great harm or great good. In one way of another, we may all at times be both perpetrators and victims of crime, at least in a moral or ethical sense.

The Open Door is about a revered grandfather who is haunted by a lynching he witnessed as a teenager. He reveals to his grandson his shame of doing nothing to help three innocent victims of racially charged vigilante injustice.

Dead Man's Parade tells the story of two black Army veterans returning home after World War II. They fought with distinction in Europe where they were respected only to return home to Jim Crow laws and unbridled racial prejudice. One will stay and one will leave.

In *The Clockmaker* a young journalist interviews an elderly German physician who is being deported back to Germany to war crimes charges. A former Nazi, the elderly clock maker wants to explain his side of the story—why he did what he did—his reasons and motivations.

Best Intentions demonstrates how wrong-headed and corrupt the quest for justice can become and how an innocent person can end up paying for someone else's mistakes and ambition.

The Price of Justice is about the plight of a single mother who is unable to pay her monthly probation fines. Working 10 hours a day and trying to provide for her two children with no child support from their father is overwhelming. The probation officer, the judge and the criminal justice system appears to operate on the principle that one size fits all.

The Mercy Seat brings together an inmate on death row awaiting execution and a corrections sergeant. They strike up an unusual friendship when the condemned inmate's expressions of integrity and compassion have a dramatic effect on the inmates and correctional officers who live and work there.

In *The Crackerjack Gospel,* a man who was the victim of high school bullying goes to the store where his nemesis works with the intention of killing him. Something happens when he arrives that tempers his desire for vengeance and justice with a taste of mercy.

As Is follows the relationship of a parolee who gets a second chance at life, though he still carries guilt after causing a girl's death in an automobile accident.

17

THE OPEN DOOR

Just about everyone called my Grandfather "Pappa Jim," although I'm not sure why. Pappa Jim and his father were both born and raised in the sleepy farming community of Ashton. My mother, who was his and Grandmama's middle child, said it was because he was kind and helpful to everyone, which was for the most part true. He was always giving away garden vegetables to neighbors and strangers alike. When a barn burned, Pappa Jim would be the first one to show up with his toolbox in hand—even if the barn happened to belong to old man Stringfellow. Stringfellow (or "String-along," as he was known by the locals) once sold a tractor he had promised Pappa Jim to someone else because the man in question had offered him five dollars more. I remember asking Pappa Jim one time why he would help somebody who had treated him and countless others so badly.

Amused, he sized up my ten-year-old indignation and chuckled.

"Stringfellow's kind needs our help the most. Maybe if he gets enough help with whatever's been sticking in his craw all these years, he'll come to realize that there's more satisfaction in helping somebody than taking advantage of them."

I can't say a young boy's logic agreed with the wisdom of my Grandfather, but that was the way he was. Pappa Jim didn't hold grudges. He forgave others their faults as easily as he seemed to forget his own shortcomings.

One afternoon, when I asked my Dad why he thought everyone referred to my grandfather as Pappa Jim, he thought for several minutes before responding. Lighting his pipe and exhaling a lazy curl of smoke, he concluded it must be because of Pappa Jim's sense of humor, and that he was a natural storyteller. He had a joke or funny anecdote for every occasion and often brought a smile to even the dourest acquaintance. When Pappa Jim told a story people seemed to laugh in spite of themselves.

I asked Grandmama the same question. She looked at me, threw her head back and laughed.

"Child, you are something. Now go get yourself one of those sugar cookies while I pour you a glass of milk."

It was always like that. Food was the currency of Grandmama's conversations and her response to most queries.

I never did figure out why everyone called my Grandfather Pappa Jim. I came to believe it was because he looked and acted like the Grandfather everyone secretly wished they had. Although everyone called me Jamie, my real name was Jim, just like his. I was proud to be named after him. He was my best friend. It's true enough we had our disagreements from time to time, but like best friends usually do, we made up in short order. Pappa Jim taught me to work and play. The hot, tedious labor of farming and gardening was rewarded in the season of ripening and harvest. He also taught me how to whittle, hunt quail and rabbits, and most importantly, fish. Nobody loved fishing more than Pappa Jim and me, and there was no place we enjoyed that vocation more than at the lake on Pappa Jim's farm. He even built a special bench near the dam where we could sit under the shade of a towering oak, which he called "Old Bertha." We would sit under that tree and while away the long hot summer, talking and laughing, and eating the sandwiches Grandmama had prepared for us. On occasion, we would catch a mess of fish, which would end up as the main course for the evening's meal. I still remember the first fish I caught—a small crappie. I was only five and couldn't believe my good fortune at catching six fish in quick succession. It wasn't until years later that I found out why I had been such a successful angler. Pappa Jim would distract my attention by showing me the ducks or some other sight while he threw the hooked crappie back into the water for me to reel in once again. I have always felt sorry for that fish. But to a five year old, it was magic.

In a way, Pappa Jim was a Grandfather to everybody in Ashton. If they needed guidance or advice, he was there for them. Of course, Grandmama didn't call him Pappa Jim. She called him Jimmy, which never sounded right to me. And his three life-long friends, Vernon, Max, and Clarence, with whom he hunted, fished, and on the first and second Friday of each month, played poker, didn't call him Pappa Jim. Vernon called him Jimbo, Max called him Big Jim and Clarence referred to him as "J." I always found it interesting that he and I were both named Jim, yet nobody called us by our real names.

I guess you could say Pappa Jim was as close to perfect as Grand-fathers go. As far as I could tell, he only had one real peccadillo that stood out: he would not let anyone open a door for him nor would he open the door for anyone else. His peccadillo even extended to my Grandmama. His daughters, including my Mother, used to occasionally chide him regarding his peculiar habit. But as always, Grandmama simply laughed and offered everyone a piece of cake, pie, or whatever other edible she had handy. When questioned about his conduct, Pappa Jim would typically respond with a shrug of his shoulders or a grunt of indifference. When con-fronted by his youngest daughter, Aunt Sue, on the occasion of en-tering the front door of the First Methodist Church for his and Grandmama's fiftieth wedding anniversary, he uncharacteristically bellowed, "Why don't you mind your own damned business?"

After that, no one, not even Aunt Sue, ever mentioned it again.

In June of 1991, I had my fourteenth birthday. In July, Pappa Jim turned 78. The week following his birthday found us sitting under the cool shade of Old Bertha, sipping Grandmama's sweet tea and fishing for catfish. Following her bout with cancer, Grandmama didn't cook as much as she used to, but she still had plenty of sugar cookies, cakes and pies, compliments of the local Piggly Wiggly.

It was one of those hot, humid, hazy summer afternoons. Pappa Jim and me weren't sure whether we wanted to fish or take a nap under Old Bertha's protective shade. When he finished the last of his tea, Pappa Jim wiped his khaki shirtsleeve across his mouth.

"Jamie, you're fourteen. Caught between childhood and manhood. You got any questions your old Pappa Jim might need to give an answer to? Like the birds and the bees? You know those girly magazines like the one your old Grandmama found under your mattress last Saturday morning don't necessarily give you the real low down."

I said nothing and looked down at my feet, gingerly holding my reel and rod. I didn't have to say anything. My beet-red face said it all.

Suddenly, Pappa Jim roared with laughter and slapped his right knee.

"Boy, don't worry about it. It's natural to be curious at your age. You know where to find me if you want to talk about it."

Pappa Jim leaned back against the trunk of the old oak tree and pulled the bill of his fishing cap down over his eyes.

"Pappa Jim, I do have one question."

I hesitated to proceed.

After a few moments, Pappa Jim raised the bill of his cap and looked at me. "Well Jamie, what is it? What's on your mind?"

"Why don't you let people open doors for you and why don't you open the door for Grandmama?"

Still reclining against Old Bertha, Pappa Jim looked at me for a long time before responding. When he did finally did, he had a far away look in his eyes, a look that made me wish I could take the question back. It was as though he was looking at something in the distance that I couldn't see.

"Jamie, meet me at the house day after tomorrow after you get home from school. I'm going to show you something. You're fourteen now. Maybe it'll do you some good. Only thing I ask is that you not tell anyone else until after I'm gone."

Wide-eyed at the prospect of our shared secret, I quickly agreed. I slept little that night, trying to imagine what the secret might be.

At the appointed time, I bounded up the steps to my Grandparent's house.

"Pappa Jim," I shouted.

Grandmama spoke from the kitchen, "Jimmy's waiting for you in his truck."

* * *

We rode in silence for a few miles before we turned into an old, ill-kept graveyard on the edge of town.

I followed Pappa Jim's quick pace to the back left corner of the cemetery. He stopped in front of three small gravestones, kneeled down and began pulling up the few weeds that had sprung up around the well-kept area. When he finished, he spread a small bouquet of fresh cut flowers in front of the three headstones. The names were barely legible.

"You know who these three fellows were?" Pappa Jim asked, rising to his feet and dusting off his pants.

"I can barely read their names Pappa Jim."

"Their names are Ben Smith, Eli Johnson and Johnny Smith."

"Ring any bells?" Pappa Jim continued, looking quietly at the headstones.

"No, Sir."

"They were the three black boys who were hung by a mob in the fall of 1933 for raping a young white girl." Pappa Jim turned and looked at me, his eyes soft and somber. "They were hung by a mob for doin' something they never did. The girl's boyfriend cooked up the whole story and she went along with it. That story ended up getting three innocent boys killed. Course, nobody around these parts likes to talk much about what happened."

"That's a really terrible thing, but what has it got to do with you?"

Continuing to look at me with a sadness I had never seen in him before, Pappa Jim fished an old, faded newspaper clipping out of his shirt pocket and handed it to me. I took it from him and read it carefully. The title of the article declared in bold print: "Three Negro Rapists Receive Their Just Rewards!"

"Like I said before, Pappa Jim, it was a terrible thing, but I still don't see what it has to do with you?"

"Look closely at the photograph Jamie. What do you see?"

I studied the faded picture as closely as I could.

"I see a mob pushing three young black men out of the jail into the street."

"See the young man holding the jail door open?"

"Yessir."

Pappa Jim sighed, "That young man is me."

Not knowing what else to do, I handed the faded clipping back to him. He carefully folded it before returning it to his pocket. We stood in silence for a long time.

"Pappa Jim, I know you feel bad about what happened, but that was a long time ago. You were barely a man. And besides, you didn't hang those boys; you just held the door open."

Pappa Jim looked at me, his eyes flashing with pain and anger.

"I was a damn fool and more importantly, I was old enough to know better."

"But Pappa Jim, you didn't hang anybody!"

"No Jamie, I didn't hang anybody, I just held the door open for the ones who did. I opened a door that I should've closed."

"But Pappa Jim...."

"No buts about it, I was a part of that heartless, murdering mob. I came to my senses when I saw them stringing those boys up in the town square. But even then, I remained silent. Those three boys, Ben, Eli and Johnny were only 15 or 16 years old. They had Mamas and Papas and dreams, just like me and you. "

Pappa Jim's voice began to crack as his eyes filled with tears. I had never seen my Grandfather cry.

"There ain't a day goes by that I haven't thought about those three boys and my part in their death. Ben proclaimed his innocence once or twice and then became silent as they placed the noose around his neck. But you could see the anger and hurt in his eyes as he looked out on that hate-filled crowd for the last time. Eli just closed his eyes and sang some kind of spiritual song until the life was choked out of him. Poor Johnny was the youngest and the most pitiful. He messed on himself and called for his Mama while the crowd laughed at him. After it was over, I cried all the way home and I've cried many a tear since. But the truth is, I was a part of that 'terrible thing' as you call it.

"My Mama was so disappointed when she saw my picture in the paper that she didn't speak to me for a long time. She and I both knew she had raised me better than that. Fact is the only honorable man in Ashton on that dark day was Arthur Johannsen. He ran a local funeral parlor and was the only person who would take the bodies. During that time, this cemetery was for whites only, but Johannsen bought the plots himself and gave the three boys a proper burial, even though it upset some of the locals. To this day, it's understood by all the black folks in Ashton that when one of them dies, they take their business to Johannsen Funeral Home.

"I come up here every year on the anniversary of the lynching and talk to Ben, Eli and Johnny."

With that said, Pappa Jim dropped to one knee and bowed his head. Standing next to him, I bowed my head as well.

After several minutes of silence, Pappa Jim rose to his feet and walked slowly to his truck.

We rode back to the farm, neither of us speaking a word. When we pulled up to the farmhouse, Pappa Jim turned off the ignition. He turned to me with a sad smile and patted me on the knee.

"So you see, Jamie, your Pappa Jim's not the man you thought he was."

From somewhere deep within, I felt the tears rising inside me. Wiping my eyes, I looked at my Grandfather, not sure what to say.

"Everyone makes mistakes."

"That's right, Jamie. But if I'm going to be real to you, you got to know me for who I am—warts and all. Lord knows I have my faults, chief among them the terrible suffering Ben, Eli and Johnny went through that I played a part in. For our bond to be strong, you and me have to be straight with each other. It's important that you learn something from my mistakes. Maybe some small good can come from the bad that I've been a part of. I know I've put a lot on you this afternoon. I'd be lying if I didn't tell you that in a way, it feels good to let you in on my secret—to maybe let you help me carry my burden in some small way. If this afternoon means anything, I need to know what you've learned from what I've told and shown you."

Pappa Jim waited patiently while I pondered what he said.

"I guess I learned a couple of things," I answered. "What appears to be ain't necessarily so. Nobody's perfect, even the ones you love. And if you love someone, you love them even if they've done something bad. Sometimes we have to carry the bad 'cause we can't make it right. We still have to try—to do the best we can even when it doesn't feel like enough."

I took a deep breath and looked into Pappa Jim's eyes. He said nothing, but his eyes were full of love and compassion. They looked like they were a thousand years old.

* * *

Now I'm thirty-four, married with a wife and two children. It's been twenty years since that afternoon and ten years since Pappa Jim passed on, but I often think about our days together.

Last night I dreamed I was fishing under the shade of Old Bertha with four elderly black men. They were talking mostly among themselves. As I rose to leave, one of them turned to me with a twinkle in his eye and said, "Jamie, have you caught any crappie lately?"

Discussion Questions

1. Can you imagine yourself as a young person caught up in the fear and anger surrounding the alleged rape of a young girl? How would it feel to be in Pappa Jim's place?
2. Imagine that you were one of the three young boys who were hanged. What would be your reaction? What if you were a member of their family and heard about what happened later? How would you feel?
3. Did it take courage and compassion for the local undertaker to give the boys a proper burial? What would the consequences be for his family and him in their community?
4. What were consequences of the hanging for the law enforcement and justice system in the community? How did you feel the hanging affected the minorities living in the area regarding their perception of justice?
5. How would you feel if you were the grandson? How would that affect your opinion of your Grandfather and the community in which you had been raised?
6. Do you feel that Pappa Jim is a "good person" despite his bad act? Does he deserve forgiveness?

18

Dead Man's Parade

"When we marched down them streets of New York City after the war with all that spit and polish and them bands playing, I swear on my Mother's grave, I could see them dead boys we left behind marching with us." Big Tiny nodded his head in agreement, but said nothing as he and Abernathy drank in silence.

A bluebird landed on a tree branch and announced its presence. Abernathy sloshed some more corn liquor into his tin cup. "Wasn't no bluebird songs on the battlefields in France or at the Bulge. Only dying songs sung there. Men screaming for their mommas. I still dream about those boys—white and black."

Big Tiny nodded once more. "Could'a been a thousand of them bluebirds and you still couldn't a' heard they song."

The row of shanties stood in a row as if standing at attention and saluting the ripe cotton fields lying before them as far as the eye could see. Weather worn and unpainted, rust covered tin roofs offered their inhabitants a modest measure of protection against the elements. The black tenant families toiled in the fields of white farmers in a nod to the past when they were considered property. Now they were free, free for the most part to be poor and submissive to the descendants of past masters—slaves to ghosts of the past.

Big Tiny turned up the jug and wiped his mouth with the back of his hand. "I woke in a sweat night before last dreamin' 'bout them damn Krauts. They 88's done took out our tank and there they was—four of them grinnin' and pointing that big gun right at me."

Abernathy took a can of Prince Albert out of his overall pocket and rolled himself a cigarette. "No need for you to run. As big as you is and as big as that 88 was, ain't no way they gonna miss."

157

Big Tiny swatted at a fly buzzing near his head. "Like I said, it was a dream. Bad as it was, I still here."

Abernathy took a long draw off his cigarette. "Truth is, they wasn't no grinning Krauts on the day you got hold o' that .50 caliber on the turret. Like the 761st motto says you 'come out fightin'. You might not 'a looked like no black panther, but from where I was, you damn sure looked like a black bear. They might 'a stopped your tank, but they didn't stop Big Tiny. How come you didn't run for cover like the rest o' us?"

"Don't know for sure," Big Tiny replied with a shrug. "They blew up our tank and killed two good boys, one from New York and the other—I can't remember where he was from. Anyways, I was trying to help Henry get off the tank and them bastards shot me in the ass. When my back was turned, they shot me in the ass. How that gonna look—me being shot in the ass?"

Big Tiny turned up the jug once more. "That made me sho' nuff mad. I be so mad I thought I would bust. I guess I was more mad than scared. Don't remember much after that. Reckon the Devil got hold o' me after that."

Rolling another cigarette, Abernathy looked at his friend and grinned. "Only devil present that day, was the devil you gave them Jerrys."

"Reckon you right," Big Tiny replied.

"Damn straight, I'm right. The Colonel hisself came down to shake yo' hand and you got a Purple Heart to boot."

Abernathy flicked a strand of tobacco off his tongue and chuckled. "Whoeee, a black man from Mississippi shoots 12 white men dead, even if they was Germans, and gets a handshake and Purple Heart for doing it. Never thought I would see such."

Big Tiny's face clouded over. "They's a couple of white men 'round these parts I'd like to join them Krauts, starting with Billy Thompson."

"He ain't but 14, Big Tiny, more like a 14-year-old beanpole."

The cloud grew darker. "He a beanpole with a mean mouth. Try to boss me 'round like his Daddy do. Cusses me and calls me a nigger. His Daddy pay my wages. He don't."

Abernathy reached over and squeezed his friend's shoulder. "Little Billy piss-pot don't know no better. He just actin' out what his Daddy thinkin'. I s'pect if he knew what you did to them Krauts, he might be more careful."

His friend's words pushed away the cloud. "I s'pect so. If'n he saw what I did over there, he wouldn't want rile me."

"Might even wet his beanpole pants," Abernathy replied, holding out his cup for a refill. "You show Tildy and your folks your medal?"

"Yeah, I showed 'em," Big Tiny nodded. "Daddy told me to hide it and he right to tell me that. Fact is, he told me not to wear my uniform home so when the bus stopped in Virginia, I put on 'share croppin' clothes and packed my uniform away. Daddy said Reverend Soloman told him 'bout a boy down in Mobile who wore his Bronze Star pinned on his uniform downtown. Three white men beat him to death on the edge o' town when he was walking home."

Big Tiny bowed his head. "Mmm. Mmm. They beat that poor boy to death right in front o' they wives and chillun."

Abernathy blew a smoke ring spiraling up into the evening air. "Heard they lynched a black soldier last month in Jackson cause someone saw a picture of a white woman in his wallet. More'n likely one of them Frenchies."

Big Tiny turned and looked at his friend. "Ab, what was we fightin' for? Our blood just as red as theirs."

The sun was beginning to set behind the tree line. "The white folk think we fightin' for them, but we—I ain't, really. What did you and me see on our leave in Paris?"

"We saw the biggest city I ever saw."

Abernathy continued. "And the people?"

Big Tiny scratched his scruff of a beard. "They was nice. They looked at us different—like we was like them. When that ol' white French lady hugged and thanked me, it 'bout scared to death. Thought maybe a lynch party might be hidin' somewhere 'round the corner."

"You told it right when you said they looked at us like we was the same as them. Me and you didn't have to look down at our feet when folks was talkin' to us and say yes suh and no ma'am. We wasn't niggers in Paris, France. We was men—fightin' men of the 761st—fightin' for they and our freedom. We was men."

Crickets began to sing in unison as night-time approached. Big Tiny's wife, Tildy walked out on the porch and placed her hands on her hips. "You two boys done had enough o' the jug. Time for y'all to come inside and eat your supper while it's hot. I already fed the chillun."

Fried rabbit and okra covered a cracked earthenware platter. Collard greens simmered in a pot on the wood stove and a pone of cornbread cooled in the cast iron skillet. A small plate was stacked high with fresh sliced tomatoes. After Big Tiny said the blessing, the friends began to eat.

"My, my Tildy, ain't no one cook like you," Abernathy said, smacking his lips. "No wonder Big Tiny as big as he is."

Tildy rolled her eyes. "Ab, you one sweet-talkin' fool, but I already married so you might as well save your shuck and jive for some other woman."

The three of them laughed. Big Tiny buttered a piece of cornbread. "Tildy shore nuff got your number, Ab."

When supper was finished, Tildy rose from the table. "You two go back out on the porch. I cook up some chicory coffee and bring you a cup."

The two of them sat on the porch steps. Abernathy rolled another cigarette and Big Tiny packed his corn cob pipe with Prince Albert. Abernathy handed his Zippo lighter to Tiny. "You hit the jackpot with Tildy. Hope you know it."

"I reckon I did," Big Tiny smiled. "She a good woman."

After Tildy brought them their coffee, they smoked and sipped from their cups in silence, listening to the sounds of the night.

"In 'bout another week, it gonna be hot in them fields," Big Tiny said relighting his pipe, "No time for resting in the shade if you want to make a few dollars from old man Thompson. He fair enough—least compared to some o' the other farmers. Lets us tenant families get vegetables from the big garden, gives us some ham and beef when butchering time comes."

Abernathy pulled a toothpick out of his shirt pocket. "Fair enough ain't none too fair considerin' the fact that you and your family be laboring from dusk 'til dark pickin' cotton and such."

"Got nothin' to do with fair. Got everything to do with puttin' food on the table and a roof over you and you family's head. What 'bout Mr. Robert Lee Higgs. How he treatin' you?"

"He a good man," Abernathy replied. "Don't talk much, but more'n fair for a white man in these parts. You remember when that Klan member, Mr. Jacob Mosely, threatened Moss Higgins with burnin' him and his family out so he could get they land? Well, Mr. Bob told Moss to turn his wagon 'round and go home. He talked to Mosely and that was that."

Big Tiny leaned back on his elbows. "I do remember. First time a white man stand up for us 'round here. Still, why he make you work on Sunday? Even sharecroppers get the Lord's day off."

Abernathy laughed. "He don't make me. He doing me a favor. He know I a better mechanic than Petey Dawson and Homer. Remember how I get those tanks and jeeps up and runnin' when we was overseas?"

"Mmhmm," Big Tiny replied.

"He also know how people 'round here feel about a black man betterin' hisself. So while I step and fetch it during the week, he open up the shop for me on Sunday after church and let me work on trucks and tractors. When he come back by at the end o' the day, he pay me in cash—the same he pay Petey and Homer."

Big Tiny's eye widened. "He do? What Petey and Homer think 'bout that?"

"They think Mr. Bob doing the work hisself," Abernathy chuckled. "Last week, I heard Petey tell Homer he can't believe Mr. Robert Lee Higgs workin' on Sunday."

Both men laughed at the thought of it.

"How them two to work with?"

Abernathy took a sip of coffee. "They no better or worse than other white folks. Homer a lot like Mr. Bob—he don't say much. Petey Dawson a little man with big man desires. He like to tease me about how the Army couldn't teach a nigger how to be a real mechanic. Little do he know."

Dogs barked in the distance.

"Ab, when you ever gonna find a woman and settle down? Ain't right a man of you age not havin' a woman and some chillun?"

Abernathy took his time responding to his friend's question. "Remember the dreams we had we was walkin' free in Paris, France. Remember how we breathed easy there?"

"Yeah, I do," Big Tiny replied. "But that dreamin' in the past. Time to put roots down. A wife, chillun' and such. 'Sides dreamin' too much in these parts can get a man in trouble—maybe even killed."

Swallowing the last of his coffee, Abernathy agreed. "Yeah it can. Yo' dream in the past. You have a wife, chillun and family 'round here. I don't 'cause I be travelin' light. My dream pullin' me toward the future."

"We be you family," Big Tiny replied, his voice full of emotion.

The two men grew quiet. Abernathy reached over and patted Big Tiny on the leg. "You always be my family. 'Though that always be, I have a need to breathe easy."

"Where you gonna breathe easy 'round here?" Big Tiny shrugged.

"I ain't," Abnernathy replied. "My dream pullin' me toward Detroit where they makin' all them cars and trucks. A good mechanic could find plenty o' work there and good wages too."

"Ab, Detroit ain't no Paris, France. I s'pect they's plenty o' Petey Dawson's up there."

Abernathy took a draw off of his cigarette. "You probably right 'bout that."

"You boys 'bout ready for bed? Tomorrow's church day," Tildy hollered from inside.

"I be hittin' the road, Tildy. Got to be at Mr. Bob's shop tomorrow," Abernathy replied, rising from the steps.

Tildy walked out onto the porch. "I ain't studyin' you walkin' them roads tonight. Saturday night's ripe with white trash drinkin' and ridin' the roads looking for a black man to gang up on. You stay with us and I fix you some breakfast 'fore we go to church meetin'."

Big Tiny looked at Abernathy. "Best do what she say when she got that tone."

Abernathy smiled. "Thank you kindly, Tildy. If you got a blanket, I just sleep out here on the porch where it cool. No need for breakfast. I ate so much supper, I won't be hungry for a while. I be leavin' early."

"Suit yourself," Tildy laughed. "Ain't no such thing as cool in these parts until just before first light breaks."

* * *

Abernathy walked along the road toward town, singing to himself. A new day was dawning. The sky was blue—not a cloud in sight. He hummed "Deep River" and thought to himself, "I don't know 'bout crossin' over into Jordan, but I sho' enough wouldn't mind crossin' over into Detroit." He smiled. "I wonder how long it would take a man to walk there."

Discussion Questions

1. It's easy to forget the lessons of history. After WWII, African-American soldiers who returned home from combat, including decorated ones, were treated badly. Not only were they not shown the respect white soldiers were shown, they often had to refrain from wearing their uniforms for fear of retaliation by local townspeople. The "Jim Crow" laws were in effect which denied members of the black community many rights, including the right to vote. How would you feel if you were a combat veteran returning from WWII and were treated the way Abernathy and Big Tiny were treated?
2. What other criminal and social injustices such as due process, education, and work-related issues did African Americans endure during this period of our country's history?
3. Why do people like Big Tiny stay in such a difficult situation when they could leave? Why do people like Abernathy leave? Can we see any common or similar issues with our current immigration challenges? What are some reasons you might decide to leave your home and friends and move to a place where you may not know anyone?
4. While we have made a substantial amount progress, there are still race and prejudice issues in today's society. What are some issues and potential solutions you can think of?

19

THE CLOCK MAKER

Sound was the first thing Walt Murphy became aware of when he entered Aldo Johann's modest brownstone. Tick Tock. Tick Tock. The three antique clocks precisely positioned on the fireplace mantle signaled the passing of time.

Meticulous was the word that came to mind as the young journalist surveyed his host's small sitting room. The room had a certain Victorian sensibility with its long dark red curtains that framed the large picture window. A small, polished antique writing table sat in the corner. Two ancient, dark brown leather wing-back chairs perched on either side of a small, ornate coffee table. Meticulous also applied to the slightly stoop-shouldered 92-year-old man who ushered him to one of the leather chairs. Aldo Johann wore a vintage tweed suit and vest. His bright blue eyes peered through a pair of gold rimmed glasses perched on the bridge of his nose. Not a hair was out of place and his goatee was trimmed close. When Mr. Johann went to the kitchen to retrieve refreshments, Walt made a mental note that the person he was to interview was a fastidious man given to fine detail.

Walt Murphy complimented his elderly host on the ornate French press that he used to prepare the coffee.

Handing a fresh brewed cup to Walt, Aldo smiled. "Yes, it is an exquisite design created for me at Buchen…." Aldo cleared his throat. "The designer in question was a true artisan. I have collected several presses over the years, but this one remains my favorite."

The two men sipped their coffee and munched on gingerbread cookies. Aldo Johann had a certain endearing quality about him. His genial manner and the twinkle of his clear, blue eyes combined with the symmetry of a disciplined smile spoke of a somewhat am-biguous distinction depending upon one's interpretation. His look could be a gesture of relaxed approval or the subtle response of seductive ridicule. Walt Murphy found the ambiguity of Aldo's masked response interesting though not surprising given the fact that Aldo wasn't his real name, but rather a mask of a different sort. The senior citizen drinking coffee and making small talk previously lived in Germany, his country of origin, as Albert Adolphus. To the inmates of the concentration camp where he was an SS physician, he was known as the "Smiling Death."

Walt Murphy placed his cup and saucer on the table in front of him. "Thank you for the coffee and refreshments, Mr. Johann."

"You may call me Aldo," his elderly host replied. "For one who likes his afternoon coffee bold with a clean finish, I have found none better than my favorite custom blend from Vienna."

Walt pulled his notebook and digital recorder from his brief case. "Given your current status, I must confess surprise that you chose to invite me to interview you."

Aldo Johann waved his hands. "No recorder, please. I prefer the old ways. You may write down anything and everything, but no recorder. To answer your question, my reasons are really quite simple. I have fondness for reading several newspapers each day, including the one for which you write. I have found your editorial commentaries to be well written and disciplined and perhaps most importantly, balanced."

Aldo leaned back in his chair. "Mr. Murphy, you are a journalist who is inclined to put your personal feelings aside in order to provide the reader with both sides of an argument. While your writing is incisive and sometimes provocative, it is always clear and within the boundaries of propriety. That kind of discipline and integrity impresses me."

"Still, given that you are in the middle of a deportation hearing for war crimes, why would you grant me an interview that could damage your prospects?"

Aldo Johann chuckled. "My prospects—what prospects, my young friend? At 92, my prospects are less than stellar no matter what the outcome of the hearing. I am confident that I will eventually be deported if I live long enough. Perhaps, I will even stand trial in the Fatherland. Whatever happens is of little matter. I have had my time and Father Time will soon come for me as he eventually does for all of us."

Walt shifted his weight in the chair. "Why an interview?"

Aldo pursed his lips in a moment of contemplation. "Much has been written about me—my past—in the last few months. Some of it is true, some not. What has not been reported is my side of the events that took place during that terrible war. There are one's actions and there are also one's intentions."

Pouring himself another cup of coffee, Aldo continued. "So here we sit, Mr. Murphy. Ask me anything."

Walt opened his notebook. "You've been accused of horrific crimes during the war, including conducting medical experiments on men, women and children at Buchenwald."

Aldo Johann waved off the question. "I will answer that and other charges in due time. To understand such claims, you must first understand something of who I am and what motivated me to do what I did." Aldo took a sip of coffee and pointed at the antique clocks that adorned his wall. "You must understand something of what makes me tick."

The young journalist considered his host's response. "So, what would you like for me to know about—how did you put it—your motivations and intentions?"

The former concentration camp doctor and current clock maker gripped the armrests of his chair and leaned to one side, staring at his favorite antique clock. "I believe in an ordered universe, a universe which desires—no requires—purity and perfection through precision. After the war I escaped to Spain for two years. During that time I fell into an abyss of despair, doubting my purpose and very being. I asked myself 'what had I done?' What had I become? I drank heavily and even contemplated ending what was left of my life."

Aldo's countenance softened. "As I drew closer to that dark appointed hour where I would exit my pitiful existence, I decided to go outside for one last look at the night sky—I always like the pristine brilliance of a star-filled night sky. And then it happened."

"What happened?" Walt asked.

Aldo Johann's eyes grew moist with excitement. "Through that bright, shining star-lit sky which illuminated the encroaching darkness, the universe spoke to me."

"Spoke to you?"

"Yes, my young friend, I know what I am saying sounds a bit preposterous. Yet, call it what you will, it penetrated my despair with an epiphany of sorts. A revelation that as terrible as the means on occasion may be, sometimes they are justified by the ends—the greater good that is served. A measure of salvation was revealed to me in that darkest of moments that while some of my actions may have been deplorable, my intentions still held some hope of virtue. What motivated me in the deepest part of my being was to improve humanity. After that life-changing experience, I eventually found my way to America and became a clock maker. I earned my living by designing, refurbishing, and repairing antique clocks. I made them operate as they were created to perform."

Aldo clasped his hands together and grew pensive. "Clocks are an amazing invention. No longer does one have to look at the position of the sun against the horizon to estimate the time of day. The clock allows us to go about our day's chores and our night's activities in an efficient and purposeful manner. Of course, such an observation only holds true if the clock operates as it was designed. The mechanics of weight-driven clocks are fascinating. The gravitational pull of carefully crafted weights, the acoustic construction of the cabinet and the hammer and rods produce a distinct sound—the sound of time and life passing."

The old man pointed to a tall, elegant grandfather clock occupying the corner of the room. "That is a 16-hammer clock with a triple chime that on every hour sounds an exquisite rendering of Beethoven's Ninth Symphony. Working on old clocks is both an art and a science. When the clock doesn't perform as it was intended, it is useless. The faulty part—be it a cog or a spring or other component—must be discarded if it cannot be repaired. In such an instance, I must conceive, engineer, and create a new part with the correct tolerance and performance characteristics to make the clock function as it was designed to do."

Walt Murphy put down his pen and folded his hands across his lap. "The law is more interested in one's actions than intentions. Judgment is rendered on what a person actually did. As the old saying goes, 'actions speak louder than words—and perhaps, intentions.' There aren't any war crimes against experimenting with broken clocks, but broken and discarded lives—that's another matter."

Aldo's brow furrowed as he toyed with his goatee. "Of course, I lived under German law which is more sensitive to one's intentions than your legal system. And you are correct in what you say—the epiphany was mine and no one else's. Still, the ways and laws of the universe are not the ways and laws of humankind. Early in my studies at the university many years ago, I experienced another revelation, an intense awareness that the universe itself chose to evolve over time through a great drama towards perfection, especially perfection of the human species. Call it nature's engineering if you wish or perhaps, the great Clockmaker in the sky, but the process as Darwin recognized was in accordance with the grand design of the universe itself. That particular revelation led me into a labyrinth where science, medical practice, and ethics converge in what is often an uneasy alliance. My personal intentions were not totally in keeping with the Reich's dogma. While it is true, I believed at the time that the Aryan race which produced the Bach's and Hegel's of the world was superior to other races, I bore no personal animosity toward other races, including Jews and Slavs."

Walt stopped writing once more and looked at the old man sitting across from him. "You speak of Bach and Hegel. What about the Einsteins, Tolstoys, Freuds of the world?"

Aldo adjusted his glasses and nodded. "You make a valid point, Mr. Murphy. I grant you that other races have their outbursts of genius. Yet, I would suggest that such individuals, while no doubt making exceptional contributions, may be, to some extent, anomalies."

Walt arched his eyebrow. "Do you still hold such beliefs?"

Aldo Johann flicked a piece of lint off his vest. "I must confess that over the years, I have moderated my thinking a bit. There is no question as a young, idealistic physician I became caught up in the resurgence of a distraught Fatherland and the charisma of its leader. As an old man, I am more circumspect and even a bit skeptical of charismatic politicians and public leaders. While I am less susceptible to idealistic naïveté than when I was a young man, I am just as convinced that the order of the universe requires—even demands—the pursuit of perfection and purity. To that end, my actions, while perhaps unacceptable by today's legal and ethical standards, were motivated by a genuine desire to perfect our species toward the improvement of all humankind."

The young journalist's skepticism was obvious. "But you, a physician, conducted medical experiments which resulted in the deaths of innocent Jewish, Slav and other men, women and children. They suffered terribly at your hand."

Aldo demonstrated little obvious emotion as he shifted in his chair. "Guilty as charged. My actions are what they are—by today's standards, perhaps even unforgivable. But my intentions—my intentions were motivated by a higher calling, a fervent desire to perfect my race and our species."

Walt observed Aldo Johann pouring himself a glass of water. He was still meticulous, but there was something else—something missing. It was as if his mind was agile enough to convince himself if no one else, that his intentions, imaginary or real, somehow trumped what he actually did. Walt wasn't sure, but there was a sense that no matter how keen Aldo Johann's intellect was, there was a lack of balance—an emptiness or void where his heart should be.

Aldo took a long drink before continuing. "As I noted before, unlike many of my party comrades, I held no personal animosity toward Jews, or that matter, Slavs. Because one believes his race to be superior, doesn't mean he holds other races to be of no value or worth. Yes, I was motivated to improve and perfect the Aryan race. My assumption was that other races would inevitably benefit from such efforts as well. Still, as you say, regardless of my zeal, ideological naïveté, and good intentions, innocent people were sacrificed."

Walt poured himself a glass of water. "You refer to it as sacrifice. I would call it murder."

"I'm certain you and your justice system do. Life is often unfair and capricious. Unfortunately, pain and suffering are often the price of progress. You might consider the fate of Native Americans or even the Orientals who died building your railroads westward, or perhaps, even your own Japanese citizens who were held in internment camps. As unfair as the march of progress can be, the greater good also has to be considered. Sometimes, the end does, in fact, justify the means. The universe, more often than not, exacts a high price from us as we move toward a more perfect state of being."

Walt Murphy could feel a headache coming on. "While I am no philosopher or legal practitioner, I would hold to the point that on a legal and more importantly, a moral level, it is still murder. I would also venture a further conclusion. While I don't claim to fathom the purpose or mind of the universe, your assumption of its requirement of the unbridled pursuit of purity and perfection seems to me to be fool's gold."

Aldo's ears perked up. "Fool's gold … interesting. Why do say that?"

Walt closed his notebook. "That's right. Fool's gold. As a physician and as a clock maker, you have been focused on the parts. You have to some extent, excused your actions based upon your perception of the purity of your intentions. You and I and all other human beings, regardless of race, have pretty much the same parts. But we are more than that. We are more than the sum of our parts. Bach composed incredible music, but you, Mr. Johann—Mr. Adolphus, you contributed to the greatest symphony of the murder of innocents that the world has ever seen."

Beethoven's Ninth began. "Ah, Mr. Murphy, our time for today is up. You see, I have a dinner engagement this evening with my lawyer. We could meet again tomorrow if you like."

Walt Murphy folded his notebook and placed it in his leather satchel. "Yes, I would like to learn more about your work and those you worked with. Context is important to me when writing a story like yours."

"Indeed, Mr. Murphy, Indeed. Same time tomorrow?"

Walt nodded in agreement. "Same time tomorrow."

＊ ＊ ＊

Walt parked his vintage VW Beetle in front of the old brownstone covered with ivy. Three crows perched on a power line watched him as he walked up the short flight of steps and rang Aldo's doorbell. Their cackling chorus seemed ominous in a strange sort of way, a grim testimony of what was past and what was to come. The door opened and there stood Aldo, immaculately attired in a cashmere navy blazer, gray flannel slacks and a pale blue silk tie.

"Walter, as I expected, you are right on time. Come in, come in."

Nobody ever called Walt, Walter. Once in the sixth grade, Johnny Spoletti did, but after a brief, surprise encounter in the alleyway on the way home after school, Johnny came to understand that Walt's proper name was 'Walt.' Instinctively Walt considered correcting Aldo, but then thought the better of it. What was the point in correcting Herr Johann. He was old school—prim and proper. Besides, he was there to find some truth if possible, not alienate his host.

Aldo Johann handed Walt a glass of Scotch and settled into his wing back chair in front of the fireplace. "Given that today's meeting is close to the five o'clock hour, I thought, perhaps, a cocktail rather than coffee might be in order. I allow myself a single glass of whiskey each day at this time. I have found over the years that a well-seasoned single malt Scotch is more suited to my palate than Schnapps."

Aldo raised his glass to Walt. "As the English are fond of saying, 'Cheers.'"

The two men drank in silence for several moments, each gathering his thoughts.

Placing his half-empty tumbler on a coaster, Aldo looked at Walt and smiled. "So, my young friend, where should we start our conversation today?"

Walt shuffled through his notes. "I would like to know more about the specifics of the experiments you and others were engaged in. Are you familiar with Karl Gebhardt and his protégé, Herta Oberheuser, and their experiments subjecting prisoners to traumatic wounds? I have a note somewhere that you and Ms. Oberheuser may have been briefly acquainted."

Aldo's twinkling eyes offered the hint of a smile. "I am impressed, Walter, with both the depth of your research and the delicate manner in which you allude to the nature of my and Herta's relationship."

Taking a sip of whiskey, Aldo continued. "Herta and I met during a seminar in Berlin. Our attraction to each other was mutual so we went on holiday together once—I believe it was Vienna in the springtime. She was a handsome enough woman, though quite needy."

The old man smiled to himself. "A neediness that I must admit, served me quite well that weekend."

Walt opened his notebook. "What about Gebhardt and the experiments?"

"Gebhardt," Aldo replied dismissively, "was a stubborn, vain fool. He was skilled in what you Americans call schmoozing. He managed to schmooz his way into being Himmler's personal physician. Because of that, he received promotions when he should have received a court-martial. He was anti-science, almost medieval in his philosophy of medical treatment. Many of us felt he was complicit in Reinhard Heydrich's death for refusing to treat his wounds with Sulfamonides, a new synthetic antibiotic that was available. He nearly killed poor Speer as well."

Walt stopped writing and looked at Aldo. "And the experiments?"

"Yes, the experiments. Although gruesome as you might imagine, they were necessary and hold some degree of virtue in that they advanced the treatment of our soldiers' traumatic war wounds with synthetic antibiotics such as Sulfamonide. Soldiers lived who would have otherwise died. The world has in fact, benefited from the development of those drugs, including American soldiers."

"Polish prisoners and children died excruciating deaths as a result of those experiments. There was a report that Ms. Oberheuser rubbed broken glass and sawdust into their wounds," Walt replied.

"Yes, yes, no doubt they did suffer great pain. And yes, the wounds were induced to mimic actual battlefield wounds. One thing about Herta, she wasn't the least bit squeamish in her pursuit of results and meeting her superior's expectations."

Aldo grew quiet as watched the blue flames dance along his gas logs. "Poor Herta. After she was released from prison, a Ravensbruck survivor recognized her and her medical license was rescinded. It seems a shame. She had served her time in prison and needed a means of supporting herself."

"What about those persons she maimed who survived the war? What means of support were they entitled to?"

Aldo looked from the fire to Walt, a weary, yet defiant flash shadowed his eyes. "Your point is taken. Most survivors were compensated by the German government, but of course, how can one who has suffered so much be adequately compensated? The circumstances of life are often unfair and the rigorous demands of scientific truth can no doubt, be harsh."

Walt ran his hand through his hair. "I believe your primary 'scientific' work was at Buchenwald. Tell me about that."

Aldo's quizzical look confirmed that Walt's edge of sarcasm did not go unnoticed.

Rising from his chair, Aldo reached for the whiskey decanter. "I believe an exception is in order to my rule of one drink. Another dollop of single malt might do us both a bit of good."

"My—our—work addressed a range of combat related issues. There were experiments that focused on phosphorous burns from incendiary devices. You might want to read about the Dresden fire-bombing raid for a more in-depth understanding of the effects of such wounds. Others worked on the effects of poisons. There were also efforts to understand bone, muscle, and nerve damage as well as the effects of gangrene. Oh yes, and there were experiments which studied the effects of freezing such as when pilots were shot down in the north Atlantic."

"All of these experiments required the use of men, women and children, most of whom died agonizing deaths."

"Not all, but yes, most of the work required human subjects, many of whom did not survive," Aldo replied with a shrug. "Of course, many more prisoners died as a result of the camp commandant and his unstable wife's decisions."

"They would be the Kochs," Walt replied, looking at his notes. "So you knew as you put it, 'his unstable wife', who was referred to by the camp inmates as the 'Witch of Buchenwald'?"

"Everyone knew Ilse Koch. The prisoners gave her that name. We thought of her more as the 'Whore of Buchenwald'."

"Why?" Walt queried.

"Let's just say that her excesses were evident when she had an extravagant indoor sports area built. Of course, her preferred sport was of a sexual nature and not a discriminating one at that. She apparently enjoyed a frequent and varied clientele that rumor had it, included Jewish prisoners. Waldemar Hoven, the Chief Medical Officer, was one of her many lovers. He apparently couldn't get enough of her. He even gave an SS officer who was set to testify against Frau Koch a lethal injection. He only escaped execution because by 1945 there was a severe shortage of doctors. Of course, that fortuitous circumstance only delayed the inevitable. He was convicted at Nuremberg and hanged in 1948."

"In the west, most women involved in the death camps escaped execution. Many weren't even brought to trial. Illse Koch was one of the few women tried for war crimes who died in prison." Walt looked at the fire. "In the east, the tribunals were less forgiving. Trials and executions were much more frequent."

Aldo drummed his fingers on the arm of his chair. "Though impervious to the greater good and driven by her desires, she was a consummate actress. I will give her that."

The old man smiled. "Of course, her respite was only temporary. I understand that she hung herself at Aichau Prison. I suppose the Grim Reaper comes for each of us at the appointed time."

Walt chewed on the end of his pen. "Your experiments focused more on chemical and biological warfare, including plagues such as typhus, cholera and smallpox."

Aldo swirled the ice around in his whiskey glass. "Yes, that was my primary area of study. I would agree with Kurt Blome's testimony at the 'doctors' trials' that our focus was on defensive tactics 'against' biological weapons and attacks. As the eastern front deteriorated, rumors abounded regarding the Bolsheviks' potential for chemical and biological attacks."

Rising from his chair Walt walked over to the fireplace and warmed his hands. "You offer an interesting rationale, especially given that there is ample evidence that the Wehrmacht's Science Section supported the use of chemical and biological weapons against England, the United States, and the Soviet Union. I believe it was referred to as 'Blitzableiter' or 'Lightning Rod.' Seventeen hundred prisoners died as a result of those experiments."

Reaching for his glass of Scotch, Aldo's eyes narrowed almost imperceptibly. "I wasn't directly associated with that work. It took place at Mauthasen. I heard rumors about plans for nerve gas to be dropped from airplanes, but remember, in 1944 times were growing desperate in the Fatherland. You might also recall that Blome was acquitted."

After taking a long drink, he continued. "As I am sure you are already aware, Karl Genzken was my superior officer at Buchenwald from 1941 through 1945. During that time period, we developed and tested the effects of vaccines for typhus, smallpox and cholera. Were our acts immoral? In hindsight, I can accept that while my intentions were good, many of the acts themselves were unethical. Were they illegal? No. In fact, we were ordered by our leaders to conduct the experiments to help with the treatment of our wounded and as a defensive measure against attacks from our enemies. Of course, history has taught us that when a war is over, the victors not the vanquished decide what is ethical and legal."

Walt rubbed the stubble on his chin. "I have one last question for you. I keep getting this nagging feeling that you and the other doctors understood that the prisoners were human on some level, but never really saw them as human beings. It is hard for me to get past that—that no matter what your orders or intentions were, how could you do what you did to innocent men, women and children."

Aldo clasped his hands together and studied them before responding. "What you say we did is in many ways unbelievable. And yet, we were taught that the Jews had caused our suffering and were themselves a dangerous contagion bent on destroying us. We were taught that the Slavs were subhuman and the Bolshevik horde was a threat to our very existence. We were a desperate and hungry people, the scourge of the west with no hope until the Fuhrer emerged. He willed a rebirth that we, not the Jews, were the chosen people. In hindsight, our new-found pride in ourselves and our nation led to a kind of collective vanity and arrogance that led to our undoing."

Taking a handkerchief from his pocket, Aldo wiped a bead of perspiration from his upper lip. "In spite of my insensitivity to the humanity of my subjects, the result of bias and prejudice I had been indoctrinated with for ten years prior to the events we are talking about, I did feel more sympathy for their suffering than you might imagine. I did what had to be done for the scientific integrity of my work and not a whit more. I did, in fact, write up official reports on two occasions regarding what I considered acts of sadism by other colleagues. One of those reports resulted in a court-martial and reduction in rank. And while it will sound strange to you, I took every opportunity to end my subject's suffering, on several occasions even risking the validity of critical experimental outcomes. Do my meager efforts pale in comparison to the suffering that was endured by prisoners? Of course. But at the very least, they do indicate that I was connected on some level to the humanity of those who suffered at my hand. On one occasion, I confided in the Camp Chaplain that I had a growing sense of melancholy that what I was doing to them, the prisoners, I was also doing to myself. Still, in the end in spite of any misgivings, I did my duty knowing that after the war, I would be pursued—that in the end, I like everyone else, could not escape my past. Now, it seems my past has come for me."

After draining the last of his Scotch, Walt put his pen in his pocket and closed his notebook. "Mr. Johann, I want to thank you for your time and hospitality. I believe I have all I need to finish the article."

"Will it be fair?"

"I hope so," Walt responded with the most subtle of smiles. "That would certainly be my intention."

Discussion Questions

1. War crimes are often the most heinous and brutal crimes imaginable. The Nuremberg Trials prosecuted many Nazi officials. What were some of the crimes they were accused of and prosecuted for?

2. War crimes trials are usually held by the victors of a war where leaders and officials of the losing side are prosecuted and judged for their actions. While the horrific actions of many Nazi officials were apparent and rightly judged, were any war crimes also committed by the Allies such as executing surrendering

prisoners, looting and such? How does the "fog of war" contribute to behavior that would likely not occur in normal society?

3. How did Aldo attempt to justify his inexcusable actions? If you were fighting in a war and believed that by causing a group of people terrible suffering and death, you could save fellow soldiers and citizens, what would you do?

4. We find that on many occasions throughout history, all sides of a war consider themselves to be fighting a "holy war." What are the moral implications and risks of engaging in war with such beliefs?

20

BEST INTENTIONS

It was a horrible murder. Not that there are any good ones. Suzanne Chart's body was sprawled on her bed, eyes bulging with petechial hemorrhaging indicating strangulation. Her face and body bore the marks of a savage beating with blood everywhere. Her three year old was evidently in the house when it happened. He was found wandering down the street, and told the neighbor that "Mommy was hurt." Before the neighbor could investigate, the husband drove up, went in, and found the body. He called 911. The strangest part of it all was the stuff piled on her body—an iron, a bunch of towels, a vacuum cleaner for Christ's sake.

"What the hell is up with that stuff?" Jim Short asked his partner, gesturing to the household items.

The bag 'em and tag 'em crew were still working, taking pictures of the body and the room and picking up items on the floor marking them as evidence. They were all waiting for the coroner to arrive to tell them what they pretty much knew already, that this young mother was dead. Strangled in her own bed before she was even dressed for the day.

"Any signs?" Carolyn Potter, Jim's partner, asked, referring to signs of sexual victimization.

"Not that I can see yet. Robe and nightgown are pushed up a bit, but that would be expected in a struggle."

So began the case.

"Who's good for it do you think?"

The cops sat in the diner shoving food in their mouths. Jim, Carolyn, and three other detectives had been assigned the Chart murder. They had spent the last month interviewing witnesses, waiting for lab reports, and developing leads. There was intense pressure in the community to close the case. Soccer moms were petrified that there was a murderer roaming their manicured neighborhoods. The police chief asked for updates daily on their progress.

"The husband. He came home from work because she wouldn't answer the phone? Come on. If my wife doesn't answer the phone when I call, I consider it my lucky day." John Morgan declared his opinion before anyone else had a chance.

They all chuckled a bit, with the two women at the table less amused at the joke. Carolyn and Jim had discovered that the husband had been having an affair with a woman at his job. He was a smarmy self-satisfied Don Juan type who thought he was God's gift to women. He cried crocodile tears at the scene and then disobeyed their orders to keep his mouth shut to the media, going on camera and tearfully asking anyone who had information to come forward. At least they had managed to convince him to keep quiet about the items found on the body. That piece of information they were keeping quiet so they could distinguish truth from fiction if any nut jobs came forward confessing to the murder. There were always a few who, for whatever reason, decided to cop to a juicy murder. Trouble was they didn't usually know that the victim was stabbed instead of shot, or found face up instead of face down. The less reported in the newspaper, the easier it was to distinguish who was telling the truth.

John had been assigned the team lead. It was unfortunate since he had a tendency to jump the gun on things, deciding who was guilty first and then finding evidence to prove his theory. All detectives had a tendency to do that; it was not human nature to collect evidence in a case without having some ideas of who was probably guilty. Besides, he was probably right. Cliché or not, it was usually the husband.

"What's Andrews say?"

Jared Andrews was the town's fierce prosecutor. He never met a criminal that didn't deserve the maximum or a lawyer who shouldn't contribute to his re-election campaign. The voters loved him. The police loved him. Defense attorneys? Not so much.

"He's leaning toward the husband too. Says we need to get something concrete though. All we have is circumstantial."

They reviewed their facts. There was the affair of the husband. Neighbors had heard arguments in the past between them although no one had seen any violence. The husband coming home in the middle of the morning was what focused the detectives on him in the first place. He said it was to check on her because she wasn't answering the phone. It could just as easily be the case that he had killed her that morning and went to work to set up an alibi and then came home to "discover" the body. The Chart couple had argued the night before. The husband said it was because it was his anniversary and he thought she wasn't being "loving" enough. After more persuasion to talk, he admitted that he wanted sex and she wouldn't accommodate him.

"But, Jeez, that doesn't mean I would kill her!"

Don Chart was aghast that he was being considered a suspect in his wife's murder. To him, the whole thing seemed like a bad dream. No one could possibly think that he could kill Mary. He loved her. They had their problems like everyone did, but he couldn't imagine why anyone would think he could kill her. He didn't know who would kill his wife. It must have been a stranger.

"Why would a stranger pick your house?"

"Why haven't there been any other murders like this one if it is a killer?"

"Why did you leave for work so early without talking to her or so you said?"

"Why did you come home that morning?"

"Have you ever hit her?"

"Did you plan to divorce?"

The detectives were relentless. They found out about his affair. A stupid thing. It didn't mean anything; it was just sex. They found out that he had a life insurance policy on Mary; but, so what? He had taken one out on himself too. They both were covered. That wasn't unusual. Only the detectives made it seem sinister.

Jim and Carolyn plodded along, putting the case together. Slowly they drew the picture of the Charts' rocky marriage. The maternal grandparents who took the little boy didn't like their son-in-law much and, after no evidence emerged that pointed to an intruder, they began to believe that Don Chart killed their daughter. Other detectives in the case, including John Morgan, contributed little bits of information to complete the puzzle.

They had nothing concrete though. The husband's finger prints were on the household items piled on the body but that could be explained since, after all, he lived there and maybe once in a blue moon helped his wife by vacuuming. She was not sexually assaulted according to the coroner, and nothing was found anywhere near the body that pointed to any suspect. The time of death was anywhere from 4 a.m. to 7 a.m. and Chart said he left for work at 6. That in itself was suspicious since his job at a printing press didn't start till 8 a.m. but he said he had some projects to get done. He had supposedly slept on the couch downstairs and didn't even see his wife before he left.

Detectives and uniformed officers combed the yard and the blocks around the house. Jim and Carolyn put in their hours coming up with nothing. Someone interviewed a neighbor that thought she "might" have seen a stranger in the neighborhood in an old truck. Sounded like someone who just wanted some attention really. There was, in short, nothing to indicate anyone had selected this house of all others, snuck in, and, for no reason whatsoever, killed the young woman in such a gruesome way. All the detectives on the squad had a gut feeling that Don Juan was tired of domestic life and wanted out.

Despite the lack of physical evidence, the Grand Jury came back with an indictment. Don Chart was arrested for murder.

The trial was the biggest thing that had happened in a long time and Jim and Carolyn were part of the line of witnesses for Andrews who tried the case himself. He and John Morgan had been especially close throughout the investigation and, truth be told, the other detectives felt like they had been frozen out of the game. Morgan had been point man on all incoming evidence and he and Andrews had many closed door sessions leading up to the trial. The other detectives didn't begrudge any of their number the small glory that came with leading a case; it was a heck of a responsibility to be team lead.

"Did you hear that the kid in the Chart murder said 'a monster' killed mommy?" Carolyn asked Jim as they were driving back to the station after interviewing witnesses in another case.

"No, where'd you hear that?"

"One of the guys. He said that the grandmother told Morgan that the boy said his Daddy wasn't home when it happened."

"Well, that's not saying much. No one is going to put a three-year-old on the stand. He probably doesn't know what he saw if he saw anything."

"Yeah, you're probably right, the DA will figure out if it's important or not I guess. I hear he's going to trial with no physical evidence. Chart refuses to take a plea. Guy still says he's innocent." Carolyn said.

"Don't they all." Her partner replied.

* * *

Don Chart's once thick wavy brown hair was now almost totally gray. Thin scars showed through on the side of his scalp from the early days when he had to fight or get punked by the toughs who saw him as an easy victim. Coming in after he was convicted of his wife's murder 18 years ago, he was a stranger in a strange land. He was appalled at the casual violence that permeated the prison and the gratuitous cruelty. He fought at least once a week at first. After broken bones and too many stitches to remember, he finally developed a rep so that the predators left him alone. He spent his time doing his work in the prison kitchen and working on his appeal. He never gave up trying to prove his innocence. A year ago, he got lucky and some big shot lawyers in New York at the Innocence Project agreed to look at his case. A young lawyer who worked for them was here now talking excitedly and Don was having trouble focusing on what he was saying because it didn't seem possible.

"What did you find? Tell me again." Don pleaded.

"It was a bandana of some sort in the evidence box. There was a note that said it was found in the vacant lot two doors down from your house. There's what looks like blood on it. We are requesting a DNA test to see if it is your wife's blood. Don't you see Don? If it is her blood, who dropped it there? It wouldn't have been you. This is the first piece of physical evidence that indicates someone else killed your wife."

"But why didn't they have this at my trial? Why didn't Becket have it?" Don referred to his defense attorney who had assured him he would be acquitted right up to the point where the jury came back with a guilty verdict.

"Don't know. We're lucky it was still in the evidence box. The testing isn't a done deal yet either. We have to ask the state for permission. The motion goes to a judge in the original jurisdiction. We've got a motion filed now and we should hear soon. I need to tell you though that the DA is contesting us."

"What? Can he do that? Why?"

"His argument is that any testing at this point after a conviction and appeal is a perversion of justice. I know, I know ..." the young lawyer calmed down his client who reacted violently to the argument that he was the cause and not the victim of a perversion of justice.

"Anyway, sit tight, but it may be the key to the whole case. Just be patient."

Four years later Don had lost patience. The young lawyer who first told him about the bandana had long since left for more lucrative activities. He was now listening dejectedly to the third associate in the seemingly never-ending stream of young freshly graduated law students who thought it would be a great thing to work with the Innocence Project until greener pastures beckoned.

"I'm sorry Don. I thought for sure the case would have gone the other way."

The lawyer had just explained that the United States Supreme Court had just ruled that prisoners did not have a Constitutional right to have post-conviction DNA testing done. This didn't bode well for their appeal in front of the state appellate court. The DA had fought their motion to have the bandana tested. They lost at the district level; they lost two different times at the appellate level and now their case was at the state supreme court. If they lost here, it would be over. Through it all Don couldn't understand why the DA fought them. Wouldn't they want to know if there was any evidence that proved his innocence? Wouldn't they want to know if they made a mistake 22 years ago?

"It's possible they'll decide on state rights. Don't give up yet."

Almost a year later, Don found out that, amazingly, the state supreme court agreed with his lawyers that the state constitution's due process guarantees created the right to have post-conviction DNA testing when it wasn't done at the time of the original conviction. Back then, DNA testing was in its infancy and used rarely in trials. It wasn't fair, according to the court, that someone did not get access to the potentially exculpatory findings just because it wasn't a common practice at that point in time. It was going to get tested. There was still a long road ahead, but at least someone was listening. At least, after all these years of fighting the DA, they won the chance to try.

"Yo, Chart, saw your mug on the news this morning. Didya know they found some other guy's DNA on that handkerchief?"

The CO had been casually filling his coffee cup from the urn kept hot in the back of the kitchen. The kitchen crew had finished serving and was sitting around the table having their little break before heading back to their housing units. Don Chart felt the earth shift beneath him.

"What'd you say Sarge?"

He stood up slowly, fists clenched at his sides, and all the inmates transferred their attention to the interchange between the Sergeant and the inmate who stood facing each other. They didn't know what was jumping off, but sensed something.

"It was on the morning news. Some DNA was found that didn't match yours. The news guys said it might mean you'll get a new trial." The sergeant almost added a dig that Chart was still in prison no matter what they found, but decided he'd leave that off. The guy looked thunderstruck. Besides, he had to admit that Chart was a model inmate and didn't deserve any crap, like some of these other guys. If he hadn't killed his wife, then he definitely got a raw deal.

It was a surreal experience seeing himself on the evening news. His lawyers were interviewed and they showed clips from the trial 23 years earlier. Somehow listening to it on the news made it seem more real than when his lawyers brought him news. First they had explained to him that the foreign DNA did not mean that he would automatically get a new trial. They had to file a motion based on new evidence that his conviction was a "manifest injustice." There might be another two years of motions and appeals before he'd get his new trial. Even then, a jury might still find him guilty despite the new evidence.

Then Mike Smith paid him a visit. Unlike the previous lawyers, he had been around for several years now and the two men had developed a close friendship. Smith wrote him almost weekly, most of the time with nothing new to report but just to give him a letter from the outside. He had doggedly pursued the case, working with the other attorneys from New York, to plan strategy and celebrate small victories. In this visit, Mike gave him the news that they had discovered that some evidence at the time was never brought out. Evidently the detective had been told by Marilyn, his mother-in-law, that Johnny told them all that "a monster" hurt his mommy.

After all these years, Don Chart broke down. His tears trickled down the creases of his face as he thought of his beautiful young son all those many years ago. Immediately after the murder, he was advised not to talk to him about anything because it was too traumatic. They couldn't stay in the house and so were staying with friends down the street and Johnny alternated between acting like everything was normal and crying for his mommy. He just tried to make it as easy as possible for his son to forget. As soon as he was arrested, Marilyn took the boy and, before he knew what happened, had got the court to terminate his parental rights. After all, a murderer didn't deserve to be a father. He hadn't seen his son now for over 23 years. He imagined what it must have been like for him to first lose his mother and then have his father disappear. He'd tried to write him through the years, but never knew where his letters ended up. He suspected that Johnny never received them. He wondered if it was possible now that he might see his son at last. Would his son want to see him? Would he remember what he saw all those years ago?

* * *

"Gentlemen, approach." Judge Weinstein waved the opposing lawyers forward.

The hearing was being held in the same court where he had been convicted and sentenced over two decades ago. He had noticed that the furniture and judge's bench had been replaced with modern Danish blonde wood which looked out of place in the old courthouse.

As the lawyers whispered with the judge in the front, Don glanced behind him. He had been brought to the small county jail from the state prison yesterday. People treated him almost like a celebrity saying, "I saw you on TV." Somehow that fact made him special.

After so many years of begging for people to listen to him, it was strange now that it was actually happening.

The hearing was to determine whether or not there was enough new evidence to justify a new trial. He had steeled himself for a disappointment. He was used to having the answer be no, followed by the appeal, and then the next appeal. Nothing had ever been quick or easy and the years bore testament to the fact that the wheels of justice moved inexorably slow.

He looked at the woman who was with his attorney and the DA in front of the judge. She had come into the courtroom this morning and, during a break in the proceedings, had asked the court clerk to see the judge. They had disappeared into the door behind his bench and when they came out, he had beckoned to the lawyers to come forward. Now they were talking in excited whispers and, as much as he strained to hear what they were saying, he couldn't make out the words.

"Step back."

The judge shuffled some papers as the attorneys came back toward the prosecutor and defense tables. He could see that his two attorneys' faces were suffused with excitement. They could barely contain their exuberance and shook hands with the woman as she made her way down the center aisle to the back exit.

"What's happening?"

"Shh, shh." Mike motioned him to be silent. "The judge is going to rule right now. I'll tell you in a minute."

"Some new evidence has been brought to my attention that totally changes the picture of these proceedings. In light of this evidence, I'm ruling that Don Chart be released immediately. Furthermore, the Court will entertain a motion to have his conviction expunged."

The judge banged his gavel as the courtroom erupted in pandemonium. Marilyn and her new husband, who had exchanged stony looks with Don as he was led into the courtroom, jumped up and ran to the prosecutor. Don could only stare stupefied at his attorney and wait to have the surprising development explained to him.

"That woman was the prosecutor from the next county. She had been following your case in the news and decided to do a little digging of her own. When she found out from the case files about the household items that were placed on your wife's body, she knew the case was similar to a cold case from her city. The murder happened only a year after your wife's murder and the house was only about 7 miles away. She took it upon herself to see if the unknown DNA from her cold case and what was on the bloody bandana matched. She just got the results—it matched!"

"It matched?"

"Yeah, so it proves that whoever killed your wife probably killed this other woman too. When the judge was presented with that evidence, he decided he didn't even need to hear any more from us or take any time to rule that a new trial was necessary. He just released you. You're free!"

Their conversation was rushed and took place amidst the other attorneys clapping Don on the back and talking amongst themselves. The prosecutor had his own group who were pushing to get close enough to hear what he was telling Marilyn and the other people who were trying to figure out what just happened.

Don was numb. After almost 25 years he was a free man.

In the weeks that followed, his case took on the nature of a circus. News teams from all over wanted interviews and his attorneys made appearances on talk shows. He refused and found it difficult to step out of his motel room. They had set him up in an extended stay motel until he got his bearings. He was having trouble adapting. At night he would wake up in a cold sweat and reach under the mattress for his weapon before remembering he wasn't in the prison any longer. Then it came out that he was owed about $800,000 from the state due to the years he had been wrongfully imprisoned. That didn't sit well with a lot of people. Some took out their anger on the prosecutor and police who put him there, but some acted like it was his fault. The money didn't seem real; hell, being out didn't seem real yet. He still couldn't get used to not hearing the clanging cell doors and the guards yelling for the men to stand by their cell doors for count.

It came out that Andrews, the original prosecutor, who was now a judge, had never shared the fact of the bloody bandana's existence with Don's defense attorney, nor the statement made by Johnny. The case file revealed that in his report to the judge, there was no mention made of these two important and potentially exculpatory pieces of evidence. There was talk of a new investigation determining whether Andrews had obstructed justice or tampered with evidence. John Morgan, the lead detective had died years before, as had the judge, but his attorneys thought they had a good case that showed serious misconduct. Other detectives would testify that they were not made aware of the bandana which, arguably, had been turned in to John Morgan who hadn't shared it with the other detectives.

Even the current prosecutor, the protégé of Andrews who succeeded him when he ascended to the bench, was the target of criticism. After all, if he hadn't fought the motion requesting DNA testing, Don might have been released years earlier. Or maybe not since the truly determinative evidence really came from the other prosecutor who had only opened the cold case review in the last year. That connection may not have ever been made if Don's case hadn't been in the news at the same time she was exploring her own case.

Talking heads pontificated about the fact that the "system" worked since an innocent man was freed. Others argued that Don's case showed the system was irretrievably broken and that nobody ever got a fair trial when the system actors held all the cards.

Andrews, the DA who had withheld the evidence, had at first refused all interviews. As the events led up to the probability of him facing some sort of formal investigation, he took to the airwaves to protest his innocence.

"I believe I have, throughout my career, served the interest of justice. I have given 30 years of my life to this county and I believe in my oath to pursue justice without fear or favor." He declared to one reporter who caught him leaving his courtroom with his judicial robes still on. His voice was strained and he seemed to have a nervous twitch to his left eye as he said his piece. "I do not remember all aspects of this case or exactly why certain decisions were made. We are only obligated to share exculpatory evidence. If I believed nothing was exculpatory, I was under no legal obligation."

He concluded the interview with his hand on his chest, staring intently at the camera.

"I have always had the best intentions to serve the people and punish wrongdoers. If I have failed in any way, it was not because

I had any bad intent. I have always had the best of intentions in serving the people of this county in prosecuting criminals."

Don sat on his bed watching the interview. He was somewhat surprised at his dispassionate reaction. He remembered how he had hated Andrews for years, believing him to be the one man responsible for Don being locked up. Now, after all this, he had no hate left. His lawyers wanted him on board to push for legal sanctions against Andrews. He supposed he owed it to them since they had stuck with him and were responsible for his freedom. He was tired though and wanted the whole thing put behind him. And he had more important things on his mind. Johnny had contacted his lawyers and had asked them to see if Don was interested in meeting with him. Today was the day that he would see his son.

[Some people may recognize some elements of this story as from the Michael Morton case in Williamson County, Texas. Although the real case sparked the idea for the story and several elements from the Morton case were used here, this is a work of fiction. None of the characters should be assumed to be descriptions of real individuals.]

Discussion Questions

1. Should Andrews be disciplined? If so, what should his punishment be?
2. Did Jim and Carolyn and the other detectives have any ethical duty to alert the defense when they knew of evidence that did not come out at trial?
3. Was the prosecutor from the other county performing her duty by exploring the connections between the cases or did she go above and beyond her duty?
4. Do you think the state owes Don Chart $800,000? More? Less?
5. How many innocent people do you think are in prison?

21

THE PRICE OF JUSTICE

Doloree hunched her shoulders against the cold December rain. The bus was late—again. She looked anxiously up the street to see if she could see its headlights through the dusky darkness. She hated the winter—not so much because of cold, but because the darkness stole a good portion of every day. Going to work and coming home in darkness made each day a chore, especially when it involved waiting for a damn bus that was always late. Finally, the crowded bus pulled up and weary workers pushed their way up the steps and into the warmth inside. Doloree stood next to the pole by the middle exit so she could brace herself to prevent falling into others who also stood in the aisle. She knew that a seat wouldn't open up for at least 20 minutes as the bus spit out its riders in twos and threes at each successive stop heading out of the central city area. She stared morosely at the passing store windows, each one more elaborately decorated for Christmas, with mannequins frozen in winter wonderlands of shimmering trees, sparkling lights, and brightly packaged presents.

There would be no presents for her children this year. She felt a growing lump in her throat and tears glistened as she contemplated how to tell her sweet Dwight that she couldn't afford the only thing he asked for—a smartphone—because "all the kids have them," he said. And she supposed they did. Denay hadn't asked for anything. Her eight-year-old eyes seemed much older as she watched Doloree slowly add up the monthly bills and subtract the amount from her paycheck, to figure out how much they could spend for groceries. She knew Denay would understand even though she was the younger of the children. Dwight was 12, but he was more like his father—wanting what he wanted when he wanted it. Which is why he wasn't with her she supposed, or at least helping to raise

Dwight, leaving her with Dwight and Denay when it wasn't convenient anymore. She knew Dwight would be disappointed and angry. Doloree had managed to put away enough money to buy some chocolates and new gloves for her two kids, but that was all. Her job cleaning downtown office buildings barely paid $10 an hour. Even with overtime she brought home about $800 every two weeks and was lucky to have the job. Still, her apartment rent was $800 even with the subsidy she received, and water and electricity was always over $100. That didn't leave much for everything else. Every month she tried to put away a little bit in a savings account toward her dream of owning a little house of her own one day, away from the drug-dealing and gangs that permeated the neighborhood where they lived. And then there was the $250 fee she owed the court every month. She sighed at the thought of it.

* * *

Jillian looked at the clock. Half past five. She could still meet the crew for happy hour if she hurried. She had one more progress report to finish and then, depending on traffic, could almost make it to Barnabee's, the bar where they all hung out at. She glanced at the file. Another non-payment person. She quickly set up the template on her computer and created the introductory paragraph indicating the probationer had not been arrested for any crimes and had not had a negative drug test in the last month. She quickly read her notes in the file. With over 100 people on her caseload it was hard to remember everyone. Ironically, the ones she did remember were the troublemakers. Everyone else kind of faded into a chronic pattern of asking the standard questions: "Have you moved?" "Do you still have your same job?" "Are you using?" and reminding them of their outstanding financial obligations to the state. She honestly could not remember this woman. A drug case five years ago, non-payment of pre-trial costs, and beginning probation with courts costs, pre-trial costs and probation fees every month had resulted in an outstanding debt of $5,500. Sporadic payments meant late fees were assessed every month on the arrears. She typed fast—it was a report she could write in her sleep. "Why don't these people just pay the fees and get on with their lives?" she wondered. Borrow if they had to, but once they paid up, she could write a recommendation for early release from probation and they'd be free of her and she'd be free of them. Of course, one gone would only be replaced by another. She and her fellow probation officers often groused to each other that they were nothing more than glorified bill-collectors. She didn't have time to do anything but write up the reports after checking arrest records and ordering random drug tests. She didn't get paid enough to worry about it though and hit the "save and close" button on the report. She was done for the day and headed to her car anticipating an enjoyable evening among friends.

* * *

Dwight let the words on the page blur and swim as he intentionally let his eyes lose their focus. What difference did it make? He didn't understand what they were saying anyway. Some dead white dudes were fighting some long-ago war that didn't have anything to do with him. He liked art and he liked science some, but this other stuff was crap. He knew momma wanted him to get his homework done before she got home and glanced at the clock. She ought to be getting home pretty soon and he was nowhere near done reading the history assignment for tomorrow, much less finished with some stupid book report about some stupid book that he hadn't read. He pushed the book away and started putting on his coat. Denay who was working across from him at the table looked up. "What you think you're doing?" she accused. "Nuthin. I gotta go out. Momma be home soon. You'll be OK." "I am not worried about me," she sassed, "But you can't go out. Remember what Momma did last time you did that. You gotta whipping and will get another for sure." "Shit," he responded, knowing she was right. But that was later and this was now and High-top and Toke would be waiting for him on the corner. He would worry about Momma later this evening when he came home and she had to decide whether to yell at him some more or let him go to bed so he could get up and go to school in the morning. If he was lucky, she'd already be asleep when he came home.

* * *

"Yes sir." Doloree answered the youth services worker who was asking if she was Dwight's mother. She was still numb. Coming home and finding her 12-year-old gone was something, unfortunately, she had experienced several times before. But coming home and getting a phone call that her 12-year-old had been picked up with some other boys for smoking pot and was now in the downtown detention center was a first for her. She spent a sleepless night after she was told she could come down in the morning and meet with some type of counselor who would "discuss options" with her. She promised to get there by noon and had anxiously watched the clock hands ticking the morning away as she waited. Finally, she was called in and the bored-looking young man was filling out a form. "Does he have a father?"

"Of course he has a father," she snapped, wondering if he thought the boy came from immaculate conception.

He looked up. "I mean, does his father live with you or provide child support?"

"No." She admitted, her defiance quickly dissipating. "No, he doesn't."

"We have a program of deferred adjudication for youth. If he admits guilt to the misdemeanor pot charge, he can get into the program. It will involve 150 hours of community service and court costs of $350. Do you want to go that route?" His pen hovered over the checkmark as if an answer was merely pro forma. "What if I don't have $350?" "We can set up a payment schedule—$50 a month is the minimum. You would also roll the community service fee into that and so after about 10 months, assuming he did his hours and didn't get into trouble again, he would be done."

"What's the alternative?" she asked wearily, knowing that $50 a month would come out of the food bill. She didn't even want to think about what would happen to her own case since she was often not even making her own payment of $250. Her monthly appointment was coming up this week and she knew that she would get threatened again with revocation because of non-payment.

"Deferred adjudication is a great deal. You don't want him to have a mark against his record do you?" The pre-trial counselor acted shocked that she would question the favor of allowing her son to escape prosecution. "He would have to be held until a hearing and the judge could make him stay in detention for several months." Doloree's stomach clenched. Dwight in jail was something she couldn't let happen if she could help it.

"Can I talk to him?"

Dwight's tear-stained face tore at her heart as she saw him enter the room. He ran to her and clutched her desperately. On the cusp of manhood, she knew this may be the last time he let her hold him. He was getting to be as tall as her and rapidly picking up the swagger and attitude of the street. Boys older than him still experienced fear but they learned to mask it with obscenities and nonchalance.

"I didn't do nuthin, momma, I swear." He pleaded. "Toke was smokin, sure, but it wasn't mine. They picked us all up though and told us we was all guilty. Why am I guilty momma, I didn't do nuthin!"

She didn't know the law. She had been asked to wait in a room and they brought Dwight to her. Now she looked around for the counselor. Maybe she could ask him if there wasn't some mistake. She believed Dwight. She had told her children more times than she could remember how drugs would ruin their lives and what happened to her. After struggling for years as a single mother, she succumbed to the temptation of using to make her problems go away, at least for a little while. She sold a little to her friends as the way to get some for herself and, sure enough, one of those "friends" was a narc. She faced a possession with intent charge and was looking at a minimum of five years. The opportunity to get into the pre-trial diversion was a God-send, but what they didn't tell her was how to make the payments when she was unemployed. She was violated and plead guilty to get a probation sentence and was now so deep in debt that she doubted she could ever escape. No, her kids wouldn't be using drugs—she was sure of it. They knew she had gone down that path and was still paying for it.

"I can't give you legal advice." The young man shook his head vigorously. "If you want to get legal counsel before agreeing to this deferred adjudication program, we'll have to hold Dwight in detention until you talk to a lawyer."

"But he says he didn't have any drugs on him. It wasn't his!" She pleaded.

"Again, I'm sorry, but I'm only here to coordinate the program. I can only put you in the program if Dwight agrees. If he doesn't, he has to go through the system and tell his story to the judge."

"But you said the judge may put him in detention for months!" She felt like she was being squeezed between two great rocks with no way out.

He shrugged. "Look, Mrs.—." Realizing he had forgotten her name, he shuffled some papers looking for it and, giving up, he just repeated, "I can't give legal advice. I'm sorry."

* * *

The beginning of a headache was starting and she rubbed her temples. Listening to the excuses every day, she wondered why the state even bothered to assess these fines. Probably a small fraction of them ever got paid. She and her colleagues were scolded in a meeting just this morning by the district supervisor. Evidently their office was the state's worst in the percentage of fines and court costs retrieved. No kidding. It stood to reason since their office serviced the inner city and outer ring. Many of their clients lived in missions for heaven's sake. They were told though that if they didn't bring up their "take," it would begin to affect their performance rating. Damn! She wished the transfer to the Riverside office would come through. Although suburban shoplifters and druggies were no fun to deal with either, at least they could pay their fees. Then after that meeting, she spent the rest of the morning listening to clients who explained why they couldn't make any payments. They had no job. Their car broke down. Their kid needed braces. The landlord raised the rent. It went on and on. She knew some of them were telling the truth, but the fact was that everyone had problems. She had to pay her car note and insurance; no one was helping her out. She had college loan bills and rent. Everyone had bills, so, good grief, if they didn't have a job—get one! If their job didn't pay enough —get another one!

"Look, Doloree. I am sorry for your troubles, but it doesn't change the fact that you haven't made a payment in four months. As far as I can see, you aren't even trying. The state has been more than patient with you and you haven't lived up to your side of the bargain. I have no choice but to file a violation report and let the judge decide what to do about your probation."

* * *

Dwight concentrated on the teacher's voice as she droned on about the Louisiana Purchase. Even though it was hard, he was determined to bring up his grades this term. He was embarrassed and ashamed that he made his momma's life more difficult. She signed those papers and he escaped the detention center. Toke and Hi-top weren't so lucky. Their parents told them that they made their own troubles and they could fix them themselves too. He shuddered thinking of that place. Some real low-down scary dudes were in there and he felt like he dodged a big bullet. He hoped his friends would stay safe.

"Dwight, that was a good effort on your paper." Mrs. Anders smiled at him as she put the paper on his desk. He acted like he didn't care, but it was kind of nice to be complimented by teachers instead of scolded. Shit, maybe this school stuff wasn't so bad after all and he could keep it up and make his momma proud.

After class, he found Denay and they walked home together. She was suspicious at first of his insistence at walking her home and helping with her homework. Finally, after a week, she decided that her big brother was through being a sullen trainee gangbanger and skipped alongside him, chattering about what she did at school that day. Merely grunting affirmatively was enough to keep her going and he did so, averting his eyes from the groups of boys they passed. Who cared if they thought he was a wimp. He was going to do what he knew was right and that was helping his momma with Denay and behaving himself.

* * *

"What does that mean, Momma?" Denay's voice trembled as she struggled to understand what Doloree was saying. She and Dwight were startled to see their momma already home when they arrived sitting at the kitchen table staring at the wall. She made them sit down on the sofa together and was telling them something that was making Dwight's jaws get all clenched up and was making her feel all jittery and scary inside.

"It means that I have to go in front of a judge. They are mad because I haven't been able to pay my fees. I told you that I owed money in order not to go to jail. Now it looks like I may have to go after all."

"NO!" Dwight stood up and threw his backpack across the room. "It ain't fair!" He yelled.

"What will happen to us?" Denay asked in a small voice, her eyes filling with tears.

"I don't want you to worry 'bout that. I'll see to it that you are going to be OK." Now both mother and daughter were crying and Dwight looked from one to the other helplessly.

"I'll get a job." He said. "I'll pay the money. Just don't worry about it momma! I'm going to get you the money!" He slammed out the door before Doloree could stop him. She literally thought she was having a heart attack as she tried running after him down the apartment corridor. What in the world was that 12-year-old boy going to do to get money?

Much later that night she heard Dwight come back into the apartment and go to the bedroom he shared with Denay who was long since asleep. She went to the door and started to enter and then heard him crying quietly. She left him alone.

* * *

Doloree shook the hand that was offered by the young public defender who was telling her he had been appointed to represent her in the motion-to-revoke probation hearing. She met him in the hallway and they immediately went into the courtroom since her case was on a docket call that began at 9 am. Now he was quickly reading the file as he asked her questions about her monthly expenses and how much she thought she could pay. Their voices dropped to a whisper as the bailiff announced the judge's entry to the courtroom and the court clerk began calling cases. Even so, the bailiff shushed them disapprovingly and motioned for them to be quiet.

"Doloree Johnson, Case number 453787."

"Here, Your honor. Stan Dearing representing Mrs. Johnson."

"Let's get this show on the road. Mr. Dearing are you ready to proceed?" The judge shuffled some papers and fixed his glare on the young man sitting next to Doloree.

"Yes, your honor."

"Then get up here and bring your client. Miss Veronica, are you ready to proceed?" The judge's voice softened as he looked at the young woman at the prosecutor's table. They seemed quite friendly and Doloree remembered someone telling her this morning that the prosecutor was the judge's daughter. She didn't think it was quite fair, but who was she to complain?

"If it please the court, the state would like to enter into evidence the violation report filed by P.O. Jillian Cruse indicating that Mrs. Johnson has not paid her court-assessed fees, fines, and court costs for the past four months and, in fact, has had a spotty record for the last four years. It is the state's position that Mrs. Johnson is willfully violating the conditions of her probation and, because of that willful disregard of her obligations, the state recommends violation and the re-instatement of the five-year sentence of prison."

How could words so evil come out of the mouth of someone so beautiful, Doloree wondered as she stared in horror at the well-dressed, elegant young woman who just recommended that Doloree be banished to prison, abandoning her babies. My God, she thought. Dwight would be 17 when she got out. Would he survive the streets? Denay was only 8. What would happen to her? She had no close relatives to take them. She begged her cousin in case things didn't go well today and the heartless heifer told Doloree she should have thought of her children before she used drugs to begin with. That was four long years ago, and she had walked the straight and narrow ever since, but no one seemed to care! Someone in the hallway had also told her that those four years meant nothing if her probation was revoked and she would still have to serve the original five-year sentence. She felt she was being pulled down into quicksand and saw her babies pulling further and further away from her. She hoped against hope that the judge would let her stay on probation.

"What say the defense, Mr. Dearing?"

"Your honor. Mrs. Johnson has had a job for the last two years. She has two children—eight years old and 12 years old—to support. The father cannot be located and there has been no child support. She has not been arrested for anything; she has had not so much as a speeding ticket, and she is trying her level best to be a good citizen. We plead for the court's mercy regarding the outstanding debt and ask that the monthly amount be reduced since she also now has financial obligations to the juvenile court for her son."

"What's that?" The judge, who had been barely listening as he shuffled paperwork, looked up and questioned the attorney. "What's the son got into?"

"He was in court for a minor possession charge and is in a deferred adjudication program. There are costs associated and Mrs. Johnson will be paying $50 a month for her son to be in the program.

Now the judge pierced Doloree with his stare. "Mrs. Johnson, you used drugs and now your son is using drugs. Do you think maybe that you haven't been a good influence on him and he'd do better without you around?"

"No SIR!" The anger grew in her belly and she felt it taking over her heart, setting fire to the worry and anxiety and depression she had been in since the hearing date was given to her.

"I am a good mother! Dwight is a good boy! He is trying hard in school and he does NOT use drugs! That charge was a mistake. My children need me and I will try to do whatever it takes to pay these bills, but please, your honor …" Her bravery fled and she burst into tears. "Please, your honor. I can't pay $250 a month. It is too much. I work 10 hour days. I am 2 hours on the bus. The children have school costs. Please, please help me!"

The courtroom was quiet. People had stopped their fidgeting and whispering and all eyes were on the judge.

"Yes, well, I've got your documents Mr. Dearing and the state's affidavit from the PO. I'll take both sides' evidence under advisement." He gathered the papers together and stood up. "There'll be a short recess and I'll give my decision."

"All rise!" intoned the bailiff as the judge exited.

Stan Dearing squeezed Doloree's shoulder. "Hang in there."

* * *

"All rise!" The judge returned to the bench and the room quieted.

"Mrs. Johnson, you have broken the laws of the state and the price you pay for that is punishment. The state has offered you an alternative to prison and you have paid very little of the total amount owed as a condition of that privilege. Ordinarily, I would not think twice about revoking your probation and letting you experience the full brunt of punishment. However, it is the Christmas season, and, also, I recognize that you have not had any other involvement with the criminal justice system, although I am concerned that it now appears your son is beginning down the same path. Be that as it may, I have decided to give you one last chance. There will be no others. I am assessing a fine of $300 for non-payment which will be added to your total arrears. You will need to find some way to make these payments or else you will be eating in a prison dining hall and your children will be in foster care, do I make myself clear?"

"Yes, your honor!" Doloree's knees gave out and she sat down hard. Her hands were shaking so bad that she could barely sign the piece of paper the court clerk was holding in front of her.

* * *

Doloree hunched her shoulders against the cold January rain. The bus was late—again. She looked anxiously up the street to see if she could see its headlights through the dusky darkness. She hated the winter—especially when it involved waiting for a damn bus that was always late.

Discussion Questions

1. Did Jillian do her duty as you see the duty of the probation officer?
2. Was there anything else Doloree could have done to pay her monthly fees?
3. What do you think about the Judge's response? Was he fair? Compassionate?
4. What do you think is going to happen to Dwight and Denay?
5. Read the following article and consider what the system could do to make treatment of poor people and those able to pay more equitable: https://www.washingtonpost.com/postevery thing/wp/2016/04/08/why-i-refuse-to-send-people-to-jail-for-failure-to-pay-fines/?wpisrc=nl_rainbow.

THE MERCY SEAT

"That's right, Jethro. Day after tomorrow, you'll be ridin' that roller-coaster straight to hell!" Elroy Perkins shouted, raising his voice like an old-time evangelist preaching his last night at a dirt-road revival. "And it'll be one hot ride." Of course, Elroy was no evangelist. He was the kind of man who made sport of disabled children and prison rape victims, and had no idea what joy or happiness felt like. The closest Elroy could come was to experience a kind of perverted pleasure in response to the pain and suffering of others, and the most genuine smile he could muster always ended up looking like a sneer.

The object of Elroy's tirade responded with a series of low moans and muffled sobs. Jethro curled up on his prison cot and tried to block out the taunts, but like all the other times, the ridicule seeped through the fingers that covered his ears and touched the fear deep within him. Elroy had his number.

"Jethro's" real name was Gerald. He was from the red clay hill country of North Georgia. Twenty-six years old and a petty criminal since he was fourteen, Gerald had been housed in Section D of the Row for a little over seven years. His most recent incarceration was the result of an incident involving him and his two older cousins, Alvin and Earl. During a night of drinking and big talk, they had come upon a high school couple having a romantic interlude in the back seat of a Ford Taurus on Hollow Leg Ridge. With the boldness that only alcohol can provide, Gerald and his cousins robbed the couple. When the boy, Lester Johnson, an All-State tight end for the local high school had resisted, they killed him and raped his girlfriend, Wanda Jean, leaving her naked and delirious on a frigid October night. Gerald was the only one who received the death sentence, compliments of his cousins turning state's evidence and the inadequacy of his court appointed attorney.

If the truth were known, Gerald was a follower, not a leader. He never initiated anything, but was always ready to go along for the ride, and more often than not, as evidenced by his numerous juvenile court appearances, he rarely knew where the ride was going. In fact, on the night in question, Gerald wet his pants at the sight of Wanda Jean being sexually assaulted by his cousins. He remained a virgin, although no one, especially the jury, believed him. Someone had to pay for the death of Lester and the rape of Wanda Jean and Alvin and Earl decided to elect Gerald. Barely able to read and burdened with an unmistakable hillbilly accent, Gerald had been renamed Jethro by his twelve fellow boarders on Section D of death row at the State Prison. Day after tomorrow, he was going to take a final ride, as Elroy had so cruelly put it. And for once, he knew where the ride was going.

Elroy was Jethro's chief tormenter on death row. Although Elroy was his birth name, he hated it. He wished his name was Elvis, like the King of Rock and Roll. Elroy saw himself as a ladies' man and a general all-around bad boy. He often addressed other men not by their given name but by the term "Honcho," or "Cacaos," or "Chief." And Elroy was more than a little proud of the crude tattoo scrawled the length of his left forearm. It read "Bad to the Bone," and few who knew him would disagree.

He had previously served twelve years in prison for beating to death the man who had taken up with his former girlfriend. Three days after he was released from prison, he killed his ex-girlfriend and was sentenced to death. He had bragged before and after he killed her that "No woman leaves Elroy T. Perkins and lives to tell about it." Of course, many had throughout Elroy's life, starting with his Mother, Eunice, when he was six years old.

There had been other assaults, physical and sexual, in Elroy's past that he had not been charged with—usually due to intimidation and on occasion, dumb luck. Elroy's Grandmother had raised him and had been heard to say on more than one occasion that Elroy himself was, more or less, an assault on the human race. Her words turned out to be prophetic. Elroy rarely passed on an opportunity to insult or harass anyone he came in contact with. When he wasn't targeting other inmates or the occasional correctional officer for abuse, he lay on his cot and sulked. While the other inmates had backed off hassling Jethro, who on a good day was an easy target for ridicule and laughter, Elroy, instead, turned up the heat.

When a death row inmate was nearing his execution date, a strange kind of solidarity encompassed his death row compatriots. Even occasional words of encouragement could be heard coming from one cell or another in the long, hot nights leading up the designated man's final walk. It was a reverent, unspoken tradition on death row—a kind of "don't speak ill of the one who is about to be dead." Of course, Elroy didn't observe traditions—especially ones that deprived him of the simple pleasures found in tormenting the doomed and the damned.

Lost in his own thoughts, a middle-aged man with a slight paunch and graying temples turned from the small window he was looking through, and faced his night shift partner, Officer Ed Jenkins, who was clearly agitated.

"The boy's carrying-on is unsettling the other men. Things are getting a little dicey. You think we ought to try to put a lid on that asshole Elroy and maybe calm the kid down? The Doc's done given him all the 'meds' he's gonna get until tomorrow."

Popping a fresh stick of chewing gum in his mouth, he looked at Ed Jenkins and replied, "I'll see what I can do."

That's really how it all started. Up until that moment, Cleve Jefferson, known by many as Bishop, was just another inmate waiting on death in Section D.

Although most men on any death row are usually low-keyed to the point of being docile, there are always one or two Elroys to contend with. Sometimes the troublemakers are mentally ill, but there are others like Elroy who are just plain mean. Of course, the former doesn't necessarily exclude the latter. One could be both mean and crazy.

The only way to deal with a primitive like Elroy was to make clear to him that the pain you were going to cause him was substantially greater than the pleasure he was experiencing. For Elroy, it was the threat of having his one hour a day on the small, interior exercise yard taken from him. To make sure he got the point, Sergeant J.T. Jones added the possibility that his canteen privileges would be suspended for a month. The threat of no Cokes, candy, or Little Debby snack cakes drove Elroy pouting to his cot in the corner of his cell.

Elroy's bullshit was contained in short order. Jethro's fragile grasp on reality proved to be another matter. What Elroy had put in motion seemed to have taken on a life of its own as Jethro's moans turned to wailing and left him curled up in a fetal position on the floor of his cell. Ed Jenkins was getting more than a little concerned.

"What are we gonna do, Sarge?"

"I'm not sure, Ed," J.T. Jones answered. "One thing I do know is that if we wake Major Dawson from his evening nap at Central Control, there will be hell to pay. I think I'll take one more shot at trying to calm him down."

J.T. Jones tried to talk to Jethro in his most soothing voice, but his crying intensified and brought curses and shouts for quiet from the other inmates who were trying to sleep.

"All right son," J.T. said to himself as much as anyone else. "I guess I'll go wake up the Major."

As he walked down the corridor to his office, a voice called out to him from cell 11. "Sergeant Jones."

J.T. stopped and walked back to Bishop's cell.

A small, bald black man with long, gray sideburns looked at him intently. "I believe I could help the young man."

"And how would you do that?" J.T. asked, picking something out of his ear.

"Me and him have been talking a lot during the last few days. I've been praying for him and I believe he might listen to me."

"Thanks for your offer, Bishop, but I doubt Jethro would listen to anybody in his present state. And with what's facing him day after tomorrow, I can't say as I blame him. Anyway, you're three cells down from him—not close enough to carry on much of a conversation."

Bishop sat down on his cot and smiled.

"Sergeant, I can't help you with the cell arrangements, but I can help you with Gerald."

J.T. looked at Bishop for a moment, then shook his head and walked back to his office.

"Good God! You can't be serious," Ed exclaimed. "We could be fired!"

"Not if you keep your mouth shut," J.T. replied, popping a fresh stick of gum in his mouth.

"If anything goes wrong, I'll take the blame."

"Damn straight you will!" Ed responded. "If the shit hits the fan, I'm deaf, dumb and blind."

As J.T. unlocked Bishop's cell door, he was amused that Bishop didn't seem to be surprised by his actions. With his tattered Bible in hand, Bishop proceeded to the chair J.T. had placed next to the condemned man's cell.

J.T. positioned himself where he could maintain a clear vision, while allowing Bishop and Jethro some measure of privacy. As Bishop pressed his face against the bars of Jethro's cell door, J.T. clearly heard only one word during his thirty-minute vigil.

"Gerald."

Even after all these years, J.T. was still amazed at the effect that one word had on the delirious young man. At the single utterance of his name, Jethro's body relaxed and he grew silent. Bishop said nothing, but sat and waited. From his vantage point J.T. could see Jethro sit up within a few minutes of Bishop's greeting and crawl on his hands and knees toward the small, black man with the long gray sideburns. What followed were whispers that sounded like praying. First Bishop, then Jethro. Then Bishop passed his Bible through the bars to the young prisoner and they clasped hands in silence, simply looking at each other for a time. Finally, Bishop smiled at Jethro, rose to his feet and walked back to the front of his cell. Once J.T. had locked the door behind him, Bishop turned and looked at him with quiet approval.

"Thank you, Sergeant Jones."

Nodding his head, J.T. went to check on Jethro and found him curled up on his cot, his face pressed against Bishop's Bible. Jethro looked up at the Sergeant for a brief moment, but said nothing and then closed his eyes.

Walking back to the office, Sergeant J.T. Jones experienced a strange sensation. He felt light-headed. Jethro's look had unsettled him and he had the strange feeling that on that particular night it was Bishop, and not him, who was in control of his domain. J.T. was grateful for the steaming cup of coffee Ed offered him.

Two days later, Jethro was executed.

Cleve Jefferson, who came to be known on death row as "Bishop," never denied his guilt. He had been a small-time drug dealer who killed two rivals in a shoot-out. That act alone would not have put him on death row—even with the list of other crimes and drug-related assaults on his rap sheet. Cleve's ticket to death row came as a result of his accidentally shooting Maria Lopez, a single mother with two young children during the same shoot-out.

During his first two years on the row, he had been an angry young man, ranting against a racist justice system and filing endless appeals. Then one day, without explanation, Cleve Jefferson gradually became less belligerent and less talkative. As he began to withdraw, Doc Hansen assumed he was experiencing the kind of depression typical for death row inmates and offered him anti-depressants, which he politely refused. Soon after, he quit talking altogether.

For six months, Cleve Jefferson said nothing. He slept, ate and sat on the edge of his cot, staring at the picture of Maria Lopez he had torn out of a newspaper. From time to time deep in the night, sobbing could be heard coming from his cell. Correctional officers on all three shifts pooled their money to see who would correctly guess the night Cleve Jefferson would take his life.

On New Year's Day of his third year on death row, Cleve Jefferson began to talk again. Over the next two years, he collected and read a variety of religious and holy books, including the Bible, the Koran, the Ramayana, the Tao Te Ching, the Tibetan Book of the Dead and Black Elk Speaks. Although Cleve seemed to prefer the Bible or his "Grandmama's Book" as he referred to it, he read and studied a wide variety of religious and wisdom traditions. He also began to share his readings and thoughts with anyone on the row who would listen. Most didn't, but a few did. Those few seemed intrigued with what he had to say and began to refer to Cleve as "Bishop." Over the years, everyone—officer and inmate alike—came to refer to him as Bishop as much out of habit as anything else. Most of the officers figured Cleve had gone a little crazy, but accepted that the men on death row coped with their predicament in different ways as best they could.

The only non-inmate who would talk with Cleve about spiritual matters was a good-natured, young Chaplain who seemed to genuinely enjoy their conversations. His two favorite expressions to Bishop were "I go to three years of Seminary to become a Reverend and you go to death row and end up a Bishop" and "I'll convert you to a Baptist yet." Each time Chaplain Smith would utter either of those phrases, Bishop's response was always the same—a smile and a chuckle. Bishop had been on death row for ten years when he thanked Sergeant J.T. Jones for letting him talk to Jethro. After that night, everything changed.

At first, their chats would only last ten or fifteen minutes, usually in the wee hours of the morning while the other inmates were asleep and Ed Jenkins was doing paperwork. Gradually, fifteen-minute chats evolved into one to two hour conversations between two men, separated by prison bars, race and a lifetime of different experiences. Their conversations ranged from prison life to sports to religion or whatever else caught their fancy. J.T. would sit in a folding chair with his coffee cup and thermos and Bishop on the edge of his cot, finishing the last of the sweet potato pie J.T. had slipped him, compliments of Margie, J.T.'s wife of twenty years.

J.T. Jones was not a particularly sentimental man. He honored the obligatory birthdays and other holidays with friendly resolve. He wasn't against such occasions any more than he was against going to the Methodist church with his wife on most Sunday mornings. Such traditions just didn't hold much appeal for him. J.T. seemed to find more solace walking in the woods on the farm that had been his Daddy's before it was his and his Granddaddy's before that. Only the occasional bird in flight could hear him singing the hymns of his youth while he pole fished from the banks of the old mill pond on the back side of his farm.

It wasn't so much that J.T. Jones was a simple man, but more that his needs and wants were simple. He had driven the same pickup truck for the last twelve years and for the most part, lived his life from the inside out. He was a careful and practical man who was at the same time, curious in a quiet sort of a way. And when a situation called for it he was willing to go against convention and take a chance. It was a mix of the three—curiosity, inwardness and non-conformity that drew J.T. to Bishop.

J.T.'s practical and careful nature required that he first review the file and background of the man who had come to be known as Bishop. The conclusion had been clear. Cleve Jefferson had become Bishop through some sort of gradual transformation, which in itself was not that uncommon on death row. J.T. had witnessed a number of men experience genuine religious conversions when facing death. Getting one's house in order, seeking some sense of forgiveness for the harm that one has done, and looking for hope in a better life beyond the grave—a fresh start so to speak—was understandable to J.T. What was different about Bishop in comparison to the others was that he didn't seem to follow any particular tradition. He didn't claim to be a Baptist, Methodist, Catholic, or Muslim. All J.T. ever heard him refer to himself as when he conversed with other inmates, was that he was one of "God's boys." In fact, every morning, seven days a week, when breakfast was served, Bishop always issued forth the same greeting to the residents of death row, Section D: "How are God's boys this morning?"

The responses to his daily query were varied and ranged from silence to complimentary replies, and on occasion, expletive-laced retorts from inmates like Elroy. J.T. smiled as he recalled a particular breakfast exchange between Bishop and Elroy, who had awaken in a particularly foul mood.

"Damn God's boys and damn you, you no-account Nigger!" snarled Elroy. "You were born a Nigger and you'll die a Nigger. A Nigger is all you'll ever be."

After the course of profanities, which echoed from other inmates toward Elroy subsided, Bishop simply chuckled and responded in a clear, calm voice.

"You're more right than you know, Elroy. I was a Nigger just as you are. We're all Niggers until we sit in the mercy seat. It's only through the mercy seat that Niggers like you and me can become men in this world and children of God."

Of course, Elroy didn't agree with Bishop's assessment and let him know in no uncertain terms before returning to his cot.

Eventually, the residents of Section D seemed to look forward to rather than tolerate Bishop's early morning greeting. J.T. and the other officers began to sense a kind of respect and even affection on the part of the other inmates toward the old man.

Numerous helpings of sweet potato pie, cooked greens and homemade cornbread later, J.T. Jones finally got around to asking Bishop the questions he had been curious about for a long time.

Handing Bishop a fresh cup of coffee through the bars, J.T. paused before he spoke.

"Bishop, exactly what kind of religious man are you? You say you are one of God's boys, but what does that mean? You got all these books about different religions and such, but you've never said what your religion is—only that you are one of God's boys."

J.T. stopped talking and took a long sip of his coffee.

"That's a pretty long question, Sergeant. Anything else?"

"Yeah, what's the 'mercy seat'?" J.T. asked, warming his hands on his coffee cup.

Bishop closed his eyes and sat quietly before answering. Finally, he spoke.

"I've read, prayed and meditated on the holy books of many faiths. The reason I keep coming back to the Bible is because it's my Grandmama's book. She called it the 'Good Book.' To me, it's 'Grandmama's Book.' You know, she raised me for the first eight years of my life, before she died of the consumption. Sitting on her front porch in the late afternoon after she had returned from working in the fields, we would drink mason jars filled with strong, sweet tea. Every afternoon, my Grandmama would read to me from the 'Good Book' and tell me stories about Jesus and the Holy Ghost. Sometimes her stories would lift me up beyond the clouds and other times they'd scare the pure hell out of me. She was a small woman with a big faith I didn't understand at the time."

Bishop paused to take a sip of coffee.

"After all my praying, reading and studying, I can't really say I know all that much 'bout anything. What I can say is that I love the Jesus my Grandmama taught me about. I guess you could say that I think of myself as a 'Jesus Man' who has a lot of friends and relatives from other faiths."

"Chaplain Smith, of course, doesn't agree," Bishop said, chuckling. "He says all my friends and relatives are going straight to hell."

Bishop drank the last of his coffee and smiled. "I like him. He's a young man with good intentions and a lot of back roads left to travel."

J.T. refilled Bishop's extend cup with coffee from his thermos. "Tell me about the 'mercy seat.'"

Bishop closed his eyes once again and grew quiet. J.T. sipped his coffee in silence and waited.

"When I was dealing drugs, violence was a way of life—nothing special. Intimidation, beatings and sexual assaults, even murder— nothing special. And then the shooting—nothing new, except this time, I killed a single mother in the crossfire. Left two small children behind. I'd seen innocent people hurt—even killed, but never by my hand."

"From the time I saw her picture at the trial, I became affected in a way that's hard to explain. It's like I was haunted. I cut that dead woman's picture out of the newspaper and carried it with me. At night, I'd dream that my Grandmama was looking at me, tears streaming from her eyes. During the day, I found myself either looking at the picture of the woman that I killed or thinking about her two children."

"When I arrived here on death row, I taped Maria Lopez's picture on the wall at the end of my cot. Then I wrote my cousin, Angela, and asked her to send me my Grandmama's Bible. Felt like I was going crazy, staring at that picture of Maria Lopez all day and dreaming about my Grandmama all night."

"When my Grandmama's 'Good Book' came in the mail, things began to change. As I began to read and to pray, I stopped dreaming about her. Then I quit talking and ate very little."

J.T. interjected, "We thought you were losing it—had you on 24-hour suicide watch."

"All I was concerned about was the picture on my wall and the hot ball of pain that was filling up my insides. I felt like I couldn't breathe … felt like I was on fire. And then one night while I was looking at that photograph, that ball of fire exploded and buried me alive in its ashes."

A thin bead of sweat broke out on Bishop's forehead.

"I felt her suffering as she drew her last breath. I felt the sorrow of her children losing their mother. I felt the loss of her parents and friends. I even felt the pain of my own Mama abandoning me when I was a little boy. It was like I was responsible for everything bad that had happened to anybody and everybody. I couldn't bear it. I was drowning in a sea of sorrow. After there were no tears left for me to cry, I began to pray to the Lord Almighty for forgiveness—for deliverance from who I was and what I had become."

"Then the big change happened."

Bishop grew quiet once more as his eyes filled with tears.

J.T. inquired softly, "What was the big change?"

In a choked voice, Bishop replied, "I finally got to sit in the 'mercy seat.' I was crying, praying, meditating and looking at that picture. I don't know how long I had been at it. I had no sense of time— it was like I was outside of time. All I know is what happened next.

"As I looked at that picture, the face of Maria Lopez began to change. Her face began to change into the face of a person I had never seen before. But I knew who it was. It was in the eyes. Not like the pictures on those funeral parlor fans. Different, like peeling off the skin to see what it hid. I been mistaking the peeling for the fruit. Those eyes were the fruit—what's behind the behind. It was Him.

"I wanted to look away, but I couldn't. Kept looking at that picture for I don't know how long. Then it changed back ... changed back to the face of the woman I killed. That picture was like a magnet. Couldn't take my eyes off it. And then ... Oh Lord ... and then ...

"The picture spoke to me. Maria Lopez's picture spoke to me."

Once again, Bishop fell silent, his head bowed.

"What did it say?" J.T. asked in a hushed tone.

Bishop looked at J.T. a long time before speaking. "She said, 'I died so that you might live.'"

Neither man spoke for a long time, each lost in his own thoughts.

Finally, Bishop took a deep breath and dried his eyes with the back of his hand. "The mercy seat's about second chances—about being forgiven when forgiveness isn't possible. Having your heart broken into a thousand pieces—then opened up and made new again."

"You got any of that coffee left?" Bishop queried with a weary smile.

Taking a swallow of the hot coffee, he continued, "If I've learned one thing from what I experienced, it's that I don't know much of anything. But—thank the Lord—I do know about the mercy seat."

* * *

Bishop's appeals finally ran out. He had plenty of letters of support, including one from J.T. and Chaplain Smith. They weren't asking for the moon, just that his sentence be commuted to life without parole, but it was an election year and everyone knows that mercy takes a back seat on election years.

The morning Bishop was transferred to the deathwatch cell, J.T. came in even though it was his day off. He came in to say goodbye. It was the last time they sat together, he in his folding chair and Bishop on the edge of his cot.

Bishop looked at him and smiled. "J.T., I guess this is it. It's all she wrote for this ol' world."

No inmate before or since ever called J.T. by his first name, but on that morning Bishop did and to J.T., it seemed only natural.

All he could say in response was, "I guess so."

He often wished his response had been more helpful, more encouraging, but that's all J.T. said—"I guess so."

Then Bishop had a final request for him, a special favor to ask. He wanted J.T. to make a promise to him.

"Promise me something."

"Promise you what?"

Reaching through the bars, Bishop gently placed his right hand on J.T.'s heart. "Promise me you'll remember that you're also one of God's boys."

J.T. couldn't speak. All he could do was nod his head.

After Bishop's death, J.T. received a package from Angela, Bishop's cousin. She wrote in a short note that Bishop had wanted him to have his Grandmama's 'Good Book.'

Sitting on his front porch, he looked at the book in his lap and smelled the supper Margie was cooking.

Opening the front screen door, Margie peered out at her husband.

"Honey, what you thinking about?"

"I'm thinking about this book—and that I'm grateful for you and the life I've had. But as grateful as I am, one thing is as certain as the sun setting over that grove of poplar trees—I miss my friend."

Discussion Questions

1. If he could go back in time, what would an older and wiser Bishop say to Cleve Jefferson, his younger self?
2. What are both positive and potentially negative aspects of religious beliefs and spiritual values regarding our justice system process? Regarding our own personal sense of justice?
3. What is the role of compassion, mercy and forgiveness when facing the consequences of one's actions?
4. What was it about J.T. that enabled him to go outside of his professional role and engage Bishop in a relationship? What did he learn from Bishop? What did Bishop learn from him?
5. It has often been said by many persons that inmates on death row should "get what they deserve." And while such a sentiment, especially from the family of the victim, may be understandable, do any of us really want "what we deserve" in life?

23

THE CRACKER JACK GOSPEL

His scarecrow-thin frame silhouetted by a dying sunset, seventeen-year-old Stanfield Huggins sprawled out in a close-cropped thatch of field grass, just beyond the pale reach of the only working headlight on his 1955 Chevy. A loaded .38-caliber pistol rested on his chest, and a sky full of stars, sparkling like flecks of rust in a moonshine still, filled his eyes.

An old sun-faded billboard advertisement for Chesterfield King Cigarettes loomed above him, its façade now serving as prime graffiti real estate for local spray-can assassins.

Stanfield stood up slowly, struggling to maintain his balance, and retrieved a Mason jar half-full of white grape juice from a pocket on his photographer's vest—a birthday gift from his uncle Lonnie, associate senior image consultant at "Smilz 4 Less" photo studio at the Baron Bend Mall outlet in nearby Ocala. Stanfield unscrewed the lid and stole two sips while walking toward the Chevy, its steady baritone rumble the only interruption in the evening's stillness.

Fireflies blinked in the cool autumn air and Stanfield traced "Sweet '73" insignia on the car's hood with his finger as he walked by. Decades ago, the moniker had been hand-stenciled by Stanfield's father, Silas, who at one time indulged in a weekend ritual of challenging other muscle car gearheads for weekend beer. Though having a thicker wallet by night's end was always a welcome reward, the more immediate pay-off for Silas and the other local white-line junkies was distraction from the sticky summer malaise that could canvas and cocoon a small county like Laramie.

It was a widely held belief that in the era of Silas Huggins, nothing could touch the '55 Chevy: Not Bigsby Tuffard's '69 Charger Supreme, not Charlie Leffler's modified Mach I, not even Woodrow McIllvain's Supercharged Camaro SS (though that particular match-up stirred up a hornet's nest of debate for decades, from dive-bars to fellowship halls).

Long after Silas retired the '55 from the backroad racing circuit, Stanfield's older brother, Reginald, added the coup de grace to the car's mystique: a simulation of the Vietnam War's Tet Offensive, staged on the Chevy's sun-warped dashboard, using miniature green plastic army figurines. Though the installation earned Reginald lifetime revocation of all rights to drive the car, the elder Huggins ultimately left the scene-in-miniature intact as a tribute to his eldest son, after he was killed during his second tour of duty in Iraq. Following Reginald's death, Silas wanted little to do with the car—or, for that matter, his youngest son, Stanfield.

Taking one more sip from the Mason jar, Stanfield placed the container on the middle of the dashboard battlefield and slipped the pistol into one of his vest pockets. Across the road, the Three Kings Gas-N-Gulp—a family-owned outpost popular with teenage hot-rodders and methamphetamine runners—rested on a curvy hip of one of the area's most infamously gnarled and ornery two-lane veins—Route 77. The humble building looked like a model train set miniature against the high-rise backdrop of the Blue Ridge Mountains, now spackled with the comforting glow and blink of distant lights.

Stanfield's shy disposition, stick-thin frame and premature male-pattern baldness, which accelerated when he turned 16, ensured that his passage from puberty to young manhood in a rough-hewn mountain farming community would be rife with every imaginable mode of psychological, physical and social torment. And it followed him everywhere, from the doorstep of his home, to daily school bus rides—to the stale metal catacombs of the high school boys' locker room, where he had found himself, only hours earlier in the day, introduced to a brand new discourse in humiliation. A teenage brood, featuring a smattering of Napier Street Baptists' finest senior Youth Ambassadors, pinned Stanfield's naked wisp of a frame on the locker room shower tile floor and tattooed, with a makeshift kit, "Pigeon Shit Bombb Zone" on his bald pate.

The local artisan whose handiwork now graced Stanfield's thin-to-gone crown was Simms Clearwater, a wiry, flame-haired juvenile hall regular and infamous schoolyard terrorist. This particular evening announced Simms' debut weekend working the night shift solo at the Three Kings Gas-N-Gulp, and for Stanfield, that meant only one thing: Simms Clearwater had to die tonight.

* * *

Stanfield slipped out of the Chevy's driver-side door, briskly made his way across the two-lane stretch and stumbled onto the Three Kings parking lot. The gravel crunch beneath his boots sounded off like miniature demolition explosives, and he turned to look back at his car, its idling engine grumble still audible from a distance. Nearing the storefront, his footsteps slowed to a creep, and he scanned with nervous eyes the old two-lane, snaking off into the darkness, determining that the anonymity of his mission was secure. Picking up speed to a slow jog (made awkward by his prominent limp, a birth defect doctors had never been able to rectify), Stanfield passed by Simms' mint green low-rider truck, its rear bumper bookended by two stickers that read "Draggin' ASSphalt Kustom Society."

He paused in front of the store entrance, his mouth dry and a hornet's nest hum ringing in his ears. He felt nausea climbing from his stomach to his throat, and gripping the store entrance door so tight his fingers ached, Stanfield willed himself inside, a trio of bells signaling his arrival.

The store was filled with an eerie calm—only the random hiss of carbonation pumps nestled near the soda fountains punctured the silence. His heart beating jackhammer loud, Stanfield approached the end shelf of the store's magazine stand and gripped it with both hands, his chest heaving in short intense intervals. He noticed an issue of *Men's Health* magazine had been opened to a dog-eared page advertising "male enhancement" pills, and he startled himself by letting loose a muted snicker. Scanning an aisle of random shrink-wrapped offerings, Stanfield placed a hand on his increasingly nauseous stomach. Colors and contents began to blur and pulse.

He exhaled deeply, wiped a patch of sweat from his brow and reached for a bag of Cracker Jacks, his brother Reginald's favorite snack.

When his brother was in Iraq, Stanfield would send him each month a personalized stash of Cracker Jack boxes—along with a narrated recording of the latest town news and gossip, and a stack of *Famous Monsters Of Filmland* magazines (a passion the two brothers shared in secrecy). Without fail, Reginald would send a return letter each month containing the prize from each Cracker Jack box. Stanfield kept every one of those prizes—25 in total—and stored them securely in the Chevy's glove compartment (and every single morning before school he counted the small square treasures to make sure they were all present and untouched.)

The task at hand abruptly shoved its way back to the front of his mind, and Stanfield closed his eyes, his breathing now slightly more manageable. He settled his hand on the cool steel of the pistol, its bulk feeling heavier in his hand than he remembered. A dull throb commandeering his skull, and an intensive series of quick, shallow breaths escaping his lungs, Stanfield gritted his teeth, slipped his trigger finger in place, and began to accelerate around the aisle-corner ice cooler display, his head a storm of feelings both fearful and enraged. But as he rounded the corner, he found his path obstructed by the long, crumpled frame of Simms Clearwater, slumped haphazardly like a ragdoll. His thick freckled arms, stained with cheap tattoos, were folded across his lap, and his back leaned awkwardly against a Trident Gum display rack. A thatch of mostly empty Budweiser bottles took up residence near his left hip. Others, with the labels peeled off, had either tipped over or rolled away, just outside his reach.

Stanfield stood frozen, his finger now sweating against the trigger; his aching knees a body's length from his intended target.

"My Daddy's dead," said Simms, his words a slurred whisper, tinged with a child-like cadence, his grief-smeared eyes slowly rolling side to side. "They told me he collapsed in the fruit aisle at the Piggly Wiggly half an hour ago."

Stanfield felt like he was separating from his body, only anchored to the moment by an ache growing in his grip.

"Betty Bivins had been talking to him," Simms continued, his raw eyes rolling over white. "She said he just stopped and looked at her for a second, and said: '*Well. Ain't that something.*' Then she said he fell to the floor, spilling apples everywhere. Said they rolled all over the damn floor and just kept goin', kept rolling—and before they stopped, he was gone."

Shaking his head, Simms bit his lower lip so hard a trickle of blood began to form. A fresh flood of emotion rushed across his face.

"He don't even like apples," he said. "Nobody in my family does—except for me. Ain't that something?"

Simms formed the shape of a gun with his right hand and pressed the barrel finger against his temple. "I swear to God, if you had a gun on you, I'd ask you to shoot me *right Goddamn now*," he said, his face distorted by grief.

Stanfield loosened his grip on pistol in his pocket and interlocked his fingers on top of his head, his eyes squeezed shut. He could feel the newborn scabs taking shape on his scalp, as well as additional residue from the morning's brutal episode.

Making a feeble attempt to sit up, Simms wiped his face with his shirtsleeve and stretched for one of the few remaining open bottles of beer.

"My Daddy was a barber at the Cut & Dried shop on Bartlett Avenue," he said, "and he always cut my hair the first Saturday of every month." He took a deep pull from the bottle and rubbed the red-hued burr of his scalp, his words trailing off. "Do you know what the three stripes on the barber pole stand for?"

"No, I don't," Stanfield answered, his face colorless, his eyes now wide and wired.

"Each color means something different," Simms continued in a slurred monotone, as if repeating a pamphlet slogan he had been familiar with his whole life. "The red means blood, the blue represents a person's veins ... and the white represents bandages used to wrap folks up when they get cut. My Daddy taught me that.

"I always thought my momma was the blue—she gave us life. I was the red 'cause I always came home bloody from somethin' or another. But my Daddy was the white. He always put everything back together again—cleaned the wounds. But now ..."

Simms slammed the back of his head against the display rack, his light blue eyes suddenly vacant and his lower jaw hanging open.

Stanfield stood quietly and began to open up the box of Cracker Jacks he had been holding in his pocket. After a few short seconds of digging around the box's contents, he retrieved a thin, small square of paper. Holding it between his fingers, he carefully leaned forward and placed it at Simms' feet, then began a slow shuffle toward the exit door.

Simms, still bleary eyed, managed a few words between hoarse dry heaves of emotion.

"What's this?"

Stanfield rubbed his eyes, exhausted.

"For a long time, it was what I used to stop the bleeding," he said. "But I think you need it more than me tonight. I'm sorry for your loss."

Stanfield walked back to the Chevy, its engine still idling steady and strong. He removed the pistol and slipped it beneath the rear bench seat. Looking at the glove box, he paused for a moment before opening it. Inside was a small cedar box containing 25 neatly stacked Cracker Jack prizes. Stanfield counted each one of them, put the box back in the glove compartment, and felt his eyelids grow heavy to the V8 engine's lullaby hum.

Discussion Questions

1. Bullying, especially in high school, has become an increasingly difficult problem in our society. Why do you think teenagers choose to bully their classmates? Have you ever witnessed or experienced such behavior?

2. The victims of bullying often choose to harm themselves or take their anger out on their oppressors. Can you think of any examples in the news of recent years?

3. Why did Stanfield spare Simms' life? Why did he give him the Crackerjack prize?

4. What can school teachers, officials, students and Criminal Justice professionals do to address the problems associated with bullying in our public schools?

24

As Is

Tommy Wills' dream was always the same, locked away deep, somewhere beneath stacks of faded denim jeans in the attic and an ashtray full of hairpins.

It would begin with a summer Saturday evening. The bathroom window cracked open. The old yellow curtain, the one she never liked, cresting and falling again.

She would let him choose the music, and he'd almost always pull out an old scratched 45 of Gram Parsons' "Brass Buttons."

She loved the 'pop' sound when the needle first hit the record. She liked that better than the song itself.

Then she would sit, perched on a stool in front of the old sink, mouthing the words, waiting for him.

Moving toward her, he'd walk as slow as he could, spirits in the old wood floor stirring, alerting them both to each footstep. He always wanted to keep the moment alive for as long as possible.

She would let him pull out her hairpins, one by one, and he'd count each one, laying them gently on the towel shelf. Sometimes he'd pull out the old ukulele that had been hibernating in her mother's attic, the one decorated with jewels from gumball machines. And she would laugh, or roll her eyes, or make up words and sing along.

He would look at her feet while washing her hair and smile at the v-shaped tan lines where she had been wearing flip-flops in the garden.

She would laugh and say, "See it through, Tommy. Stay on course and see it through."

He would dry her off, then wrap her up in an apricot-colored towel, the one with the Corvette Stingray parked in front of a palm tree, the one they got that weekend it rained at the beach.

Then he would lean against the doorway and watch her walk around the hallway corner, to the bedroom. She would always turn and smile just before disappearing, and he'd count each footprint on the floor, left in her wake.

And then she would be gone.

* * *

"Wake up sunshine. Break's over. There's a new shipment of Jr. Miss thong sandals with your name on it that's ready to be unloaded and stored in the stockroom."

Tommy lifted his head off his desk and slowly peeled his eyes open, his right hand still wrapped around a Styrofoam coffee cup, wisps of steam drifting from its top.

Ford Fennel, Tommy's 23-year-old assistant manager at the On The Good Foot Shoe Shack, was hovering over him, eyebrows arched and finger tapping against a gold-plated Swiss Army watch.

"Hey listen, I need to cut out a bit early today," he commanded, wiping off his "Get On The Good Foot" sales award pin, which he always wore, even after hours. "Would you mind wrapping up the paperwork, honcho? Got some bidness to tend to."

Tommy took a deep breath, sipped his coffee and glanced over at a small corkboard covered in Polaroid photos of employees. Half of them were of Ford posing with various family automobiles, and more than a few had been "artistically manipulated" by mischievous co-workers wielding Sharpie pens. It was widely known, at least within the confines of The Good Foot, that Ford's parents had named their six children after automobile brand names. Anytime this fact was brought up in conversation among employees, someone would crack, "Which one is Yugo?" or "Is the younger sister named Hyundai, or is that the older sister?" And on and on.

Tommy rubbed his eyes and took a sip of his coffee before standing up.

"Yeah, I can take care of that for you."

"That'd be outstanding."

"Before you leave, though, I'd like to clarify a few things about my history, and perhaps kick a bit of wisdom your way, if you don't mind," Tommy politely asked, sneaking another sip.

Ford, looked at his watch, irritated, and exhaled a deep breath.
"Sure. Shoot."

"For the record, the reason I'm wearing this lovely ankle bracelet
here," Tommy said, lifting his khaki pant leg and pointing at the
GPS tracking device wrapped around his ankle, "is between me
and my parole officer, and it involves neither the rape of someone,
nor murder by crowbar."

Ford stood still as a stone, his jaw slack, his eyes frozen wide
open. He slowly began reaching for the breakroom door to exit.

"Oh, and Ford …"

"Yessir."

"If I ever hear again of you passing off your conspiracy theories
as fact concerning why I'm wearing this lovely accessory, I'll find a
reason to have a matching one on my other ankle. Clear?"

"As a bell, sir."

* * *

Jim "Dandy" James had only been working as a salesman at The
Good Foot for four months, but he was already a legend. Dressed
immaculate in a suit (even on casual Fridays), The Dandy would
hand pick customers on which to work his self-described "mojitsu"
persuasion technique he claimed to have picked up during a dubious
tenure in the Orient. He even carried his own personalized Brannock
foot measuring device.

In the month of April alone, he convinced 131 customers that
orange suede clogs were the harbingers of a nower-than-now
Dutch-influenced fashion wave that was still "top seek(ret) in
Milan."

The kid was *that* good.

Tommy always tried to guess which color combination The Dandy
would assemble for the day's seduction, and this time he was on
the money: Khaki linen suit, chocolate & white duotone loafers.
He looked sharp as a guillotine and could jaw so well that area car
salesmen were known to come in and buy a cheap pair of Adidas
just to hijack some of his game.

"Feelin' it today, Tommy boy, rollin' thunder!" The Dandy spoke
in a singsong voice, waltzing into the store.

He pulled out a single stick of Juicy Fruit gum from his inside coat pocket, tore it in half, placed one half in his mouth and the unopened piece on the cashier's counter.

"TomTom, visualize with me," he directed from behind the checkout counter, his eyes closed and arms extended out like a televangelist during sweeps week. "Athletic department, third aisle, second shelf. Blonde mother of two. Blue New Balance with Pink trim. Full Retail. A wink and a giggle. Sold, three minutes tops."

The Dandy then shimmied his hands and shot both forefingers toward the more upscale women's shoes selection.

"I see a Steve Madden limited edition boho-stiletto set walking out of here in about five … wait," he said, hesitating. "Scratch that. Gimme the Madden bohos, and gimme an additional pair of eggplant-colored aqua socks for the lady at 9 o'clock. By the time the flavor is gone in the gum I'm chewing, it'll be D-U-N, done."

Tommy shook his head and clapped his hands.

"The Dandy do right," he said, smiling. "Make the magic happen, son."

"Yes sir, where you headed?"

"Dinnertime—gonna sample some fine Food Court cuisine and see if I can fatten up this stunning specimen," Tommy answered, patting his generous midsection. "Figured an extra large order of fried won tons will do the trick."

*　*　*

Tommy grasped the escalator's handrail and began his descent, his fingers tapping in rhythm to the cover version of a cover version of some forgotten song trickling out of the shopping center's speaker system. He looked at the faces of those riding in the opposite direction. Some looked familiar, and most wore what he called "the mall mask"—an expression that's a combination of impatience, anxiety, boredom and frustration.

"Ah, so many choices," Tommy whispered to himself, scanning the Food Court's neon and candy-colored marquees beckoning hungry stomachs. "And so many ways to make your arteries explode."

But he knew which one he'd choose. The same one he always chose (Asian Au Go-Go). At the same time (6:15 p.m., sharp). For the same reason (Celia Skye was the manager, and had provided for the last few weeks, the best dinner companionship he'd had in a long, long time).

Tommy and Celia eased their chairs up to a rare empty table, and that unmistakable Mall Buzz, consisting of pubescent chatter, scattershot laughter, screaming babies and innumerable parental pleas—all wrapped up in a white noise casserole, fell deaf on their ears.

It was just the two of them.... and two Moo Goo Gai Pan combo specials, on the house.

Celia tested the heat of the sauce with her index finger and noticed Tommy's tie selection for the day.

"A bolo tie today, huh?," she said, scooping a fork full of food in her mouth. "Looks sharp, Texas Pete."

Tommy smiled, shaking his head.

"My grandfather gave me a collection of these ties when I was a kid. He had a whole wall devoted to 'em. Used to just stand in his room in the summertime, and look at them hanging there, shimmering in the light. Got one for each state. Today is North Dakota's moment in the sun."

"I'm impressed."

"I'm repressed."

Celia laughed out loud, nearly spilling her Coke.

"What is that, a 98 ouncer?" Tommy asked, "They should outfit that thing with a diving board."

"Noooo, it's only a 32 ouncer."

"Oh, *only* a 32 ouncer; that's a sugar O.D. waiting to happen."

Celia smiled and picked at her food a moment.

"Can I ask you something personal?" she asked.

"Shoot."

"For weeks, we've been gathering at this table together, you and I, and I'm looking at that wedding ring on your finger. And I take it that, from the direction our conversation has been flowing here, you're not married—am I right?"

"Mmhm. That's true."

"So, may I ask why you still wear the ring?"

Tommy pulled his straw out of his cup lid and poked at the luke-warm remnants of his Moo Goo Gai Pan. The dinner rush was beginning to fade a bit.

"My wife passed away five years ago next week. Cancer."

Celia shook her head, tucking her hair behind her ears.

"I'm so sorry."

Tommy carefully pushed his plate aside and held up his left hand.

"She made this ring for me. She was an artisan—stained glass, pottery. A real hands-on type," Tommy continued, putting the straw back in his cup. "After she passed, I went out of my mind, pretty much. The usual TV Movie Of The Week-type stuff. Heavy drinking, lost the big job, lost the house. Lost it all. Thank God we didn't have kids."

Celia crumpled her napkin and placed it on her near-empty plate of food as Tommy continued.

"So one night, after celebrating my grief—*yet again*—I drove my 1987 Mercury Cougar into the broadside of a parked car. Two young ladies were inside, gussied up for an evening out. The impact of my car killed the girl in the passenger side. Michelle Dubois. 20 years old. Economics major at Georgia Tech. On the verge of everything.

"Such a beautiful girl," his voice trailed off. "A real beaut."

"I was sentenced to five years in prison. Michelle's family, understandably, wanted my throat slit in front of the television cameras. My friends turned into ghosts ... but I did the time, and here I am—an ex-convict salesman, fourth best in the bunch, for The Good Foot, with a boss half my age ... and this lovely little fashion accessory."

Tommy lifted his left pant leg to reveal a black, belt-like strap just above his ankle.

"It's a GPS tracking device, a Global Positioning Satellite tracks my every move and reports to my probation officer," he said. "Very James Bond, huh?"

Celia wiped her hands on her napkin and reached to graze the strap with her finger.

"Is it heavy?"

"Was at first, but you get used to it. Thought I might debut it at the beach this summer, start a new fashion trend."

"I'd love to see that," Celia answered, laughing. "Next stop: the runways of Par-eeee!"

Tommy and Cecilia both laughed out loud, the Food Court's buzz now a post-dinner rush hum.

"So, anyway, the only connection to her I had left was this ring, which the boys in blue slipped into a little Ziplock bag for safekeeping while I was in prison. And when I was released, it was the first thing I saw that reminded me of the life I had outside—of life with her. It's all I have left."

Celia leaned in toward Tommy and tucked her hair behind both ears.

"I think you have a little more left than you realize," she said.

A faint smile cracked across Tommy's face. He reached to pull his pant leg down over the strap strangling his ankle.

"No, don't," Celia said, waving his hand away from his pant leg. "Leave it as is."

Tommy paused for a moment and looked at Celia. He thought about her voice. It was warm and cozy as a lap.

Celia took a long sip of coffee, and Tommy watched a wisp of steam rise from its lid, smeared with lipstick.

She unfolded one of the crumpled napkins on her dinner plate, pulled out a pen and began writing.

"Do you think about her often," she asked, still writing.

"She's always there," he said, "kind of like a loose shoe string that keeps clicking against the floor when you walk."

Celia folded the napkin neatly, removed a hairpin from her tangle of brown curls, and clipped the napkin onto Tommy's bolo tie.

"You been walking in those shoes a long time, Tommy," she said, standing up. "Maybe it's about time for a new pair."

Tommy unfolded the napkin.

It read: "Wanted: Tall ex-convict. Brown eyes, bald. Bad taste in ties. Will take him as is. If interested, call Celia at 770.881.3224."

After carefully folding the napkin and slipping it in his shirt pocket, Tommy held Celia's hairpin up to the light and smiled.

"770.881.3224," he repeated to himself, over and over, humming the numbers as if they were words in the melody of a song he thought he had forgotten to sing.

Discussion Questions

1. Why did Tommy Wills not hesitate to show his "ankle bracelet" to his store manager?
2. What kind of role does prejudice play in the story?
3. Why did Tommy continue to wear his wedding ring, even after his wife had passed away?
4. Given Tommy's past, why do you think Celia accepted him?
5. How do our past transgressions affect/shape who we are?
6. Do you think tolerance (or prejudice) is something we learn through experience, or is it ingrained in us at birth?

References

Angelou, M. 1983. *I Know Why the Caged Bird Sings.* New York: Bantam Books.

Braswell, M., McCarthy, B. and McCarthy, B. (eds.) 2002. *Justice, Crime and Ethics (4th ed.)* Cincinnati, OH: Anderson.

Carlson, P. and Hawkins, P. (eds.) 1994. *Listening for God.* Minneapolis, MN: Augsburg Fortress.

Clark, W. and Wright, W. (eds.) 1968. *The Complete Works of William Shakespeare (vol. 2).* New York: Nelson Doubleday.

Crane, Stephen. 1990. *The Red Badge of Courage.* New York: TOR Books.

Daly, R. 1984. *Prince of the City.* New York: Berkley Press.

Hawthorne, N. 1961. *The Scarlet Letter.* New York: MacMillan

Lee, H. 1960. *To Kill A Mockingbird.* New York: Popular Library.

Lozoff, B. 1988. *Lineage and Other Stories.* Durham, NC: Human Kindness Foundation.

Maas, P. 1973. *Serpico.* New York: Viking Press.

Maas, P. 1983. *Marie: A True Story.* New York: Random House.

MacIntyre, A. 2001. *Dependent Rational Animals: Why Human Beings Need the Virtues.* New York: Open Court Publ.

Maggio, R (ed.). *Quotations on Education.* Paramus, New Jersey: Prentice-Hall.

Masters, J. 1997. *Finding Freedom.* Junction City, CA: Padma Publishing.

Miller, A. 1976. *The Crucible.* New York: Penguin Books.

Morris, N. 1992. *The Brothel Boy and Other Parables of the Law.* New York: Oxford University Press.

O'Connor, F. 1999. "Greenleaf" In *The Best American Short Stories of the Century,* eds. J. Updike and K. Kenison, 348–368. New York: Houghton Mifflin.

Pollock, J. 2004. *Dilemmas and Decision: Ethics in Crime and Justice:.* Belmont, CA: Wadsworth/ITP.

Pollock, J. 2012. *Ethical Dilemmas and Decision in Criminal Justice:.* Belmont, CA: Wadsworth/ITP.

Tannebaum, J. 2000. *Disguised as a Poem.* Boston: Northeastern University Press.

Author/Subject Index

Angelou, Maya, 5

Bentham, Jeremy, 8
Braswell, Michael, 9, 10, 231

care, 9, 29, 33, 49, 83, 117,
  128, 136, 138, 197, 199,
  201, 224
Carlson, Paula, 4, 231
caseworker, 105–107, 110, 112
chaplain, 84, 107–112, 177,
  209, 212, 214
Churchill, Winston, xii
compassion, 10, 11, 29, 147,
  148, 155, 156, 215
connectedness, 9
correctional officer, 109, 205
Crane, Stephen, 231

Daly, Robert, 4
death row, 148, 204, 205,
  208–210, 212, 215
Dickinson, Emily, xv
duty, 7, 8, 21, 41, 51, 55, 83,
  110, 123, 127, 177, 190,
  201, 218

education, 96, 108, 129, 132,
  144, 163, 231
ethics, 4–10, 82, 139, 169,
  231, 232
execution, 148, 175, 205

fiction, 3–5, 180, 190

Gandhi, Mahatma, xv, 9, 10
Grisham, John, 4

Hawkins, Peter, 4, 231
Hawthorne, Nathaniel, 231
Hemingway, Ernest, xiii
Hersey, John, xiii
homelessness, 5

injustice, 4, 5, 124, 139, 147,
  185

juvenile delinquent, 5, 219
justice, 4–6, 8–10, 14, 31, 66,
  81, 96, 108, 112, 114, 120,
  129, 133, 147, 148, 156,
  170, 184, 187, 189, 191–
  201, 208, 215, 222, 231, 232

Kant, Immanuel, 7
King, Jr., Martin Luther, 6,
    9–11

lawyer, 40, 84, 118, 120, 125,
    126, 171, 180, 183, 184, 195
Lee, Harper, 4
loyalties, 13, 31, 57, 87
Lozoff, Bo, 4, 231

Maas, Peter, 4, 231
Masters, Jarvis, 4, 231
McCarthy, Belinda, 9, 10, 231
McCarthy, Bernard, 9, 10,
    231
Miller, Arthur, 4
mindfulness, 9
moral action, 9
Morris, Norval, 5
Mother Teresa, 9, 10

O'Connor, Flannery, 3, 232

peacemaking, 9
policing, xvi
Pollock, Joycelyn, 5–7, 232
prison, 6, 69, 84, 107, 108,
    110, 113, 124, 129–131,
    133, 173, 175, 183, 185,
    186, 188, 190, 199–201,
    203, 204, 209, 228, 229
prostitution, 83, 93
poverty, 100

racism, xvi, 3, 36, 107, 147,
    208
redemption, 147, 148
relationships, 10, 13, 14, 66
religion, 209, 211
retribution, 3

Shakespeare, William, 231
Shute, Nevil, xiii
spiritual, 147, 154, 209, 215
substance abuse, 25, 85, 223
stories, 1, 3–11, 36, 61, 83,
    211, 231, 232

Tannebaum, Judith, 4, 232
truth, 26, 44, 64, 84, 88, 95,
    98, 112, 117, 131, 132,
    141–146, 154, 158, 172,
    174, 180, 182, 196, 204
Turow, Scott, 4

utilitarianism, 8

values, 6, 7, 9, 24, 82, 133, 215
violence, 3, 5, 24, 33, 181,
    183, 212

Weil, Simone, xv
whistleblower, 31, 77, 141
wisdom traditions, 9, 208
Wright, W. Aldis, 231